DECISION MAKING IN
BEHAVIORAL
EMERGENCIES

DECISION MAKING IN
BEHAVIORAL
EMERGENCIES

Acquiring Skill in Evaluating
and Managing High-Risk Patients

Phillip M. Kleespies

AMERICAN PSYCHOLOGICAL ASSOCIATION

WASHINGTON, DC

Published by
American Psychological Association
750 First Street, NE
Washington, DC 20002
www.apa.org

To order
APA Order Department
P.O. Box 92984
Washington, DC 20090-2984
Tel: (800) 374-2721; Direct: (202) 336-5510
Fax: (202) 336-5502; TDD/TTY: (202) 336-6123
Online: www.apa.org/pubs/books
E-mail: order@apa.org

In the U.K., Europe, Africa, and the Middle East, copies may be ordered from
American Psychological Association
3 Henrietta Street
Covent Garden, London
WC2E 8LU England

Typeset in Minion by Circle Graphics, Inc., Columbia, MD

Printer: Maple Press, York, PA
Cover Designer: Berg Design, Albany, NY

The opinions and statements published are the responsibility of the authors, and such opinions and statements do not necessarily represent the policies of the American Psychological Association.

Library of Congress Cataloging-in-Publication Data
Kleespies, Phillip M.
  Decision making in behavioral emergencies : acquiring skill in evaluating and managing high-risk patients / Phillip M. Kleespies.
    pages cm
  Includes bibliographical references and index.
  ISBN 978-1-4338-1664-2 — ISBN 1-4338-1664-4 1. Psychiatric emergencies.
2. Crisis intervention (Mental health services) 3. Mental illness—Risk factors. I. Title.
  RC480.6.K57 2014
  616.890025—dc23
                              2013028466

British Library Cataloguing-in-Publication Data
A CIP record is available from the British Library.

Printed in the United States of America
First Edition

http://dx.doi.org/10.1037/14337-000

Contents

CONTENTS

Preface

Clinical work with patients or clients who are deeply troubled holds many challenges, but perhaps none so great as when the patient or client is at risk of suicide, of violence toward others, or of becoming a victim of violence. Over the course of my career as a clinical psychologist, I have had the opportunity to work with mentally and emotionally disturbed patients (primarily veterans) in inpatient psychiatry, in an emergency room, and in an urgent care clinic. In each of these settings, I have had to make or participate in decisions about the management of patients who had varying degrees of risk for life-threatening behavior. These decisions had to do with whether someone at risk should be hospitalized, voluntarily or involuntarily; whether the person could be treated on an outpatient basis, and if so, how closely he or she should be monitored; whether a patient's ability to exercise self-control had been temporarily lost and he or she needed to be restrained for the safety of self or others; whether to advance the privileges of an inpatient who had been considered a threat to self or others just a few days earlier; and so forth.

In the course of my work, I have also had the opportunity to observe how professional colleagues made these decisions, and I found that when there was time pressure and pressure from staff, as well as from angry or agitated patients, to make a decision, some clinicians were able to make seemingly sound decisions quite quickly and with limited information. These observations led me to think about what process these clinicians, myself included, went through in such circumstances. This book is about decision making under this type of pressure and about how clinicians can acquire the skills needed to make these often difficult and trying decisions. In this sense, this book differs from (but complements) my previous book, *Behavioral Emergencies: An Evidence-Based Resource for Evaluating and Managing Risk of Suicide, Violence, and Victimization* (Kleespies, 2009). Whereas the previous book provided a knowledge base for use in evaluating and managing behavioral emergencies, the current book focuses on how the practitioner can acquire the actual clinical skills needed to work effectively with high-risk patients.

Acknowledgments

I consider it a privilege to have had a career in public service providing psychological care and treatment to some of our most emotionally wounded veterans. I have learned a great deal from these patients, who have presented with a wide range of crises and emergencies. I have also been fortunate to have been able to work with and train many psychology interns and postdoctoral fellows in emergency psychological services at the VA Boston Healthcare System. Training interns and fellows in a setting that can be tense and anxiety provoking has prompted me to devote considerable thought to what may be needed to assist them in becoming competent in this area of practice. I have learned a great deal from observing their efforts to acquire the necessary skills. I have also learned a great deal in consulting with colleagues about some of their more challenging cases.

In addition, I am indebted to several professional colleagues. My thanks to Alisa Angelone, PhD, a postdoctoral fellow in clinical psychology, and to Shimrit Black, MA, an intern in clinical psychology, both of whom—concurrent with their rotation in the Urgent Care Clinic at the VA Boston Healthcare System—reviewed and provided comments on the case vignettes in Chapter 4 ("Mental Practice for Decision Making During Behavioral Emergencies"). My thanks also to Dale McNeil, PhD, for reading and commenting on Chapter 5 ("The Use of Decision-Support Tools in Behavioral Emergencies") and, particularly, to Glenn Sullivan, PhD, and Bruce Bongar, PhD, for their review of Chapter 7 ("The Stress of Legal and Ethical Issues in High-Risk Cases"). My thanks as well to the two anonymous peer reviewers and to APA Books development editor Harriet Kaplan for their very helpful comments and suggestions. They have enriched and improved the book.

As always, I am grateful to the multidisciplinary staff from nursing, psychiatry, and social work whose assistance in working with cases in the VA Boston Urgent Care Clinic at the Jamaica Plain campus has been invaluable.

My special thanks also to my grandson, Declan Hugh O'Dwyer, who provided many a pleasant and needed distraction playing whiffle ball and building fortresses as I worked on this book.

DECISION MAKING IN
BEHAVIORAL
EMERGENCIES

Introduction

This book is about acquiring skill in the area of practice known as *behavioral emergencies* (i.e., in evaluating and managing patients or clients who are at risk of suicide, violence, or victimization). In particular, it is about acquiring skill in making difficult decisions in clinical situations in which there is the possibility of patient life-threatening behavior. As such, it is intended as a companion book to the volume *Behavioral Emergencies: An Evidence-Based Resource for Evaluating and Managing Risk of Suicide, Violence, and Victimization* (Kleespies, 2009). Whereas that book was about a proposed knowledge base for this area of practice, the current book is about the development of the skills and attitudes needed to practice competently when assessing and working with high-risk patients.

Tension is inherent in any situation in which a patient or client appears to be at risk, and the decisions that the clinician makes could have life-or-death consequences. The clinician may worry about his or her

http://dx.doi.org/10.1037/14337-001
Decision Making in Behavioral Emergencies: Acquiring Skill in Evaluating and Managing High-Risk Patients, by P. M. Kleespies

ability to understand the patient's emotional distress and form a working alliance with the patient. He or she may have only limited information about the patient and limited time in which to gather additional information. In the real world, clinicians must deal with other stressors, including other patients who are in crisis, management demands to limit the time spent on any one individual case, and additional professional and administrative duties.

Maltsberger and Buie (1974), in a well-known article, posited that clinicians who work with suicidal patients can develop what they referred to, in psychoanalytic terms, as *countertransference hate.* They posited this construct because they felt that the clinician's reactions to suicidal patients can be particularly intense and can lead to aversion and malice toward the patient. However, when Jobes (2006) and several of his doctoral students attempted to study countertransference reactions that were unique to suicidal patients through both analogue and survey studies, they found but scant empirical support for Maltsberger and Buie's theoretical construct.

Although the terms *hate* and *malice* may be somewhat extreme when applied to the reactions of most clinicians to suicidal patients, there is long-standing evidence indicating that clinicians often view such patients as stressful to manage and anxiety arousing. In a survey of 279 professional staff, psychology interns, and psychology practicum students at 14 VA Medical Centers and 12 university counseling services, Rodolfa, Kraft, and Reilley (1988) found that clinicians rated suicide attempts and suicidal ideation as the second and third most stressful events, respectively, that they had confronted. In a national survey of psychologists, Pope and Tabachnick (1993) found that 97% of the respondents reported being afraid of losing a patient to suicide.

In the survey by Rodolfa et al. (1988), participants rated patient violence directed at the clinician as the most stressful event. In addition, 89% of Pope and Tabachnick's (1993) sample reported episodes in which they had been afraid that a patient might physically attack a third party, and 61% reported having had a patient who actually did. In their work with victims of violence, clinicians' stress reactions have been frequently reported and referred to as *vicarious trauma* (McCann & Pearlman, 1990) or as *secondary traumatic stress* (Figley, 1995; see Chapter 8 of this volume for further discussion of the potential stress that can result from clinical work with behavioral emergencies).

This book is about how clinicians can increase their ability to manage this level of stress and decrease its negative impact when making decisions about the assessment and care of patients who are suicidal, potentially violent, or at risk of becoming victims of violence. Chapter 1 provides an overview of the area of clinical practice that comprises behavioral emergencies and crises. The chapter describes some of the difficult decisions that mental health clinicians face when confronted with a patient or client who may be at imminent risk of harm to self or others. Evidence is presented indicating that, despite the fact that nearly all mental health clinicians at times work with high-risk patients, and despite the potential gravity of these cases, psychology practitioners (and clinicians from other mental health disciplines as well) need, but do not typically receive, education and training specific to this area of practice.

Clinicians usually have very limited time to assess a patient or client who is distressed, agitated, and potentially at risk to self and/or others, so it is important to understand what decision-making strategies are most appropriate under such conditions. Chapter 2 reviews three broad categories of theoretical models for decision making: (a) rational and normative, (b) descriptive, and (c) naturalistic decision-making. I have concluded that the rational and normative models of decision making—in which one considers all alternatives and generates a large option set—are not particularly useful in the high-pressure crucible of behavioral emergencies. Although rational models are widely used by scientists and in management decisions, naturalistic decision-making models are more consistent and effective with the task of evaluating behavioral emergencies when there is limited information about the patient as well as time and procedural pressures. The chapter discusses the following naturalistic decision-making models: the recognition-primed decision model, the recognition/metacognition model, the situation awareness model, and the hypervigilant decision-making strategy. Although each of these models has something to contribute to understanding the process of decision making in behavioral emergencies, recognition priming through clinical experience (i.e., using past experience to quickly understand a current situation and decide on a course of action) is presented as particularly relevant to achieving competence in decision making under these conditions.

Chapter 3 examines the effects of stress on decision making and discusses the need for stress training. Stress training has its roots in the stress inoculation training (SIT) program of Donald Meichenbaum (1985). In this model, the effort is not to eliminate stress but to encourage a view of stressful events as problems to be solved. SIT was developed as a clinical treatment program. Johnston and Cannon-Bowers (1996) modified the SIT model for use in training professionals in the cognitive and behavioral skills needed to perform tasks under high-stress conditions. They refer to their model as *stress exposure training* or SET. SET has the professional or professional-in-training practice the acquired skills under conditions that increasingly approximate the potentially stressful circumstances. This graduated approach to skills training is seen as ideally suited to training in the evaluation and management of behavioral emergencies.

Mental practice with case scenarios is an early step in a gradated approach to developing skill in dealing with behavioral emergencies. In Chapter 4, I present 10 emergency case scenarios that are based on actual events. Details have been changed to protect the identity of the individuals involved. The cases were chosen to represent a range of high-risk situations from intimate partner violence, to adolescent suicide, to the psychotic patient at risk to others, to combat veteran suicide, to the elderly suicidal patient with physical illness, and so forth. As noted in the chapter, these cases do not necessarily have a *correct* answer. They are intended to reflect the complexity of real clinical life when possible emergency situations arise. Following each case scenario is an *Author's Comment* section. Before reading the comment, the reader is encouraged to read the case, placing himself or herself in the role of the clinician, and to think about (and perhaps write down) his or her thoughts about managing the case. The author's comments are provided for comparison with the reader's ideas about the case and to stimulate further thought and discussion.

Given the difficulties of estimating the risk of suicide or violence, clinicians need whatever assistance may be available. Typically, they have turned to evidence-based risk and protective factors as a basis for making decisions about the level of risk. In Chapter 5, I discuss this approach and list some of the better known risk and protective factors for suicide. Interestingly, there have been some promising developments in the short-term prediction of violence through an approach referred to as *structured professional judgment* (Borum, Lodewijks, Bartel, & Forth, 2010).

In terms of violence prediction, it has long been known that actuarial methods have had a higher level of accuracy than unaided clinical judgment. There have, however, also been problems with strict actuarial methods. For example, they can involve a rather rigid process that overlooks clinical and situational changes that can modify the estimate of risk.

The structured professional judgment method attempts to incorporate the strengths of both the clinical and actuarial approaches. It has involved the development of decision-support tools (which are not formal psychological tests) in which an expert-selected set of key risk factors is used to guide the clinician's judgment about the risk of violence. The risk factors are viewed as an aid to the clinician's judgment, but the clinician's judgment and consideration of clinical and situational factors are clearly part of the process of arriving at an estimate of risk. Several of the decision-support tools that have been more thoroughly assessed for reliability and predictive validity are presented in this chapter. Although they may not be immediately applicable in an actual mental health emergency situation, I argue that a working familiarity with them can be of great use when one is under pressure to arrive at a decision about a patient's level of risk for violence.

In Chapter 6, the evaluation and management of behavioral emergencies is conceptualized as a functional competency as defined by the American Psychological Association (APA) Task Force on the Assessment of Competence in Professional Psychology (2006). *Functional competencies* are clusters of integrated knowledge, skills, and attitudes needed to perform a particular task. In this chapter, I present the outline of a knowledge base for behavioral emergencies as well as a supervisory model and a model training program for acquiring the skills and attitudes needed to work with patients at risk to self and/or others. Consistent with the APA Task Force report, I argue that the training for and the assessment of competence are best accomplished in real-life encounters with actual patients or clients while under supervision and, especially in the case of behavioral emergencies, while receiving stress training. In this way, both training and assessment maintain the value that the APA Task Force has placed on training in which there is fidelity to practice. The use of *experience near* simulated patient interactions or actual patient interactions is recommended for the assessment process.

Another stressor for those who have patients who are at risk of life-threatening behaviors is the knowledge that these are cases that can have a serious negative outcome. A life or lives can be lost, and that can lead to legal, ethical, and professional consequences for the clinician. Perhaps the best way to manage this type of stress is to practice in ways that are informed by the legal and ethical issues involved. In Chapter 7, the legal and ethical issues associated with malpractice claims based on negligence are discussed. In addition, certain legal caveats for clinicians who have either outpatients or inpatients who are potentially suicidal are presented. Further, issues related to patient violence toward others and the clinician's possible duty to protect the potential victims of his or her patient are also reviewed.

Although there have been improvements in the evaluation and management of behavioral emergencies, and some of the decision-support tools mentioned earlier hold promise for the short-term prediction of violence, the reality, of course, is that patient suicides and patient violence to others continue to occur. Patient suicides, for example, have been referred to as an occupational hazard for psychologists and psychiatrists (Chemtob, Bauer, Hamada, Pelowski, & Muraoka, 1989). In Chapter 8, I review the potential emotional impact of such events on the clinician or clinicians who may have evaluated or treated patients who commit suicide, who seriously harm or kill others, or who are the victims of violence. I also review those methods that have been found to be helpful in coping with the emotional aftermath of such events.

Finally, in a brief Afterword, I call for improved training for professional psychologists in the skills needed to work with patient life-threatening behaviors.

1

Evaluating and Managing Behavioral Emergencies and Crises: An Overview

A 29-year-old man is accompanied by a friend to the clinic where you are doing intakes. The friend looks very concerned. The patient has told him that he has thoughts of killing his supervisor at work, and his friend has convinced him to come to the clinic to talk with someone. You meet with the patient and find that he is enraged, and he angrily paces the interview room. His supervisor has frequently been critical of him and has now told him that he is giving him an unsatisfactory performance rating. He has threatened to have the patient reassigned to a position that will mean a substantial cut in pay. The patient pays child support for a 6-year-old son and lives at a subsistence level on his current salary. He states that he has appealed for help from his union, but it has been ineffective in attempting to represent him. He emphasizes that he will not accept this reassignment and, in the most graphic of terms, states that he has thoughts of brutally killing his supervisor. He adds that he will also kill himself rather than spend the rest of his life in prison.

http://dx.doi.org/10.1037/14337-002
Decision Making in Behavioral Emergencies: Acquiring Skill in Evaluating and Managing High-Risk Patients, by P. M. Kleespies

There are few, if any, responsibilities that weigh so heavily on a clinician as the need to deal with a patient such as this one, a man who seems at great risk of engaging in life-threatening behaviors. In reference to such cases, Pope and Vasquez (1991) made this point very succinctly in the following statement: "This aspect of our work focuses virtually all of the troublesome issues that run through this volume [*Ethics in Psychotherapy and Counseling*]: questions of the therapist's influence, competence, efficacy, fallibility, over- or under-involvement, responsibility, and ability to make life-or-death decisions" (p. 153).

This scenario is what I refer to as a *potential behavioral emergency*. The possibility of a negative outcome (in this case, a murder–suicide) is stress inducing in itself, but the clinician may be simultaneously attempting to cope with a number of other stressors, such as another patient or client in crisis in the waiting room, a report that his or her child is sick at the day care center and needs to be picked up, or both. Some clinicians respond to such heightened stress with improved performance, but many experience a performance decline. It is at times like this that there is an increased risk that the decision-making process will be degraded and poor decisions will be made. This book is about acquiring the skills to evaluate and manage behavioral emergencies under the stressful conditions that often occur in real clinical life.

In this first chapter, I present an overview of the area of practice referred to as *behavioral emergencies and crises*. The overview includes a definition of the term *behavioral emergency* as well as a discussion of an integrative perspective on behavioral emergencies. The incidence of behavioral emergencies and the need for training in this area of practice are also addressed. The management of each of the three major behavioral emergencies (as described in the next section) is considered, with a particular emphasis on the decisions that need to be made in situations where there appears to be imminent risk.

For a more extensive presentation of behavioral emergencies and related issues, the reader is referred to the book *Behavioral Emergencies: An Evidence-Based Resource for Evaluating and Managing Risk of Suicide, Violence, and Victimization* (Kleespies, 2009). Whereas that book presents a knowledge base for behavioral emergencies, the major focus of the current book is on acquiring skill in decision making about behavioral emergencies under the stressful conditions that often occur in clinical practice. The topics that pertain to this process are discussed more specifically in the chapters that follow.

DEFINING BEHAVIORAL EMERGENCIES

A *behavioral emergency* exists when (a) a client or patient is at *imminent* risk of intentionally inflicting serious physical harm or death on himself or herself or others, or (b) a client or patient is at *imminent* risk of being a victim of intentionally inflicted serious harm or death by another. There are relatively few situations in mental health practice that would be considered behavioral emergencies. They include (a) serious suicidal states, (b) potential violence to others, (c) situations of grave risk to a potential victim (e.g., as with a battered wife), and (d) states of very impaired judgment in which the individual is endangered.

There has been considerable discussion in recent years about the difficulties of defining the term *imminent risk* (as used in the definition presented here; see, e.g., Berman, 2011). R. I. Simon (2006) argued that *imminence* defies definition and that, at least in regard to suicide risk, there are no known short-term risk factors that identify when, or if, a patient will attempt or complete suicide. Although that statement may be true, potential behavioral emergencies (such as the one described at the beginning of this chapter) nonetheless happen, and when it appears that there is a high risk of life-threatening behavior, the mental health clinician cannot be unresponsive. He or she must decide whether there is reason to intervene immediately. One hopes that the clinician forms an opinion about the likelihood of imminent risk on the basis of the available evidence and does not simply make a "gut" decision. It should be clear, however, that a clinician's statement that a patient or client is at imminent risk for harm to self or others is based on a clinical judgment that there appears to be great risk of serious harm or death "in the next few minutes, hours, or days" (Pokorny, 1983, p. 249). It is not, however, a prediction. The prediction of statistically rare events such as suicide, violence, or victimization is beyond our current capabilities. Suicide, for example, has a rate of 12.4 per 100,000 in the general U.S. population (McIntosh, 2012), whereas the homicide rate is far lower at 4.8 per 100,000 (U.S. Department of Justice, 2011). It has been estimated that the suicide rate in the psychiatric population has been 5 or 6 times that of the general population, or approximately 62–74 per 100,000 (Tanney, 1992). Unfortunately, our clinical acumen and our assessment instruments do not have the sensitivity and specificity to detect such statistically rare events.

In attempting to understand what is meant by a behavioral emergency, it may be helpful to contrast the terms *behavioral emergency* and *behavioral crisis*. As Callahan (1998, 2009) and Kleespies (1998a, 2000) have pointed out, these two terms have frequently been used interchangeably in the literature. I prefer to distinguish between them, given that the term *crisis* has been used to refer to a wide range of problems (e.g., a midlife crisis, a relationship crisis, a financial crisis), most of which would not necessarily be considered life-threatening emergencies in themselves. Its use as a term to refer to emergency conditions, therefore, seems more subject to misunderstanding. In addition, the distinction between the two terms is often what drives our thinking, our decision making, and our interventions when confronted with potential emergencies.

A behavioral crisis is a serious disruption of an individual's baseline level of functioning, such that his or her usual coping mechanisms are inadequate to restore equilibrium. It is an emotionally significant event in which a state of anxiety may develop and in which there may be a turning point for better or worse. It does not necessarily imply danger of serious physical harm or life-threatening danger.

A behavioral emergency, on the other hand, implies exactly that; that is, there is a risk of serious harm or death to self or others. At times, a behavioral crisis may contribute to, or be a precursor to, the development of a behavioral emergency, but such a crisis never fully accounts for life-threatening events like suicide or serious violence. Events such as these are usually multidetermined and have several levels of explanation. When patients present in a crisis, however, part of the work for the clinician is to distinguish between crises that are likely to lead to an emergency situation and those that, in all likelihood, are not.

It is likewise important to distinguish between an *emergency intervention* and a *crisis intervention* (Callahan, 2009). A crisis intervention usually implies that a response is made within 24 to 48 hours, whereas an emergency intervention implies a more immediate response; that is, the risk typically needs to be resolved in a single encounter with the patient. In contrast, when engaging in a crisis intervention, the clinician has several meetings with the patient over a 4- to 6-week period. The focus of the sessions is on restoring the patient's ability to cope and his or her emotional equilibrium. A resolution of the crisis is expected within that time period. An emergency intervention, on the other hand, needs to address what appears to be a situation in which there is imminent risk of serious harm or death to self and/or others. The clinician needs to assess the risk and may make efforts, in meeting with the patient, to reduce it. If such efforts fail, however, he or she needs to make a good-faith effort to manage the patient and the situation to prevent harm or death.

AN INTEGRATIVE PERSPECTIVE ON BEHAVIORAL EMERGENCIES

As Lutzker and Wyatt (2006) pointed out, suicide research, violence research, and, I might add, research on interpersonal victimization, have tended to be regarded as relatively independent areas of study. There is evidence, however, that there may be considerable overlap and inter-relatedness among these major behavioral emergencies. Of course, it goes without saying that interpersonal violence begets victims. As Kilpatrick (2005) pointed out, however, victimization can also be a contributing factor in the emergence of suicidality and the perpetration of violence in the future. In analyses using data from a large National Survey of Adolescents (Kilpatrick et al., 2003), it was noted that after controlling for risk of depression, posttraumatic stress disorder (PTSD), and drug use disorders, a history of victimization significantly increased the risk of suicide attempts. It was also found that after controlling for other mental health problems, a history of victimization significantly increased risk for the perpetration of violence. In addition, in a 7- to 8-year follow-up of this study, it was found that young women who were victimized as adolescents and developed PTSD were at higher risk for revictimization.

To test the relationship between childhood maltreatment, power-assertive punishment in childhood, and exposure to violence between parents on subsequent risk for adult partner violence, Ehrensaft et al. (2003) gathered prospective data on a community sample of 543 children over a period of 20 years. They found that physical injury by a caregiver directly increased the probability of their using similar violent tactics to resolve conflicts in future intimate relationships. Moreover, exposure to violence between parents was found to be the greatest independent risk factor for being a victim of future partner violence. Exposure to violence between parents and power-assertive punishment were found to be additional and potent predictors of the future perpetration of violence on partners.

The findings of Kilpatrick et al. (2003) and Ehrensaft et al. (2003) are supported by earlier work (e.g., see Plutchik, Botsis, & van Praag, 1995), as well as by extensive literature reviews by Kolko (2002) on child physical abuse and Berliner and Elliott (2002) on the sexual abuse of children. Thus, Plutchik et al. (1995) presented evidence of an overlap of suicidal and violent behavior in hospitalized psychotic adolescents, incarcerated juvenile offenders, and adult psychiatric inpatients. In addition, Mann, Waternaux, Haas, and Malone (1999) studied 347 consecutive admissions to a psychiatric hospital and found that rates of lifetime aggression and impulsivity were significantly greater in suicide attempters than in those who had never attempted suicide. These findings led the investigators to conclude that lifetime aggression and impulsivity should be considered a risk factor for suicidal behavior. In a similar vein, Apter et al. (1995) assessed 163 consecutive admissions to an adolescent psychiatric inpatient unit for depression, suicidal behaviors, and violent behaviors. They found that depression and violent behavior both correlated significantly with suicidal behavior, but there was no significant correlation between violent behavior and depressive symptoms. They speculated that there are two types of suicidal behavior that occur with adolescents: (a) suicidal behavior related to depression and (b) suicidal behavior related to problems with aggression and impulse control.

In the literature review by Kolko (2002), it was found that there were many studies demonstrating that a history of being physically abused as a child put individuals at greater risk of future aggression, poor anger modulation, impulsivity, and violent behavior. Likewise, Berliner and Elliott

(2002) found numerous studies indicating that sexual abuse in childhood could lead to greater risk of depression, anxiety, lower self-esteem, and suicidal behavior. Interpersonal victimization in childhood and adolescence thus seems to be a distal risk factor for the development of future suicidal and violent behavior.

INCIDENCE OF BEHAVIORAL EMERGENCIES IN PRACTICE

Almost all mental health practitioners encounter patients or clients who may be on the verge of one type of behavioral emergency or another.[1] Those who work on inpatient psychiatry units see patients who are at some risk of suicide or violence on a daily basis; those in outpatient clinic or private practice settings are also likely to encounter such patients or clients.

In a survey of former psychology interns from a variety of internship sites, it was found that 97% of the sample had provided care to at least one (and often several) patients with some form of suicidal ideation or behavior during their training years alone (Kleespies, Penk, & Forsyth, 1993). Of this sample, 29% reported having had a patient or client who made a suicide attempt, and 11% reported having had a patient or client who committed suicide. In a national survey of psychologists, Pope and Tabachnick (1993) found that 29% of their respondents reported that at some point in their career one of their patients or clients had committed suicide. Ruskin, Sakinofsky, Bagby, Dickens, and Sousa (2004) conducted a survey and found that 50% of their sample of psychiatrists had experienced at least one patient suicide. Feldman and Freedenthal (2006) surveyed clinical social workers and reported that 87% of the respondents had worked with a suicidal patient within the past year, and Sanders, Jacobson, and Ting (2008) found that 55% of the clinical social workers in their sample had at least one patient or client who attempted suicide during their career. Moreover, in a large random sample of social workers, approximately one third of the participants reported having

---

[1]For a more detailed discussion of this topic, see Kleespies and Hill (2011) and Kleespies and Ponce (2009).

interns/suic

had a patient or client die by suicide (Jacobson, Ting, Sanders, and Harrington, 2004).

In addition to having patients or clients who may attempt or complete suicide, mental health professionals may also have patients who threaten or pose a risk of violence to others (Pope & Tabachnick, 1993), as well as a risk to the clinician himself or herself. Statistics gathered by the Bureau of Justice between 1992 and 1996 revealed that 80 of every 1,000 mental health workers were victims of some form of nonfatal workplace violence (Arthur, Brende, & Quiroz, 2003). In this same survey, 29% reported that they had feared for their lives at least once during their professional careers. In a national survey of psychologists, J. Guy, Brown, and Poelstra (1990) reported that nearly 50% of their sample had been threatened with physical attack by a patient or client, and 40% reported actually being attacked. Fortunately, most of these assaults did not result in serious injury, but they often caused considerable emotional distress.

In the past 2 decades, there has also been increasing evidence that psychologists and other mental health clinicians can be the victims of stalking, or what Meloy and Gothard (1995) referred to as *obsessional following. Stalking* is said to occur when one individual intrudes on another repeatedly and to an extent that the other person fears for his or her safety. At times, these intrusions have led to violence.

Gentile, Asamen, Harmell, and Weathers (2002) conducted a large survey of randomly selected psychologists who were practitioners and members of the American Psychological Association. They found that 10.2% of their sample reported being stalked by a patient or client at least once in their careers to that date. In a large mail survey of randomly selected psychologists in the State of Victoria, Australia, the investigators found a lifetime prevalence of stalking by clients of 20% (Purcell, Powell, & Mullen, 2005). Significantly higher rates were found with forensic psychologists (32%), clinical psychologists (24%), and counseling psychologists (20%) compared with educational psychologists, neuropsychologists, and organizational psychologists. Nine percent of the psychologists in this survey reported that they were physically assaulted during the course of the stalking. In a smaller study of multidisciplinary mental health staff members affiliated with an urban, university-based, psychiatric inpatient unit, 53% reported that they had been the target of stalking outside of the hospital or other locked setting during their careers (Sandberg, McNiel, & Binder, 2002). In this study, 4% of the participants reported being physically attacked, 4% reported destruction of property, 18% reported threats of harm, 50% reported harassing phone calls and letters, and 46% reported unwanted following, approach, or surveillance.

As noted in the preceding section of this chapter, victims of interpersonal violence are at increased risk of experiencing a range of negative outcomes. The most common adverse consequences may be extreme anxiety and depression, as well as impaired social and occupational functioning. Fortunately, most people are resilient, and these symptoms only last for a few days or weeks (Bonanno, 2004). It is estimated, however, that up to 33% of adult and adolescent victims of interpersonal violence go on to develop more chronic problems, such as PTSD, major depression, and substance abuse (Kessler, Sonnega, Bromet, Hughes, & Nelson, 1995; Kilpatrick et al., 2003). Although we do not have data on the percentage of these victims who seek mental health treatment, it seems safe to say that it is not uncommon for clinicians to see such patients or clients in individual or couples treatment.

A National Violence Against Women Survey indicated that almost one fourth of women and one of every 12 men have been victims of intimate partner violence at some point in their lifetime (Tjaden & Thoennes, 2000). Women, and at times men, who are victims of intimate partner violence are often at risk of ongoing threat and revictimization (Riggs, Kilpatrick, & Resnick, 1992). Studies have indicated that between 35% and 50% of those who have been physically or sexually assaulted have been victimized more than once (Basile, Chen, Black, & Saltzman, 2007) and may be in circumstances where it could happen again. These victims often present for medical treatment in an emergency department or primary care clinic (Resnick, Acierno, Holmes, Dammeyer, & Kilpatrick, 2000) where they may also be referred for immediate mental health evaluation and follow-up care. The mental health clinician needs to be prepared to offer support and work on basic safety planning for those who feel unsafe and/or at risk of revictimization.

THE NEED FOR TRAINING IN THE MANAGEMENT OF BEHAVIORAL EMERGENCIES

Given the incidence of behavioral emergencies in clinical practice, and given that behavioral emergencies involve situations that may be life threatening, one might assume that mental health practitioners are routinely trained in evaluating and managing them. Surveys on education and training over the past 30 years, however, have shown that this is not the case. In the area of suicide risk assessment, an early survey of psychologists by Berman (1983) indicated that the average amount of formal didactic training in the assessment and treatment of the suicidal patient was 2 hours. Bongar and Harmatz (1991) reported that only 40% of graduate programs in clinical psychology offered any formal training in the study of suicide. Kleespies, Penk, and Forsyth (1993), in their survey, noted that approximately 55% of graduate students in clinical psychology had some form of didactic instruction on suicide, but the instruction was quite limited (i.e., one or two lectures). Ellis and Dickey (1998) found that training in the study of suicide seemed to be lacking in both quantity and quality in many psychology internship and psychiatry residency programs. In the survey by Dexter-Mazza and Freeman (2003), approximately half of the psychology interns had been in graduate programs that did not offer training in the assessment and management of suicidal patients. Finally, Jahn et al. (2011) reported that only 3.8% of graduate programs that responded to their survey had a suicide-specific course and that the majority of the responding programs relied on passive training in which information about suicide was mentioned in other courses or was to be gained in practicum experiences or workshops.

In 1999, the U.S. surgeon general (Dr. David Satcher) declared suicide to be a public health problem and issued a document titled *The Surgeon General's Call to Action to Prevent Suicide* (U.S. Public Health Service, 1999). As part of a comprehensive strategy to reduce the suicide rate in the United States, one of the goals stated in this document was to increase the proportion of psychology graduate programs and medical residency programs that include training in the assessment and management of suicide risk by 2005.

In 2010, the Suicide Prevention Resource Center and the Suicide Prevention Action Network USA collaborated on a review of the surgeon general's national strategy and published a report titled *Charting the Future of Suicide Prevention: 2010 Progress Review of the National Strategy for Suicide Prevention.* Sadly, after reviewing the training standards for 11 different mental health professional groups (psychology included), it was found that only the Council for the Accreditation of Counseling and Related Educational Programs had placed increased attention on the issue of suicide in its 2009 standards compared with its previous standards. In addition to the surgeon general, the Joint Commission (2010), the Institute of Medicine (2002), the U.S. Department of Health and Human Services (2001), and the United Nations/World Health Organization (1996) have all made statements about the critical need to improve the capabilities of mental health professionals in assessing and managing suicide risk. Yet, there has been little indication in the literature of a significant effort on the part of most mental health disciplines and their training programs to respond to these important statements and calls to action.

I believe that a similar gap exists in regard to training for violence risk assessment and management and for the assessment and management of victims of violence. In a national survey of psychologists, J. Guy, Brown, and Poelstra (1990) reported that those in their sample had a mean of 1 hour of clinical training in the management of patient violence during their predoctoral years. In the postdoctoral years, the mean increased to 2.3 hours. In a national sample of over 500 psychiatric residents, Schwartz and Park (1999) found that a third of the respondents received no training in assessing and managing the risk of patient violence, and another third described their training as inadequate. In terms of training to assist victims of violence, such as abused children, Alpert and Paulson (1990) conducted a review and reported that most professional degree programs in psychology did not incorporate child sexual abuse in their training. Moreover, in a national sample of psychologists, Pope and Feldman-Summers (1992) found that "very poor" was the rating most frequently given to graduate school and internship training in the area of sexual and physical abuse.

Those who offer training in the major behavioral emergencies (i.e., suicide risk, risk of violence, and risk of interpersonal victimization) might use the three broad categories suggested 25 years ago by Lomax (1986) in regard to the suicidal patient: (a) knowledge, (b) skill, and (c) attitude. These categories for training psychologists have also, more recently, been supported by the APA Task Force on the Assessment of Competence in Professional Psychology (2006).

In the book *Behavioral Emergencies: An Evidence-Based Resource for Evaluating and Managing Risk of Suicide, Violence, and Victimization,* I proposed a knowledge base for behavioral emergencies. The contents of the book are organized as a potential curriculum for teaching about these emergency situations and related topics. Skill development and attitude, however, come with supervised clinical experience, increased clinical confidence, and a sense of mastery. Work with patients who are in a state of crisis or a state of emergency can be anxiety arousing for seasoned professionals, let alone for those who are in training and less certain of their clinical abilities and status. The clinician needs more than a knowledge base and more than training through typical supervisory sessions. It is a premise of the current book that the clinician needs training to make decisions under the actual stress of behavioral emergency conditions—that is, when a negative outcome could be tragic and have far-reaching consequences for the patient, for the patient's family, for others in the community, for the clinician himself or herself, and for the clinic or hospital.

DECISIONS IN MANAGING BEHAVIORAL CRISES AND EMERGENCIES

There are often many decisions that must be made in the course of managing a behavioral emergency. Some of the more crucial ones are discussed next.

Decisions in Managing the Acute Risk of Suicide

There is no absolute rule for when a suicidal patient can be managed on an outpatient basis or when the clinician must make an emergency intervention and hospitalize the patient. Treatment providers need to be guided by a carefully considered estimate of the level of risk and by a weighing of the risks and benefits of each way of proceeding. The sections that follow offer some guidance for making the, at times, difficult decision to maintain the patient as an outpatient or to have him or her hospitalized.

When Can Suicide Risk Be Managed on an Outpatient Basis?

Clinicians may be inclined to hospitalize patients with suicidal ideation because they feel it is safer and because they have a high index of concern about liability issues should the patient commit suicide. These are legitimate concerns, but many patients with suicidal ideation can be treated successfully on an outpatient basis, and the estimated level of risk is the key issue in making this decision. Level of risk is often determined by a careful weighing of empirically supported distal risk factors, proximal risk factors, and protective factors (Kleespies & Hill, 2011). Alternatively (or perhaps concurrently), the clinician might consider level of risk from the perspective of *static* (or unchanging) risk factors and *dynamic* (or modifiable) risk factors. Static risk factors are typically dispositional and historical factors such as gender, race/ethnicity, or a previous suicide attempt, whereas dynamic risk factors are typically clinical or situational factors such as hopelessness, an acute episode of depression, or a financial crisis. Depending on the level of the dynamic risk factors, the clinician may adjust the overall level of risk upward or downward.

Generally, outpatient management for patients determined to be at either mild or moderate risk has been found to be feasible and safe (Rudd et al., 2001; Sullivan & Bongar, 2009). Stanley and Brown (2012) recommended that the management of such patients include a Safety Planning Intervention (SPI). An SPI consists of a prioritized written list of coping strategies and sources of support, developed collaboratively by the clinician with the patient and for use by the patient preceding or during a state of heightened suicidality.

The SPI consists of six steps, the first of which involves helping the patient to identify and pay attention to the warning signs that occur when he or she begins to think about suicide. These warning signs, which may be thoughts, behaviors, or moods, are listed in the safety plan in the patient's own words. Second, the patient is asked to identify internal coping strategies that he or she might use to take his or her mind off of problems. These strategies might include going for a walk, exercising, or reading. Third, if the internal coping strategies are ineffective in reducing suicidal ideation or intent, the patient's safety plan should include a list of social contacts that might serve as a distraction. Such contacts might include going to coffee shops or places of religion. Patients should be advised to avoid environments where alcohol may be present or served. Fourth, the patient is asked to designate family members and/or friends whom he or she could talk with and inform that he or she is having thoughts of suicide. This step differs from the third step in that the patient is to explicitly tell the family member or friend that he or she is having such thoughts. Although it is not considered mandatory, the clinician could work collaboratively with the patient to see if he or she would feel comfortable actually sharing the safety plan with someone whom he or she trusts. Fifth, in the event that the previous coping strategies are ineffective, the patient should generate a list of clinicians or professional agencies that he or she could contact. This part of the plan should include contacts that can be reached during nonbusiness hours, such as the National Crisis Hotline (1-800-273-TALK [8255]). Because some patients may fear being hospitalized or rescued in a way that they do not want, potential obstacles to rescue efforts should be discussed when making the safety plan. Finally, the clinician should discuss with the patient what means he or she might use in a suicide attempt and then work collaboratively with the patient on eliminating or limiting access to lethal means such as firearms.

Whereas Stanley and Brown (2012) focused on the management of suicidal states by helping the patient to develop coping strategies, Rudd and Joiner (1998) suggested that the clinician who is working with a suicidal outpatient might wish to consider the following contingencies: (a) an increase in outpatient visits and/or in telephone contacts, (b) frequent assessment of suicide risk, (c) recurrent evaluation for hospitalization while the risk continues, (d) 24-hour availability or coverage, (e) reevaluation of the treatment plan as needed, (f) consideration of a medication evaluation or change in regimen, and (g) use of professional consultation as warranted. For patients at milder risk, recurrent evaluation and monitoring of suicide potential may suffice.

In regard to treatment, there is some accumulating evidence that cognitive–behavioral approaches have been successful in reducing suicidal ideation and the risk of suicide attempts (Rudd, Joiner, Trotter, Williams, & Cordero, 2009). These approaches tend to emphasize learning of problem-solving and adaptive-coping skills. Linehan (1993) advocated an approach oriented toward changing patterns of dichotomous thinking and learning skills to help regulate strong emotions. She has reported that, with such treatment, patients with borderline personality disorder who are suicidal can be treated as outpatients without a high frequency of hospitalization (Linehan, Armstrong, Suarez, Allmon, & Heard, 1991).

When Might a Decision to Hospitalize Be Necessary?

Emergency intervention is necessary when the level of suicide risk becomes severe. It often begins with an effort to resolve or reduce a crisis that has precipitated an increase in suicidal intent. At times, it is possible to achieve such a resolution and have the patient continue to pursue outpatient follow-up. As Comstock (1992) pointed out, however, hospitalization is indicated when it is not possible to establish or reinstate a treatment alliance, when crisis intervention techniques fail, and/or when the patient continues to have intent to commit suicide in the immediate future. Although there is no evidence that hospitalization ultimately prevents suicide, it does provide a relatively safer environment during a period of heightened suicide risk. Typically, a 1- or 2-hour encounter with a patient who maintains imminent suicidal intent is sufficient to convince clinicians to hospitalize the patient.

Because most suicidal patients seem to have ambivalence about taking such a final action as suicide, many who require hospitalization agree to a voluntary admission. When patients evaluated at imminent risk refuse to be hospitalized, however, the clinician must make a decision about involuntary commitment. This decision can be difficult because the estimation of suicide risk is not always reliable, and involuntary hospitalization involves overriding the individual's wishes while possibly creating barriers to effective treatment (i.e., creating heightened resistance to forming or maintaining a therapeutic alliance; Comstock, 1992). As Kleespies, Deleppo, Gallagher, and Niles (1999) pointed out, however, it nonetheless remains the clinician's responsibility to decide whether hospitalization is needed. In the final analysis, the decision to hospitalize involuntarily must be based on sound clinical judgment that considers the risk–benefit ratio and the estimated imminence and severity of the risk. In making such trying decisions, it may be helpful to keep in mind that once hospitalization has occurred, resistant patients often begin to perceive the caring nature of the clinician's actions and become ready to reestablish a treatment alliance.

Decisions in Managing the Acute Risk of Violence

If a clinician has made an informed clinical judgment that a patient or client is at risk of becoming violent to others, he or she must formulate a plan for managing the risk. The plan will, of course, depend on the level and immediacy of the risk and the capacity of the patient to exercise or gain self-control. As with suicide risk, the level of risk for violence should be estimated by a careful consideration of evidence-based (distal and proximal or static and dynamic) risk factors and protective factors (see Borum, 2009; Elbogen et al., 2010; McNiel, 2009). Distal or static risk factors might include dispositional and historical factors such as age, gender, and history of violence, whereas proximal or dynamic risk factors might include such clinical and situational variables as active alcohol abuse, anger, and homelessness.

What Are the Options for Managing the Risk of Violence?

Depending on the estimated level of risk, Monahan (1993) suggested three types of intervention for working with the potentially violent patient or client: (a) intensifying treatment, (b) hardening the target, and (c) incapacitating the patient or client.

With the patient or client who is estimated to be at mild to moderate risk and has some capacity to modulate or modify his or her behavior, it is possible to *intensify treatment* in the community as a way of managing risk. Thus, the clinician can increase the frequency of therapy sessions, have telephone safety checks with the patient, have the patient enter a more structured outpatient or partial hospitalization program, have the patient enter a substance abuse treatment program (if needed), develop a plan for 24-hour emergency coverage, and make frequent reassessments of the level of risk. The focus of therapy sessions can be on techniques or methods that might reduce the likelihood of violence—for example, increasing insight, teaching anger management techniques, increasing frustration tolerance, improving affect regulation, and so forth.

Of course, as VandeCreek and Knapp (2000) cautioned, it behooves the clinician to be aware of his or her state's statutes that may regulate what actions a treatment provider is to take in managing a patient's or client's risk of violence. Some jurisdictions may require that the intended victim be warned in addition to intensification of treatment.

Warning the intended victim(s) and/or alerting law enforcement has become known as *hardening the target.* In the case of the potential victim, it makes it possible for him or her to take protective measures. After the *Tarasoff* case in California, warning the intended victim became known to clinicians as the *duty to warn* (*Tarasoff v. Regents of University of California,* 1974). What is often not well understood by clinicians, however, is that the same California court reviewed the *Tarasoff* case 2 years later, vacated the duty to warn ruling, and revised their opinion to what has now become known as the *duty to protect* (*Tarasoff v. Regents of University of California,* 1976; Welfel, Werth, & Benjamin, 2009). In effect, the court's revised opinion was that therapists have a duty not simply to warn but also to protect the intended victim or victims of their clients or patients, and there can be a number of ways to do so. Warning the individual in question may be one way, but it is not the only way or, depending on the circumstances, necessarily the best way.

Borum (2009) noted that warning the intended victim can be frightening to the individual or engender retaliatory anger and should be reserved for those times when other interventions have been rejected by the patient or are not feasible. If a warning is given, Borum's advice is that the clinician be careful in reviewing the nature and seriousness of the threat and then work with the individual to find sources of assistance and develop protective measures.

The *incapacitation* of a patient or client means using measures that directly decrease the person's ability to act out in a violent manner. These measures can include involuntary hospitalization, sedating medication, and physical restraints or seclusion. These are obviously very intrusive interventions and should only be used in situations where the danger of serious harm is great and less restrictive means have failed or will not be effective. The use of these means is typically regulated by law and institutional or agency policy. Their use is sometimes necessary to avoid a worse alternative (i.e., serious harm to or death of an intended victim). They are not a solution to the longer term risk of violence, but they prevent immediate harm. They may also allow for a diagnostic evaluation and the initiation of treatment that may have longer lasting benefit.

Using such restrictive measures can be a difficult decision because they are intrusive and involve depriving an individual of personal freedom. Clinical experience also indicates, as with the suicidal patient, that the use of involuntary hospitalization or the use of restraints can damage the patient–clinician relationship. The patient may feel betrayed or become angry with the therapist. This damage, however, can often be repaired once the patient has become more emotionally stable. It may also be possible to lessen the risk of such damage if the patient has been informed early in the treatment relationship that there are limits to confidentiality and that, if the patient is considered to be at imminent risk of seriously harming himself or herself or others, the therapist is ethically and often legally obligated to break confidentiality and initiate actions to protect the patient or others who may be at risk from the patient.

What If Aggression Is Directed at the Clinician?

If a clinician works with patients who have the potential to lose control in his or her practice setting, the safety of the patient, the clinician, other patients, and colleagues are all of critical importance. In addition to a patient's aggressive verbal statements or threats, there are certain behavioral signs of potential loss of control or dangerousness that have been learned from clinical experience. These may include (a) psychomotor restlessness such as pacing, fidgeting, clenching fists, startle response, grinding teeth, or inability to sit down; (b) affective and facial changes that reflect hostility, fear, or paranoia; and (c) an increase in the tone and loudness of the patient's speech. The clinician should pay careful attention to such behaviors.

It may be helpful to develop an internalized algorithm for making decisions about how one might respond if levels of aggression or threat increase. An initial response might be to observe that the patient or client seems upset and ask if it is something that can be discussed. Putting an emphasis on the benefits of collaboration in dealing with the patient's issues can make the interaction seem less adversarial. At times, taking a break can also reduce tension.

If a patient or client is not responsive to verbal efforts to reduce tension or set limits, the next level of response will probably depend on the setting and the availability of assistance. Those who work in a counseling center or a private practice may wish to terminate the session and/or contact security officers. If the situation is serious enough, the clinician might complete a temporary involuntary commitment so that local police can take the patient to a more secure setting, such as an emergency room where he or she can be evaluated further. In such instances, the assistance of a colleague who can make the appropriate phone calls or stay with the patient while the clinician calls can be invaluable.

Those who work in more secure settings, such as an emergency room, a hospital, or an urgent care clinic, typically have more options for response. In these settings, medical staff can offer the patient tranquilizing medication (if appropriate) or the patient might agree to voluntary hospitalization. If the patient is losing control, there is typically a code team that can be called, and if worse comes to worst, the patient can be incapacitated as noted previously (see Kleespies & Richmond, 2009, for a more complete discussion of this topic).

If a patient or client has threatened a treatment provider, after the patient and the situation have been stabilized, the provider should examine his or her feelings toward the patient to determine if further work together is feasible. Threats, of course, can engender negative reactions such as fear and/or anger and make for tension in any future therapy relationship. After being threatened, the clinician may not feel comfortable in broaching particular topics or issues for fear of angering the patient again. If such a situation exists, the therapist should consider the possibility of responsibly transferring the patient to another treatment provider.

Decisions in Managing Incidents of Interpersonal Victimization

In most U.S. jurisdictions, mental health clinicians are mandated reporters if, in the course of evaluation or treatment, they suspect or have reason to believe that a patient or client is engaging in child abuse, elder abuse, or abuse of the disabled. The laws governing mandated reporting typically do not require anything further in terms of evidence. The protective services agency to which the clinician reports is obligated to conduct a more complete investigation.

Despite the mandated nature of this reporting, however, there is evidence that clinicians can have difficulty with these decisions. In a large survey of child abuse reporting behavior, Zellman and Fair (2002) noted that almost 40% of the respondents admitted that, at some point in their career, they had suspected child abuse or neglect but had decided not to report it. The most frequent reason given for not reporting was that the clinician felt that there was insufficient evidence that abuse or maltreatment had occurred. He or she exercised discretion about reporting or not. What distinguished these discretionary reporters from others in the study was their negative opinion about the professionalism and ability of the protective services staff, whom they often saw as overburdened with cases. Most of these respondents had experience in treating cases involving child maltreatment. They felt that reporting would risk termination of treatment and loss of the opportunity to provide the support and education that they felt could reduce the likelihood of further abuse.

There is evidence that in homes in which there is child abuse, there is an increased probability of partner abuse and vice versa. Using data from two National Family Violence Surveys, O'Leary, Slep, and O'Leary (2000) found that when child abuse was present, the conditional probability of partner abuse was 31%. Likewise, when partner abuse was present, the conditional probability of child abuse was coincidentally also 31%. It is noteworthy that arguments over child rearing have been found to be one of the most common precipitants of partner violence (O'Leary & Woodin, 2006).

Clinical work with couples or with a member of a couple in which there is the threat of intimate partner violence can be trying. At least one of the partners is very likely to have problems with anger and aggression as well as issues with power and control. If therapeutic efforts have failed and the violence or abuse is continuing or escalating, one of the partners may wish to separate in the hopes of bringing the violence or the threat of violence to an end. Unfortunately, it comes as no surprise that there can also be heightened risk in ending a violent relationship. As Riggs, Caulfield, and Fair (2009) pointed out, estranged wives or partners have been found to be at substantially higher risk of being killed by their partners than wives in an intact relationship or those who are divorced. Moreover, incidents in which a female partner was killed have been found to be approximately three times as likely as nonfatal assaults to be precipitated by the woman's leaving a relationship or attempting to do so.

Battered or abused partners frequently seek the counsel of their therapists during the tense times leading up to and during a separation or divorce. The therapist may be involved in helping the patient or client come to decisions about how and when to terminate the relationship. If there is a risk that the other partner may become violent, the first step is to identify the abuse victim's immediate needs. The clinician and the victim may need to work together to ensure that the victim has a safe place to stay (e.g., a safe house) and to identify any potentially dangerous situations that he or she might encounter in the community. They can then collaborate on formulating plans for how the victim might keep himself or herself safe if dangerous situations arise. Emergency phone contacts would, of course, be a part of such a plan. Because some victims can become suicidal or may wish to retaliate in a violent way against a perpetrator, it is also important for the clinician to inquire about such thoughts or plans and, if necessary, work to prevent harm to self or others.

Offering such practical assistance (i.e., so-called psychological first aid) can help to counter the feelings of helplessness and hopelessness that victims often experience. Assistance with contacting social service agencies that can offer financial aid, information about accessing legal services, or information about housing can help to relieve many worries and concerns. Any victim with physical injuries or possible physical injuries should be encouraged to seek medical attention.

CONCLUDING REMARKS

In this chapter, I have given an overview of the area of practice referred to as *behavioral emergencies.* I have also attempted to emphasize some of the difficult decisions that clinicians must make when faced with a suicidal or potentially violent patient or with a situation in which a patient is at risk of becoming a victim of serious violence. As noted earlier, working with such patients can be very stressful in and of itself, but the demands may be even greater if there are other patients in need or other issues competing for the clinician's attention. What a clinician learns about suicide risk or violence risk in the controlled setting of the classroom or the workshop is clearly helpful, but the ability to maintain performance under the stress of situations in which decisions can lead to life-and-death consequences is ultimately learned in the doing. In the chapter that follows, we examine models of decision making and how they might apply to the decision-making process during behavioral emergencies. The remainder of the book is focused on acquiring the skills for sound clinical decision making under the stress of dealing with behavioral emergencies.

2

Decision Making Under Stress: Theoretical and Empirical Bases

There are many theories and models of decision making in the literature. Research has supported the proposition that people adapt and change their decision-making strategies on the basis of the task with which they are confronted and because of time pressure. Payne, Bettman, and Johnson (1988), for example, showed that under increased time pressure, individuals will accelerate their information processing, filter what information they will process, and change the method that they use for decision making.

In this chapter, I briefly review several of the major models of decision making and then discuss the theoretical paradigm or paradigms that seem most consistent with decision making under the stress of a behavioral emergency—that is,

- when there is great concern about the patient's condition,
- when information about the individual is incomplete,

http://dx.doi.org/10.1037/14337-003
Decision Making in Behavioral Emergencies: Acquiring Skill in Evaluating and Managing High-Risk Patients, by P. M. Kleespies

- when there is uncertainty about what the best course of action may be,
- when the situation is emotionally charged,
- when there is time pressure, and
- when the stakes are high if there is a negative outcome.

DECISION-MAKING MODELS

There are at least three broad categories of theoretical models for decision making (Polic, 2009; Shaban, 2005): (a) *rational* and *normative* models, (b) *descriptive* models, and (c) *naturalistic decision-making* models.

Rational and Normative Models

Rational models of decision making focus on how decisions should be made in an ideal world. They assume a clearly defined problem in which, as Driskell and Johnston (1998) stated, "the decision maker undertakes a systematic, organized information search, considers all available alternatives, generates a large option set, compares options, and successively refines alternative courses of action to select an optimal outcome" (p. 205). In these models, the decision maker is to impartially analyze, compare, and contrast options and, presumably, be fully rational in his or her choice (Polic, 2009). Models such as these are often used in management for allocating financial resources or in the military for evaluating alternative system designs. They are likely to be the preferred model of the scientist who needs to try to be very deliberative and analytical in making decisions about research design or in drawing conclusions from data.

Normative models are rational procedures that are based on probabilities. Perhaps the best known of these models are the Bayesian inference model (or Bayes theorem for judgments) and subjective expected utility theory. In these models, there is an analysis of all possible choices and associated risks, and the risks are assigned weights. Each choice is assigned a probability and, factoring in the associated risks, the option with the highest utility for the decision maker can be determined. The effort is to quantify the probability of the events and determine which choice will be most useful for the individual to make given his or her objectives (Shaban, 2005).

In the past, deviations from a pattern of rational decision making were viewed as a breakdown in the decision-making process (Janis & Mann, 1977). Increasingly, however, it has been noted that there are several limitations and criticisms of these rational and normative models. First, it takes a relatively long time to structure the decision problem and arrive at a judgment. The models are best used for long-range planning, and they are not well suited to the fast-paced decision making that is sometimes needed in clinical emergencies and other scenarios such as on a military battlefield. Second, in dynamic and changing situations in which decisions must be made with incomplete knowledge, it is not possible to adequately fulfill the requirements of the model for a complete quantification of risks. Third, it has been amply demonstrated that, in practice, human decision making often does not occur according to the processes described in rational and normative models (Kahneman, Slovic, & Tversky, 1982). This latter point gave rise to interest in descriptive models or models that attempt to demonstrate how individuals actually do make judgments and decisions.

Descriptive Models

It was the research of psychologist and economist Herbert Simon (1957) who initially challenged the notion that people attempt to evaluate all available response choices as called for in rational models of decision making. He proposed the concept of *bounded rationality,* which suggests that, in decision making, people use a limited rationality in which they consider only as many alternatives as needed to find one that satisfies them. Simon's theoretical writings and empirical findings motivated psychologists like Daniel Kahneman and Amos Tversky to investigate and describe more closely the processes by which individuals actually arrive at decisions (Kahneman et al., 1982). The work of these authors has been called *descriptive* because they initially placed a greater emphasis on describing what actually occurred in the decision-making process rather than on offering an explanatory theory of decision making.

Tversky and Kahneman (1974) provided empirical support for the proposition that under conditions of uncertainty, people frequently rely on a limited number of heuristic principles (or strategies) that reduce the complex tasks of decision making to simpler judgmental operations. Thus, in numerous studies, they demonstrated that when making choices in which conditions were uncertain, naïve subjects (but also experienced researchers) tended to ignore probability issues such as the base rates of events or the sample size of groups and based their decisions on heuristics (or rules of thumb). These heuristics included representativeness (or similarity to a set of characteristics attributed to certain groups of people or things), availability (or the ease with which an option can be recalled), and adjustment to an anchor (i.e., adjustment to a particular starting point or value).

To give an example taken from Kahneman et al. (1982), if Steve is described as shy and withdrawn, always helpful, tidy, with little interest in people, but with a need for order and structure, and people are asked to assess the probability that Steve's occupation is that of an attorney, a physician, a salesman, a librarian, or an airline pilot, they typically state that the probability is that Steve is a librarian on the basis of his similarity to a stereotype of a librarian. One thing that they typically ignore is that the base rate of librarians who are male is low. This type of representativeness heuristic often serves the decision maker well, but it can also lead to serious biases and errors in judgment. In the model, a better understanding of heuristics, as well as an awareness of the biases to which they can lead, is seen as the means to improve decision making in situations of uncertainty.

Kahneman (2011), in his book *Thinking, Fast and Slow,* has now placed the heuristics model within a larger, two-system framework for thinking and decision making. In this framework, what he refers to as System 1 consists of thinking and perceiving that operates automatically and quickly with little or no effort. It is the system that includes the innate abilities by which we recognize objects and see causality, and think intuitively. Heuristics, as rules of thumb for decision making, are a function of this system. System 2, on the other hand, consists of thinking that involves effortful mental activity that includes critical thought and analysis. It runs in a "low effort mode" much of the time but is activated when events are encountered that require analytical and logical reasoning.

Other psychologists (e.g., S. Epstein, Pacini, Denes-Raj, & Heier, 1996) have also posited that we have two independent but interrelated modes of processing information: intuitive experiential and analytical rational. They have hypothesized that the two systems normally interact in a seamless and integrated manner but occasionally conflict. The dominance of one or the other may be determined by the demands of a particular situation, by the preference of the individual for relying on one way of thinking or the other, or by the degree of emotional involvement in the outcome.

Gore and Sadler-Smith (2011), while accepting that two separate systems underlie human thinking, cautioned that the thinking and decision-making process may be still more complex. They argued that System 1, or intuition, is not a unitary construct and may contain many subsystems. Thus they have theorized that there may be a *problem-solving* intuition, a *creative* intuition, a *social* intuition, and a *moral* intuition. Problem-solving intuition is described as a type of intuition that involves pattern matching or recognition of a situation or condition learned through repeated training and practice. It is triggered by structured problems such as whether to, or how best to, evacuate a burning building. Creative intuition, on the other hand, involves combining knowledge in novel ways. It may involve a conjecture that could lead to a scientific discovery or an artistic endeavor. Social intuition refers to the rapid and automatic evaluation of another person through the perception and not necessarily conscious processing of verbal and nonverbal cues. Finally, moral intuition refers to the automatic, rapid, and affect-based judgment that we often make in response to an ethical dilemma. It is the *gut feeling* type of reaction to a moral quandary that is subsequently rationalized or justified with post hoc reasoning.

Naturalistic Decision Making

Although descriptive models of decision making such as that of Kahneman and Tversky are more in keeping with the process of decision making in everyday life, they are based on studies done "in the laboratory," so to speak. As Zsambok (2009) pointed out in regard to rational models, descriptive models also fail to take into account the effects of the context that can accompany decision making in the real world, where, as mentioned at the beginning of this chapter, the decision maker may confront many different pressures. As a result, decision researchers and theorists started to question how experienced decision makers who worked in dynamic, uncertain, and fast-moving natural environments went about assessing their situation and making decisions. This direction of theory and research is more consistent with the decision-making process that occurs when evaluating and managing behavioral emergencies such as situations in which a patient or client appears to be at acute suicide risk and/or acute risk of violence.

Several naturalistic decision-making (NDM) models have been proposed: (a) the recognition-primed decision (RPD) model, (b) the recognition/metacognition (R/M) model, (c) a situation awareness (SA) model, and (d) the hypervigilant decision-making strategy. A brief review of each model follows.

Recognition-Primed Decision Model

Klein (2009) proposed the RPD model to explain how experienced decision makers can identify a situation and generate a course of action without needing to analyze multiple options. It has three functions: *simple match, diagnose the situation,* and *evaluate a course of action.* The simple match occurs when a decision maker identifies a situation as similar to situations that he or she has experienced in the past, and also recognizes a typical course of action. If the individual is confronted with a situation for which he or she has no match, the diagnostic function is activated. Two common diagnostic strategies are what Klein referred to as *feature matching* and *story building.* In feature matching, the decision maker identifies relevant features of the situation in an effort to place it into a known category, whereas in story building, he or she tries to mentally synthesize the relevant features into a novel causal explanation of the situation. In complex cases in which there is incomplete information and uncertainty, the evaluate a course of action function involves conducting a mental simulation to see if the course of action under consideration will encounter difficulties and, if so, whether they can be remedied or whether a new course of action may be needed.

The RPD model asserts that people can use their experience to understand a current situation and make a decision on a course of action without generating large option sets. Expertise and experience with the task or situation can allow one to find a plausible option as the first one considered.

It also asserts that time pressure need not have a negative effect on the performance of experienced decision makers because they use pattern matching, which can occur very quickly. This model is consistent with the notion of problem-solving intuition as described by Gore and Sadler-Smith (2011) and noted previously.

Klein (2009) cited various studies as empirical support for the RPD model. Thus, for example, Randel, Pugh, Reed, Schuler, and Wyman (1994) studied electronic warfare technicians while they were performing a simulated task. They found that 93% of the decisions involved non-comparative deliberations in keeping with the RPD model. Only two of 38 decisions were found to involve comparisons between options. In another study, Calderwood, Klein, and Crandall (1988) investigated the quality of chess moves by chess masters and Class B chess players under tournament conditions (2.6 minutes per move) and blitz conditions (6 seconds per move). Under the extreme pressure of blitz chess, they found that the rate of blunders increased for the Class B players (from 11% to 25%), but not for chess masters, whose blunder rate remained essentially unchanged (from 7% to 8%). The more experienced chess masters presumably had a greater range of, and/or more easily accessible, matches to the chess board situation.

Recognition/Metacognition Model

In the R/M model, when an individual who is experienced in his or her field is involved in a situation or event requiring a decision, there is an initial level of pattern recognition that activates schemas (or mental structures) related to past situations with similar elements (M. Cohen, Freeman, & Thompson, 2009). In the theoretical model, the schemas are under metacognitive level control. At the metacognitive level, there is a process of critiquing that identifies if there are problems with the recognitional schemas and the developing situation model.

In general, critiquing can uncover three types of problems with an assessment: *incompleteness, conflict,* or *unreliability.* An assessment is incomplete if there are key elements of the situation model or plan missing. There are conflicts if there are arguments that lead to contradictory conclusions. Finally, there is unreliability if an argument from evidence to conclusion is based on doubtful assumptions. The critiquing may lead to processes of correcting that include additional observation, additional information retrieval, and a reinterpretation of cues to bring about a more satisfactory situation model.

The R/M model attempts to show how critical thinking can be an effective part of situation assessment and decision making without using relatively inflexible rational and normative models. Proficient and experienced decision makers work with evolving situation models or scenarios while continuing to investigate gaps and conflicts that may require modifications to the model or scenario. In a small study with active duty army officers, the authors (M. Cohen et al., 2009) found evidence that these critiquing or critical-thinking skills can be enhanced by training. Participants were given a pretest and a posttest with a military battle scenario. For some participants there was training in R/M methods between the tests, and for others there was a discussion of traditional situation assessment techniques. The R/M trained participants considered significantly more factors in their evaluations of the battle situation than the control group. Moreover, they placed greater value on the factors that more experienced senior officers also valued.

A Situation Awareness Model

As Endsley (2009) pointed out, many human errors that are said to be due to poor decision making are better attributed to the SA portion of the decision-making process and not to the choice of action. Individuals may make the correct decision given their perception of the situation, but their perception may be where the flaw is. In the field of naturalistic decision making, therefore, SA has received considerable attention. Endsley's model of SA involves three levels: (1) perceiving critical factors in the environment, (2) understanding what those factors mean, and (3) understanding what is likely to happen with a dynamic or changing situation in the near future.

At Level 1, the decision maker needs to perceive the relevant elements, attributes, and dynamics of the environment or situation. An automobile driver needs to be aware of the road, of the position of other vehicles in the vicinity, and of the movements of those vehicles in relation to his or her own. A mental health clinician working with a patient in crisis needs to be aware of the patient's emotional presentation (e.g., sad, tearful, anxious) and of his or her behavior (e.g., restless, tense, agitated). Level 2 goes beyond simple perception to understanding the significance of the elements or attributes of the situation. A holistic picture is formed in which the various components of the field are integrated. At Level 3, the decision maker is able to project the likely future actions of the people or objects in the situation. He or she achieves this through knowledge of the status and dynamics of the elements in the environment and a comprehension of the overall meaning of the situation. The experienced decision maker is typically capable of achieving Levels 2 and 3 of this model, but the novice decision maker may fall short at these higher levels.

In this model, experienced decision makers use long-term memory stores of schemata or mental models (representations of similar situations or events) to aid in understanding the current situation and coming to a decision. In effect, they look for a best fit between the characteristics of the situation and the characteristics of known categories of events or prototypes. If scripts have been developed for prototypical situations, the load is reduced in terms of the mental operations needed to generate alternative courses of action. Of course, the decision maker needs to guard against becoming too automatic in responding because he or she may become susceptible to missing novel aspects of the situation.

The Hypervigilant Decision-Making Strategy

In proposing a naturalistic decision-making strategy, Klein (1996) argued (as did the other theorists noted previously) that, in many task settings, decisions must be made under time pressure with ambiguous and conflicting information. Under such conditions, decision makers do not have the luxury of conducting a painstaking search for information. Nor do they have the time to weigh all alternatives and eliminate each until they arrive at a solution (as they would with a *vigilant* [rational-analytic] decision-making strategy). Rather, they must conduct a less-than-exhaustive information search, do an accelerated evaluation of the data, consider a limited number of alternatives, and come to rapid closure on a decision. Johnston, Driskell, and Salas (1997) referred to this type of decision-making process as a *hypervigilant* decision-making strategy, and in contrast to earlier uses of this term (see, e.g., Janis & Mann, 1977), they contended that it does not represent a defect in the decision-making process but rather an adaptive and effective response given the time-limited nature of the task.

Johnston et al. (1997) tested whether, with a naturalistic task, such a hypervigilant strategy might lead to more effective decision making than the use of a vigilant strategy. They had 90 U.S. Navy enlisted personnel from a technical training school perform a computer-based simulation of a real-world navy task. The participants were initially trained in either a vigilant or hypervigilant decision-making strategy. They then had to monitor a radar screen with their own ship at the center and with numerous other unidentified contacts or potential threats that popped up on the screen. The task was to access three information fields or menus to classify the type of craft that had appeared on the screen, whether it was civilian or military, and whether its intentions were hostile or peaceful. Participants were told to work as quickly and as accurately as they could to identify and engage or clear each contact before it reached their ship. The researchers also manipulated stress levels (normal vs. high stress) with auditory distractions, task load, and time pressure.

The findings from this study indicated that those who used a hypervigilant decision-making strategy made a significantly greater number of accurate target identifications. Performance was degraded under high stress with both the vigilant and hypervigilant strategies, but those using the vigilant strategy still performed significantly worse under high-stress task conditions. The investigators concluded that the ideal pattern of decision making is likely to be dependent on the nature of the task demands, and that under some conditions (e.g., time pressure, incomplete information), a hypervigilant approach (as described previously) can be the more effective strategy.

NATURALISTIC DECISION MAKING AND BEHAVIORAL EMERGENCIES

Several of the NDM models for expert decision makers clearly have common ground. The RPD model, the R/M model, and the SA model all see experience and long-term memory as crucial to the recognition (in the present) of similar patterns or representations of situations or events from the past. In most cases, this type of recognition is seen as enabling the individual to make relatively quick decisions about a course of action when there is time pressure to do so. The R/M model tends to stress the role of critiquing to a greater extent than either the RPD model or the SA model, whereas the SA model stresses situation awareness to a greater extent than the other two. The hypervigilant decision-making strategy is one that seems to describe how, in naturalistic task settings with time pressure, it is necessary to rapidly evaluate the limited information and data that can be gathered. It does not, however, invoke experience, long-term memory storage, and pattern recognition as explanatory concepts in the development of decision-making expertise.

Kahneman (2011), with his two-system model of thinking and judgment, seems to be in essential agreement with the major concepts found in the RPD, R/M, and SA models. In regard to his concept of System 1 (the system of intuitive thinking), he cited Herbert Simon as follows: "The situation has provided a cue: this cue has given the expert access to information stored in memory, and the information provides the answer. Intuition is nothing more and nothing less than recognition" (p. 237). Kahneman (2011) also noted what he found to be the two conditions necessary to acquire skill as an expert decision maker: (a) an environment that is sufficiently regular to be predictable and (b) an opportunity to learn these regularities through prolonged practice.

I contend that the NDM models of decision making and the conditions in the previous paragraph (noted by Kahneman) are crucial for understanding what must be learned to acquire the skills necessary to become competent in the evaluation and management of behavioral emergencies. When a clinician works with patients who may be at imminent risk of suicide or violence, a life or lives can be in the balance, and the time for evaluating and managing the situation can be very limited. The clinician needs to have good situational awareness (i.e., he or she needs to be aware of the patient's demeanor and behavior as well as the resources he or she may have to cope with the patient's behavior should problems escalate). He or she needs to rapidly gather and analyze the information that can be obtained in a limited period of time. Because time is limited, the focus must be on gathering information that is essential to the decision at hand. He or she needs to be able to call on past experiences (or be *recognition primed*) in evaluating the situation and deciding if something preventive needs to be done. The clinician also needs to be able to critique and detect gaps or inconsistencies in the recognition schema that seems to be a good fit. Part of the process of critiquing is checking on biases to which he or she might be vulnerable. In Kahneman's terms, the clinician needs to learn to recognize situations in which mistakes are likely and try to avoid them, particularly when the stakes are high.

Situation Awareness in Behavioral Emergencies

In working with patients or clients who present as potential emergency cases, the clinician needs to remain aware of the mental and emotional state of the patient, of his or her own reactions to the patient, and of the characteristics of the setting in which they are meeting.

In terms of the patient's condition, I noted in Chapter 1 of this volume that when a patient or client is in a crisis or emergency state, the clinician needs to pay particular attention to the patient's behavior for signs of risk of self-harm or risk of harm to others. The clinician should make mental notes of behaviors such as agitation, restlessness, and pacing, as well as hostile or paranoid comments, as potential signs of decreased self-control.

Difficult or uncooperative patients can evoke a range of feelings in the clinician, including anger, anxiety, discouragement, and avoidance. It can be difficult to acknowledge such feelings, but if they are not dealt with adequately, clinical judgment and decision making can be affected (Pope & Tabachnick, 1993). Patients who are manic or have narcissistic features, for example, are often adept at finding the sensitivities of the clinician and devaluing him or her. One way of managing the impact of such negative remarks is to observe your own reactions and use them as a resource for understanding the patient. Thus, if you feel the patient is devaluing you, it is likely that he or she is attempting to bolster self-esteem or compensate for a perceived narcissistic injury.

Patients who are at serious risk of self-injury or suicidal behavior may need to be monitored or observed in a safe environment, one that is relatively free of objects and means by which they can harm themselves. If there is concern that a patient or client who might be at high risk for suicide will resist going to a safer setting such as an emergency room, the clinician should consider how he or she might obtain assistance in dealing with the situation. When working with patients who have problems with anger management and who could potentially lose control, it may be wise to review the safety of your office or work setting. In other words, check for items that could be used as weapons, such as heavy paperweights, scissors, and letter openers, and have them out of sight. Think about the seating arrangement in your office and whether it can be arranged so that you have access to an exit if necessary. Think about ways that you might communicate a need for help to others (e.g., panic button, emergency code or signal) should the need arise. If you are seeing someone at high risk for violence, let colleagues know so that they can be alert to signs of trouble.

A Hypervigilant Strategy in Behavioral Emergencies

As with the SA model, the hypervigilant strategy with behavioral emergencies emphasizes how the clinician must be alert to the patient's behavior and to his or her own reactions for cues to the patient's current condition. Questioning of the patient and review of the medical record must focus on obtaining essential psychodiagnostic information as it relates to risk to self and/or others. The model does not appear to place great emphasis on experience and memory that might lead to relatively quick pattern recognition. Rather, it relies on gathering information during the immediate encounter with the patient. The attention of the clinician is narrowed but highly focused. Given the emergency circumstances, this narrowing of attention is considered adaptive in the interest of efficient decision making. It is not viewed as a failure to follow a more analytic or rational model.

Recognition Priming for Behavioral Emergencies

As noted earlier, developing a store of memories or schemata of behavioral emergencies comes with multiple experiences in dealing with patients or clients who are at risk of suicide or violence. With experience and available schemata, the clinician can approach most emergency situations with thoughts about what may need to be done and what a reasonable plan may be. The completely novel and surprising event will be rare.

The skilled but less experienced clinician or clinician-in-training may find behavioral emergencies more intimidating because of lack of experience. It may be this lack of experiential knowledge that accounts for findings in the literature that the risk of patient violence directed at the mental health clinician is greater for those who are newer and less experienced in the field. Thus, in a national survey, Jayaratne, Croxton, and Mattison (2004) reported that young and male social workers were at greater risk of patient assault, and J. Guy, Brown, and Poelstra (1990), in another national survey, found that 46% of all attacks on psychologists involved graduate students or trainees and another 33% occurred in the first 5 years after completing the doctoral degree. These data suggested that nearly 80% of patient assaults on psychologists occurred in the first 8 to 10 years in the field. There are several hypotheses to explain these findings. One is that less experienced clinicians may be less attuned or less alert to cues of potential violence. Another is that they may be less aware of when it might be good to set limits and may consequently allow aggressive behavior to escalate. In any event, the findings suggest that clinicians or therapists in training need close supervision and guidance in learning to manage behavioral emergencies, a topic that we revisit in more detail later in this book.

Critiquing Recognition-Primed Schemata in Behavioral Emergencies

Making decisions on the basis of the recognition of cues to prior events or experiences is often efficient and serves the clinician well. While the NDM models describe how decisions are typically made in fast-moving and dynamic situations, this type of decision making is not without risk. As noted earlier, Kahneman and Tversky have highlighted how, as decision makers, we are vulnerable to many biases through the heuristic shortcuts that we often use. Even (or perhaps particularly) in fast-paced and quickly changing scenarios, it is important to critique and check one's decision-making process if possible.

One of the more obvious heuristics that can lead to biased decision making is what Kahneman and his colleagues have referred to as the *affect heuristic*. With the affect heuristic, judgments and decision making are guided primarily by feelings of liking or disliking, and little deliberation and reasoning are used. Earlier, I cited other heuristics, such as the availability heuristic in which, for example, judgments of the frequency with which an event occurs are based on the ease with which one can recall similar instances from past experience. There are also apparently unconscious ethnic/racial and gender biases that could be implicated in African Americans and women receiving unequal access to health care (Schulman et al., 1999; Smedley, Stith, & Nelson, 2003; Wilson, 2007). It is because of such biases that Kahneman (2011) presented the following principle: "The confidence that people place in their intuitions is not a reliable guide to their validity. In other words, do not trust anyone— including yourself—to tell you how much you should trust their judgment" (pp. 239–240).

It is for these very reasons that it is important to critique decisions in situations such as behavioral emergencies when time is limited and the stakes are high. Kahneman's (2011) guidance is that we can regard our judgment to be skilled or expert in nature when the two conditions noted earlier apply—that is, the environment in which we are working is sufficiently regular to be predictable and the decision maker has had the opportunity to learn these regularities through prolonged practice. In this regard, Kleespies (2009) argued that psychologists and other mental health providers (who, as noted in Chapter 1 of this volume, almost all encounter patients at risk of suicide and/or violence) need training in a setting where such patients are seen with some regularity.

With emergency cases, the clinician himself or herself needs to think through and critique the proposed decision and plan of action. If he or she works as part of a clinical team, the opinions of other team members can provoke further thought about how to proceed. With complex or difficult cases, it can be very useful to seek the consultation of a peer or of someone more expert. In so doing, the clinician either gets confirmation or a different perspective and opinion that may bring to light other aspects of the case.

CONCLUDING REMARKS

There is a great deal to be learned from the NDM models in regard to how best to approach the decision-making process when dealing with behavioral emergencies. In an acute clinical situation involving questions of risk to self or others, the task demands typically do not permit the painstaking approach of the rational and normative models of decision making. In fact, as we have seen, efforts to apply such models in time-limited, dynamic, and rapidly shifting circumstances can lead to poorer performance (Johnston et al., 1997). In some sense, we can take something from each of the NDM models that we have discussed in this chapter and find that it applies well to the evaluation and management of behavioral emergencies.

In evaluating and managing high-risk patients or clients, the mental health clinician clearly needs to be very situation aware in terms of the patient's mental and emotional state, the patient's behavior, the presence or absence of colleagues who might assist if necessary, and issues related to office safety. Given the pressure of time and sometimes the pressure from the acuity of the patient's condition, he or she must be hypervigilant (so to speak) in primarily searching for psycho-diagnostic information that is essential for quickly making a determination of the patient's level of risk. With increasing experience, the clinician becomes recognition primed to observe certain combinations or constellations of symptoms and behaviors that may indicate higher risk. He or she may have developed a personal algorithm for how to respond to different types and levels of risk. Finally, the clinician needs to critique his or her formulation of the patient's condition while being aware of the value and risk of certain heuristics and biases that he or she might use and while being alert to aspects of the case that may not be a good fit and, consequently, might trigger a modified or different formulation.

3

Training to Reduce Stress in Dealing With Behavioral Emergencies

In 1988, the U.S. guided missile cruiser *Vincennes* had been in a battle in the Persian Gulf against small armed boats manned by the Iranian Revolutionary Guard. Intelligence reports had informed U.S. naval forces in the area that the Iranians might be planning an incident to embarrass the United States. An Iranian plane in the commercial airline corridor was coming directly at the *Vincennes,* and although it was climbing as a commercial plane would after takeoff, two console operators in the command center of the *Vincennes* reported that it was descending (as a fighter jet might when zeroing in on a target). There was limited time to make a decision. Repeated radio warnings from the *Vincennes* to the aircraft apparently were ignored. The crew, thinking that they had detected an aircraft with hostile intent, then shot down the airliner, killing the 290 people on board (Collyer & Malecki, 1998). There was a congressional hearing into the incident, and as Hammond (2000) pointed out, research interest in

http://dx.doi.org/10.1037/14337-004

Decision Making in Behavioral Emergencies: Acquiring Skill in Evaluating and Managing High-Risk Patients, by P. M. Kleespies

the potential influence of stress on judgment or decision making seemed to greatly increase after that time.

Although there has been debate about the causes of the *Vincennes* tragedy—Klein (1999), for example, argued that system weaknesses were more to blame than human error—the conclusions of the official report stated that stress and unconscious distortion may have played a major part in the incident. The report suggested that there was an expectancy bias, which in this case meant that there was a belief among crew members that an attack was underway. On the basis of that belief, it was suggested that facts were either misinterpreted or there was selective attention to facts that supported the belief. One of the recommendations of the official report was that there was a need for further research into the effects of stress on decision making, particularly under navy combat conditions. The incident and the official report, however, spurred broader (not simply military) interest in the topic.

In this chapter, we discuss what is meant by *stress*, what stresses may exist with behavioral emergencies, what we know about the potential effect of stress on decision making, and how mental health clinicians can be trained to cope with these stresses better, particularly in the case of dealing with behavioral emergencies.

THE MEANING OF STRESS

As Woolfolk, Lehrer, and Allen (2007) noted, the concept of stress has a long history that includes many variations in meaning. For example, in the past century, we have moved from the physiologist Walter Cannon's concept of stress as a disturbance in homeostasis induced by external threats and resulting in the fight-or-flight response to Hans Selye's stages of the stress response (i.e., the alarm stage, the adaptive-resistance stage, and the exhaustion stage) to the more contemporary cognitive-appraisal model of stress offered by Richard Lazarus (1994). In the model proposed by Lazarus, stress is not solely induced by events in the environment, nor is it solely a response in the individual. Rather, stress involves an interaction between the person or group and the environment in which the demands of the situation are appraised as taxing or exceeding the coping resources available to deal with those demands. As a result, the individual feels distressed and under pressure to find a way to cope, meet the demands, and relieve the distress.

The model proposed by Lazarus introduced cognitive or psychological factors into the conceptualization of stress. In his model, it is the individual's perception and assessment of his or her ability to manage the situation that can lead to stress, particularly if the person is uncertain or doubts that he or she has the resources to cope with or control the unfolding events. The awareness of stress can protect the individual if it prompts an effective response to a problematic or threatening situation. It can also be harmful if the person's response is inadequate, the stress persists, and the individual feels overwhelmed and helpless. This cognitive-appraisal model of stress is the one that will be used in this volume.

THE STRESS OF DEALING WITH BEHAVIORAL EMERGENCIES

The incidence of patient suicide has been referred to as "an important occupational hazard for psychotherapists" (Chemtob, Bauer, Hamada, Pelowski, & Muraoka, 1989, p. 294). In a national survey of psychologists (Pope & Tabachnick, 1993), 97% of the respondents reported being afraid of losing a patient to suicide. As noted in Chapter 1 of this volume, having a patient or client who is, or becomes, suicidal is practically a universal experience for mental health clinicians. Because our knowledge of who will commit suicide is clearly incomplete, however, there can be anxiety and concern about decisions to give privileges or increased freedom to suicidal inpatients who appear to be improving or to treat suicidal patients at mild to moderate risk on an outpatient basis.

In the survey by Kleespies, Penk, and Forsyth (1993), the participants completed the Impact of Event Scale (IES; Horowitz, Wilner, & Alvarez, 1979), with instructions to respond to items on the IES in regard to how they felt immediately after a particular patient of theirs had either reported suicidal ideation, made a suicide attempt, or committed suicide. The results indicated that there was a significant graduated increase in impact (i.e., an increase in intrusive thoughts about the event and/or efforts to avoid such thoughts) as a function of the increasing severity of patient suicidal behavior (i.e., from suicidal ideation to suicide attempt to suicide completion). Many of the participants gave anecdotal accounts of feeling very stressed not only when a patient had committed suicide but also when a patient had made a serious suicide attempt or had intense suicidal ideation and seemed to be at risk of making a suicide attempt.

Rodolfa, Kraft, and Reilley (1988) surveyed staff and psychology trainees at 12 American Psychological Association (APA)–approved counseling centers and at 14 VA Medical Centers. Participants were asked to rate 19 client behaviors and 24 therapist experiences on a scale of 1 (*not stressful*) to 9 (*extremely stressful*). The two client behaviors that were ranked most stressful by all groups (i.e., by psychology staff, psychology interns, and psychology practicum students) were physical attack on a therapist and a suicide attempt by a client. These two types of incidents were followed (in rank order of stress-inducing events) by client suicidal statements, a client reporting a current crime, and a client expressing anger toward the therapist. In a study by Whitman, Armao, and Dent (1976), it was reported that during a 1-year period of practice, 81% of their sample of psychologists perceived a patient of theirs as a threat to others. In the survey by Pope and Tabachnick (1993), it was also found that 89% of a national sample of psychologists reported experiencing episodes in which they were afraid that a patient might attack a third party. Moreover, as mentioned previously, patient threats to clinicians themselves, or actual patient assaultive behavior toward the clinician, can induce significant stress.

There is also evidence in the literature indicating that clinicians who treat victims of interpersonal violence (e.g., victims of assault, rape, or torture) over a prolonged period of time may suffer negative effects that have been termed *vicarious trauma* and *secondary traumatic stress*. McCann and Pearlman (1990) defined vicarious trauma as the effect that a patient's graphic and painful description of victimization can have on the therapist's beliefs and assumptions about self and others. The concept of secondary traumatic stress, on the other hand, focuses more on the emotional or social disturbances that trauma clinicians may suffer (Figley, 1995; Jenkins & Baird, 2002). These disturbances can include reexperiencing the patient's or client's trauma event or avoidance or numbing in response to reminders of the patient's trauma.

Of course, stress may also be experienced by mental health clinicians who, as noted in Chapter 1, must be involved in reporting child abuse, elder abuse, or abuse of the disabled, or who work with a battered spouse who wishes to leave a violent partner (or who may wish to return to a violent partner). If a child or elder needs to be separated from an abusive family situation, emotions can run very high. Likewise, if a partner in a relationship in which there has been violence wishes to leave, intimidation, stalking, and further violence can be serious risks that can induce tension in all concerned. These situations need to be managed with great care.

EFFECTS OF STRESS ON DECISION MAKING

Theorists such as Hammond (2000) have questioned whether stress actually has a negative effect on decision making. In fact, as discussed in Chapter 2 of this volume, it has been found that people adapt and change their decision-making strategies to simpler operations depending on the intensity of task and time demands, and these more abbreviated operations (e.g., the naturalistic decision-making strategies) have been found to be more effective under conditions of task and time pressure than lengthier, more complex rational strategies—at least with decision makers who are expert in their field. It therefore seems feasible that the performance of some people, particularly those who are experts, might not be degraded and, in fact, might improve under stressful conditions. The question remains, however, whether stress has a deleterious effect on the decision making of those who are not so expert or who are novices at a particular task or in a particular field in which there can be uncertain knowledge, a variety of pressures, and high stakes in terms of the outcome.

The study of chess players mentioned earlier in this volume (Calderwood, Klein, & Crandall, 1988) has a bearing on this question. As noted, the "blunder" rate of the less expert players increased significantly under blitz chess conditions (i.e., 6 seconds per move) as opposed to tournament conditions (2.6 minutes per move), but the blunder rate of the more expert chess masters remained low and unchanged under both tournament and blitz conditions. There have been at least two other laboratory studies that have examined the effects of anticipatory stress on decision making (Preston, Buchanan, Stansfield, & Bechara, 2007; Starcke, Wolf, Markowitsch, & Brand, 2008). In both studies, a gambling task was presented to naïve subjects and anticipatory stress was induced by informing the experimental group that following the gambling task, they would need to deliver a public speech (either about their physical appearance in one study or about their cognitive abilities in the other). The control groups filled the induction time by either thinking of their next vacation or informally talking with the examiner. Both studies used the same standardized questionnaires about anxiety and affect to measure stress before and after the induction phase. Both studies also used a physiological measure of stress—that is, a measure of heart rate in the study by Preston et al. (2007) and an endocrine measure of salivary cortisol (which has been found to rise during psychosocial stress) in the study by Starcke et al. (2008). In the study by Preston et al., the experimental group learned the contingencies of the choices in the gambling task significantly more slowly, whereas the results of the Starcke et al. study clearly indicated that the stressed participants as a group scored significantly lower on the gambling task than the comparison group, and performance on the task was negatively correlated with an increase in cortisol. Starcke et al. concluded that stress can lead to disadvantageous decision making.

The previously cited laboratory study by Johnston et al. (1997) also seems pertinent to this issue. In that study, U.S. Navy personnel had to identify (on a radar screen) simulated threats and other unidentified contacts with their ship. The investigators trained subjects in either vigilant or hypervigilant decision-making strategies and manipulated stress levels (normal vs. high stress) by using auditory distractions, task load, and time pressure. Although those trained with a hypervigilant strategy did better under high-stress conditions, it was nonetheless found that performance was degraded under high stress with both vigilant and hypervigilant decision strategies.

In yet another simulation study, LeBlanc, MacDonald, McArthur, King, and Lepine (2005) had flight paramedics from two levels of certification participate in either a low-stress or high-stress study condition. In the high-stress condition, the participants were in a simulated ambulance with an adult-sized mannequin on a stretcher. The mannequin was programmed to replicate many human physiologic functions, such as heart rate, pulse in limbs, breath sounds, and so on. The paramedics had to diagnose and manage respiratory failure, including doing a tracheal intubation. They then completed an anxiety inventory and were required to complete a set of drug dosage problems. Those in the low-stress condition completed a study questionnaire and then completed the anxiety inventory and the set of drug dosage problems. Those in the high-stress condition reported a significantly higher level of anxiety and did significantly worse on solving the drug dosage problems. The investigators concluded that when paramedics had to calculate drug dosages after experiencing a highly stressful situation, their performance was impaired.

Further, several studies have examined issues pertinent to decision making under stressful and real-life conditions. In a case control study, Gawande, Studdert, Orav, Brennan, and Zinner (2003) investigated the occurrence of an adverse medical event—that is, when a foreign body such as a gauze swab or an instrument is accidentally left in the body of a patient following surgery. Although overall such events are rare, the investigators found that the probability of such an event was 8 times higher when the operation was performed under emergency conditions and 3 times higher when the operation involved an unexpected change in procedure. They attributed these increased risks to the abandonment of routine procedures and to the time pressure that exists during an emergency operation.

In a related study, Koh, Park, Wickens, Ong, and Chia (2011) examined the experience-related differences in attention management between novice and experienced surgical scrub nurses who are responsible for keeping track of and counting the swabs and instruments used during surgical procedures. These scrub nurses must also perform multiple other tasks that impose heavy demands on their cognitive resources. Using a mobile eye-tracking system, the investigators found that experienced nurses gave significantly more visual attention to the incision area during the procedure, whereas novice nurses were more likely to switch their attention to other areas of interest. The findings support the notion that novices (as opposed to experts) are more vulnerable to distraction and loss of focus under high-demand conditions.

As noted in the model proposed by Lazarus (1994), stress is induced by an interaction between the demands of the situation and the appraisal of the individual. An example of this type of interaction is seen in a study by Gaba, Howard, and Jump (1994) that examined the effects of production pressure on anesthesiologists. These investigators conducted an anonymous survey of members of the American Society of Anesthesiologists residing in California. They defined *production pressure* as "overt and covert pressures and incentives on personnel to place production, not safety, as their primary priority" (p. 488).

Survey respondents reported that they had felt pressures within themselves to work agreeably with surgeons, avoid delaying surgical cases, and avoid litigation. They further reported overt pressure from surgeons and hospital administrators to proceed with cases instead of canceling them and to hasten anesthetic procedures. Some of the results of this survey indicated that nearly half (49%) of the respondents had observed an anesthesiologist pressured to administer anesthesia in what they considered an unsafe fashion. Thirty-one percent had seen patients undergoing surgery with significant contraindications for either the surgery or the anesthesia. Thirty-four percent had observed a colleague perform anesthesia on a patient for whom anesthesia had just been refused or canceled by another anesthesiologist for safety reasons. Gaba et al. (1994) concluded that production pressure from internal and external sources was perceived by survey participants as having resulted, at least in some cases, in decisions to proceed with anesthesia under unsafe conditions.

TRAINING TO DEAL WITH STRESS

As noted earlier, evaluating and managing patients or clients who may be acutely suicidal, possibly close to becoming violent, or at great risk of becoming a victim of violence can be stressful, and as we have seen, stress can negatively affect decision making in high-demand situations. Unfortunately, as reported in Chapter 1, the mental health disciplines have generally not made training in this area of practice a routine and integrated part of their educational and training process (see, e.g., Schmitz et al., 2012), and they have clearly not made consistent efforts to assist clinicians in dealing with the stress that can accompany work with high-risk patients or clients (Kleespies & Ponce, 2009).

Although it might seem obvious, it is nonetheless reasonable to ask if training and/or experience with the evaluation of behavioral emergencies actually makes a difference in the management of patients. There has been very little research on this topic, but a recent study by Teo, Holly, Leary, and McNiel (2012) has provided some relevant information. As part of a larger study, these investigators examined whether unstructured violence risk assessments completed by experienced attending psychiatrists were more accurate than those completed by psychiatric residents. Using a retrospective case-control design, the research team selected 151 patients from four locked psychiatric units of a county hospital who had physically assaulted staff during the years 2003 through 2008. They also selected an equal number of nonviolent patients matched for psychiatric inpatient unit and month of admission. On admission to these units, physicians rated each patient on a 4-point assault precaution checklist that ranged from 0 (*no clinical indication for violence precautions*) to 3 (*strong intent is present or unable to control impulses*). It was found that the clinical assessments by attending psychiatrists had a moderate degree of predictive validity, whereas those completed by residents were no better than chance. The violence risk assessments by the attending psychiatrists were significantly more accurate than those by residents. The investigators concluded that less training and experience is associated with less accurate violence risk assessment.

In recent years, there have been several efforts to provide models or programs for training in the behavioral emergencies or in a particular type of behavioral emergency. The aforementioned book by Kleespies (2009) and an earlier book (Kleespies, 1998b) were organized to provide a curriculum for teaching about mental health emergencies and related topics. McNiel and his colleagues in two separate publications (McNiel, Chamberlain, et al., 2008; McNiel, Fordwood, et al., 2008) reported on a study in which they provided a 5-hour workshop on evidence-based assessment and management of risk of violence and risk of suicide to a group of psychiatry residents and psychology interns. A comparison group attended a 3-hour workshop on the application of evidence-based medicine to psychiatry that was not focused on risk assessment for violence or suicide. The investigators found that, after the training, the study group participants were able to identify in a more systematic way the evidence-based variables that pertain to violence risk and suicide risk. They were also able to be more explicit about the significance of risk and protective factors when they developed plans for intervention to reduce risk. In relation to the comparison group, the training group's improvements were described as substantial. Further, the risk assessment training was associated with increased confidence in risk assessment skill.

Focusing more exclusively on training in suicide risk assessment, Oordt, Jobes, Fonseca, and Schmidt (2009) also demonstrated that training in a workshop format with an empirically based assessment and treatment approach to suicidal patients could significantly impact the professional practices and confidence of U.S. Air Force mental health professionals when dealing with suicidal patients. Further, those who have been concerned with training in the evaluation and management of suicidal patients have developed what they consider to be core competencies needed to become a clinician capable of working with individuals at risk for suicide (Rudd, Cukrowicz, & Bryan, 2008; Suicide Prevention Resource Center, 2006; see Table 3.1 for a listing of these core competencies). In addition, there have been at least two workshop-type programs that have been developed for teaching content that is consistent with these core competencies. One is a 6-hour program titled *Assessing and Managing Suicide Risk: Core Competencies for Mental Health Professionals* (AMSR; Suicide Prevention Resource Center, 2011), and the other is a 16-hour program called *Recognizing and Responding to Suicide Risk* (RRSR; American Association of Suicidology, 2011).

An outcome study of the RRSR (Jacobson, Osteen, Jones, & Berman, 2012) was recently published. In this study, 452 participants in RRSR training workshops were assessed at three points (pretest, posttest, and 4-month follow-up). The assessments included a variety of measures related to attitudes toward suicide prevention, confidence to work with clients at risk for suicide, and change in clinical practice behaviors. Only those who provided complete data for the three assessments were included in the analyses. The results suggested that training in this workshop format can improve clinicians' attitudes toward working with suicidal clients, confidence about

Table 3.1

Core Competencies for the Assessment and Management of Individuals at Risk for Suicide

Section	Competencies
A. Working with individuals at risk for suicide: Attitudes and approach	1. Manage one's own reactions to suicide.
	2. Reconcile the difference (and potential conflict) between the clinician's goal to prevent suicide and the client's goal to eliminate psychological pain via suicidal behavior.
	3. Maintain a collaborative, nonadversarial stance.
	4. Make a realistic assessment of one's ability and time to assess and care for a suicidal client as well as for what role the clinician is best suited.
B. Understanding suicide	5. Define basic terms related to suicidality.
	6. Be familiar with suicide-related statistics.
	7. Describe the phenomenology of suicide.
	8. Demonstrate understanding of risk and protective factors.
C. Collecting accurate assessment information	9. Integrate a risk assessment for suicidality early on in a clinical interview, regardless of the setting in which the interview occurs, and continue to collect assessment information on an ongoing basis.
	10. Elicit risk and protective factors.
	11. Elicit suicide ideation, behaviors, and plans.
	12. Elicit warning signs of imminent risk of suicide.
	13. Obtain records and information from collateral sources as appropriate.
D. Formulating risk	14. Make a clinical judgment of the risk that a client will attempt or complete suicide in the short and long term.
	15. Write the judgment and the rationale in the client's record.
E. Developing a treatment and services plan	16. Collaboratively develop an emergency plan that assures safety and conveys the message that the client's safety is not negotiable.
	17. Develop a written treatment and services plan that addresses the client's immediate, acute, and continuing suicide ideation and risk for suicide behavior.
	18. Coordinate and work collaboratively with other treatment and service providers in an interdisciplinary team approach.

(continued)

Table 3.1

Core Competencies for the Assessment and Management of Individuals at Risk for Suicide (*Continued*)

Section	Competencies
F. Managing care	19. Develop policies and procedures for following clients closely, including taking reasonable steps to be proactive.
	20. Follow principles of crisis management.
G. Documenting	21. Document the following items related to suicidality (informed consent, bio-psycho-social information, formulation, plan, management, interaction with professional colleagues, progress and outcome).
H. Understanding legal ethical issues related to suicidality	22. Understand state laws pertaining to suicide.
	23. Understand legal challenges that are difficult to defend against as a result of poor or incomplete documentation.
	24. Protect client records and rights to privacy and confidentiality following the Health Insurance Portability and Accountability Act of 1996 that went into effect April 15, 2003.

Note. These core competencies are reproduced with the permission of the Suicide Prevention Resource Center.

doing so, and clinical practice skills as measured by response to suicidal client vignettes both posttest and at 4-month follow-up. The practice skills assessed were ability to identify risk and protective factors, ability to make a formulation of risk, and ability to make a management plan in response to the risk. A limitation of the study was the lack of opportunity to observe actual clinical practice in the assessment and management of suicidal clients.

As informative, useful, and well constructed as these workshops appear to be, Pisani, Cross, and Gould (2011) recently conducted a rather sobering review of workshops that met the following three criteria: (a) the target audience was primarily mental health professionals, (b) the program's educational objectives targeted clinical competence in the assessment and management of suicide risk, and (c) there was at least one peer-reviewed article that described or evaluated the training or explicated the clinical model. Twelve workshops met these criteria (including the AMSR and the RRSR). The investigators gave a cross-program description of the objectives and methods of the workshops. They also reviewed the training, qualifications, and feedback for trainers who deliver the workshops, and they reviewed published studies about training outcomes (the study cited previously by Jacobson et al., 2012, was of course not available for this 2011 review). They found that research was very limited in terms of documenting real-world outcomes for those mental health professionals who participated in these workshops. The available studies indicated that clinician knowledge and attitudes improved with the workshop training, but with the exception of the workshop done by McNiel, Fordwood, et al. (2008; and now with the study by Jacobson et al., 2012), there was little evidence of improved clinical skill and, most important, no evidence of improved real-life clinical care for suicidal patients.

Clearly, acquiring knowledge about suicide risk and violence risk, improving one's ability to do a formulation of the risk, and having practice in risk evaluation and management under controlled conditions (such as those in a workshop) can be a very valuable training experience. As noted earlier in this book, however, I contend that it is only under real-life conditions that one can learn to meet the challenges of these high-stakes situations in which there is risk of suicide or violence to others. Real-life conditions are situations that are often stressful in themselves, but there can also be many other associated stressors (e.g., time pressure, other concurrent demands on the clinician, the needs of other patients). That is why it is important to have not only training but also what has been referred to as *stress training* (Driskell & Johnston, 1998).

Stress training has its roots in the stress inoculation training (SIT) of Donald Meichenbaum. In terms of his view of stress, Meichenbaum (1985, 2007) is in the tradition of the cognitive-appraisal or transactional model of stress discussed at the beginning of this chapter. With regard to training to cope with stress, he has noted that the object of any stress management training is not to eliminate stress "but to encourage clients to view stressful events as problems-to-be-solved rather than as personal threats. The goal is to make clients better problem solvers to deal with future stressful events as they might arise" (Meichenbaum, 1985, p. 30). In addition to helping people be better problem solvers, however, he has also emphasized learning techniques designed to relieve distress and foster emotion regulation. As he has stated, "Rather than conceiving their stressors as being overwhelming, uncontrollable, unpredictable, debilitating, and hopeless, the SIT trainer helps clients develop a sense of 'learned resourcefulness'" (Meichenbaum, 2007, p. 513).

The SIT model has three phases: (a) a conceptualization phase, (b) a skills acquisition and rehearsal phase, and (c) an application and follow-through phase. In the conceptualization phase, the focus is on attaining a better understanding of the nature of stress, its effect on emotion and performance, and on reconceptualizing it into transactional or cognitive-appraisal terms. The skills acquisition and rehearsal phase focuses on developing and rehearsing a variety of coping skills, primarily through imaginal and behavioral rehearsal. Finally, the application and follow-through phase focuses on transitioning from the imaginal and behavioral rehearsal to graded in vivo or real-life exposure to stressors.

Although it has been applied with some professional groups, the SIT model was originally developed as a clinical treatment program for individuals who had difficulty dealing with problems such as physical pain, anger, and phobic responses. It has retained an association with treatment for clinical conditions. In an effort to extend stress training beyond the clinical domain, Johnston and Cannon-Bowers (1996) developed a modification of the SIT model (i.e., stress exposure training or SET) to be used in training professionals who must perform tasks under high-stress conditions.

STRESS EXPOSURE TRAINING MODEL

As presented by Driskell and Johnston (1998), the SET model has three objectives. The first is to convey knowledge of the stressful task and environment. This objective is based on the assumption that stress is reduced by giving an individual information about what to expect in performing under stressful conditions. The second objective is to emphasize skill development. This objective involves training people in the behavioral and cognitive skills needed to perform the task or tasks effectively under stress. The third objective is to build confidence in the ability to perform under stress. This objective is only achieved when the person in training experiences success or task mastery under actual stressful conditions.

Consistent with these objectives, the SET approach has three stages: (a) an initial stage in which information is provided about the importance of stress training and what stressors are likely to be encountered, (b) a skills-training phase in which cognitive and behavioral skills for performing the task or tasks under stress are acquired, and (c) a final stage of applying and practicing the acquired skills under conditions that increasingly approximate the potentially stressful environment or circumstances.

I propose that this three-phase model (with modifications) be used as a guide for training clinicians in dealing with behavioral emergencies. Thus, there is a Phase 1 or a phase in which information is provided about what stressors may be involved when a behavioral emergency arises, but in this phase the clinician-in-training also learns, through lectures, readings, and/or workshops, about suicide risk, violence risk, and the risk of interpersonal victimization. Such preparatory information can begin to lessen the buildup of stress by clarifying misconceptions, reducing fear of the unknown, and increasing the clinician-in-training's understanding of this area of practice. It can provide a preview of the stressful events and make them less unfamiliar.

Phase 2 consists of cognitive and behavioral skills training through case conferences in which high-risk situations are discussed and/or through scenario-based training in which potentially stress-inducing clinical situations are presented and can be used for mental practice in decision making about high-risk patients (see Chapter 4 for some suggested scenarios). As Meichenbaum (1985) suggested, it is in this phase that the clinician-in-training can rehearse how he or she might attempt to cope and then receive feedback or hear how others might have responded.

In Phase 2, there are also certain stress-training strategies that can begin to be integrated into the training process (Driskell & Johnston, 1998). *Mental practice* or *mental simulation* is most consistent with the scenario-based training noted previously. It refers to cognitive rehearsal without actually performing the task. It is a technique by which the mind creates a mental representation of a cognitive skill or a motor skill with the intent to mentally practice and enhance performance. In a metareview of studies of mental simulation, van Meer and Theunissen (2009) concluded that "the general effectiveness of MS (mental simulation) for both motor and cognitive tasks has been established beyond reasonable doubt" (p. 104). Of course, it should not be used instead of actual practice, but it can be an excellent training adjunct. There is a debate in the literature about whether mental practice is as effective with *open skills* as with *closed skills;* an open skill requires one to improvise and be reactive to changes, and a closed skill is exercised without much interference from external influences. With open skills, the investigators suggest reducing complexity and practicing components of the task. Behavioral emergencies certainly require open skills. A clinician-in-training, however, might think through and mentally practice how he or she would respond in a scenario in which a patient was feeling hopeless and expressing suicidal thoughts or in a scenario in which a patient was feeling disrespected, angry, and having an urge to become violent to others.

Furthermore, in complex situations in which there are often competing demands, it can be crucial to learn *prioritization skills.* If there is time pressure and/or high stakes, the clinician may need to think through what is most important to deal with or accomplish first. Time and attention cannot be devoted to low-priority tasks when one may lose the opportunity to deal with more critical issues. In scenario-based training with behavioral emergencies, he or she can mentally rehearse how multiple tasks or multiple patients might be prioritized in terms of the urgency of each person's condition.

Phase 3 involves applying and practicing skills under conditions that increasingly approximate the potentially stressful task or situation. With suicidal or potentially violent patients, applying and practicing evaluation and management skills is best initiated under close, on-site supervision. In fact, it can be an excellent learning experience if a more senior clinician or supervisor initially has the trainee or intern observe him or her doing an evaluation. On a subsequent case or two, they can switch and let the trainee or intern take the lead in the interview or evaluation while the supervisor is there to inquire further if needed or to assist in managing the case. In cases that follow, the trainee can do the evaluation more independently, but with supervisory consultation before the case is completed and a management plan is decided. In this way, the clinician-in-training can have a graduated experience leading to increasing mastery and autonomy.

This graduated approach to skills training allows the clinician-in-training to become more familiar with the stressors that he or she may face with patients who are at risk without feeling overwhelmed. It also gradually builds confidence and is less likely than immediate exposure to an intensely stressful situation (without guidance or support) to interfere with learning and mastering the task.

In Phase 3, the trainee or intern can practice additional stress-training strategies. Thus, he or she can work on increasing his or her cognitive control while being involved with actual cases. Control can be improved by recognizing when task-irrelevant thoughts and emotions start to occur and then replacing them with task-focused cognitions. Attention can be consciously directed to task-relevant issues and away from distractions. The clinician can also use physiological control strategies, such as relaxation through deep-breathing exercises. Of course, use of relaxation techniques is based on the premise that relaxation and stress are incompatible. If someone is relaxed, he or she is less likely to experience the negative feelings and reactions brought on by stress.

Overlearning has also been found to be a good training procedure for dealing with high-stress situations. The term refers to deliberate overtraining of a task beyond the level of proficiency. It is training to the point that aspects of the task become automatic and require less attention. Because stress can restrict attention in a negative way, making certain tasks automatic can compensate, to some degree, for the effects of stress. Of course, with overlearning and multiple experiences, the clinician-in-training also develops his or her store of memories or schemata of behavioral emergencies; that is, he or she becomes more recognition primed to understand a high-risk situation and quickly decide on a course of action to manage it.

CONCLUDING REMARKS

The model (noted in this chapter) for stress exposure training with behavioral emergencies is presented in three phases. It should be noted, however, that these three phases are not intended to be strictly sequential. Clearly, the clinician-in-training can be acquiring a knowledge base in behavioral emergencies while simultaneously learning cognitive and behavioral skills through participation in case discussions and scenario-based training. Likewise, one can be learning cognitive and behavioral skills in simulated clinical scenarios while beginning to engage in the application of skills by doing evaluations with close supervisory monitoring. The model is presented in phases to emphasize the importance of taking a graduated approach to acquiring the skills needed to evaluate and arrive at decisions with high-risk patients under what are often stressful conditions. The three-phase model is also consistent with the position that a clinician-in-training is not fully competent until skills learned in more controlled settings are put to the test in real-life situations with real-life consequences that can be life threatening.

4

Mental Practice for Decision Making During Behavioral Emergencies

One of the major goals of stress training is to reduce stress or make it more manageable by providing practice under conditions that begin to approximate those likely to be encountered in the real world. In complex situations, however, such as when someone may be at risk to self or others, the individual's condition can be uncertain. It can shift in unexpected ways, and our ability to predict how events will unfold, and what we may be faced with, can become very difficult. It is, therefore, important to know if stress training with one set of circumstances can be said to generalize to novel task or stress conditions.

Driskell, Johnston, and Salas (2001) investigated this issue. Initially, they examined whether the benefits of stress training would generalize from the stressor experienced in training to a novel stressor. Next, they investigated whether it would generalize from one task to another.

http://dx.doi.org/10.1037/14337-005
Decision Making in Behavioral Emergencies: Acquiring Skill in Evaluating and Managing High-Risk Patients, by P. M. Kleespies

In the first study, a sample of U.S. Navy technical school trainees was asked to participate in a three-phase protocol. In Phase 1, the participants were trained in either a spatial orientation task or a memory search task, both of which were computer based. They then performed each task under conditions of either auditory distraction or time pressure. In Phase 2, all participants received stress exposure training (SET) consisting of (a) preparatory information, (b) skills training, and (c) application and practice. Preparatory information included information on the type of stressor they would encounter in performing the task and information on the reactions they were likely to feel under stress. Skills training consisted of an attentional intervention in which participants were informed about avoiding distractions and focusing selectively on task-relevant stimuli. Those who would experience auditory distraction were instructed on how noise can be distracting and how it is important to ignore noise, and those who would experience time pressure were instructed on how time pressure can be distracting and how it is important to ignore time pressure. The participants then performed the respective tasks. In Phase 3, the participants applied their skills by performing the task under either noise stress or time pressure. On a third trial, they performed the task under the other stressor (i.e., time pressure if training had been with noise stress and vice versa). The findings indicated that the improvement in performance from Trial 2 to Trial 3 was sustained when participants performed under a novel stressor. In addition, a reduction in subjective stress was also sustained when participants performed under a novel stressor.

In the second study, a similar pattern of results was found when participants performed a novel task while the stressor remained constant. The investigators concluded that the overall pattern of results strongly supported their hypotheses that stress training would be maintained and generalized when participants performed under novel stress conditions and under novel task conditions.

Meichenbaum (2007), in the stress inoculation training (SIT) model, noted how exposing individuals to milder forms of stress can bolster their coping resources and preparedness for dealing with similar but more intensely stressful and complicated events. In this chapter, I offer a series of crisis and/or emergency case scenarios that are intended to present clinicians with some potentially stress-inducing situations that they can use for mental practice in evaluating and managing patients or clients who are at some risk to self or others. As is elucidated in Chapter 6, such mental practice is only one component of training for competence in dealing with behavioral emergencies. The cases presented are based on real events, but certain details of each case have been changed to protect the identity of the individuals involved. The cases do not necessarily have a single *correct* answer but are intended to provoke thought about possible approaches to resolving the crisis or emergency nature of the situation. It should also be noted that the cases do not necessarily include what might be considered "complete" information about the individual or the circumstances involved. Rather, in an effort to present the reader with more realistic crisis or emergency conditions, the information about each case may be less complete than the clinician would like, yet decisions about management must be made according to what, in fact, is known. The reader should approach each case as though he or she were the clinician involved.

Following each case scenario, I provide a comment in the section titled *Author's Comment*. The reader is encouraged to formulate his or her own thoughts about managing the case before reading the comments. Again, these comments are not intended as the correct or only response to the case but to stimulate further discussion.

The reader should keep in mind that an actual suicide or violence risk assessment should ideally occur within the context of a more complete clinical evaluation (see Kleespies & Richmond, 2009, for an example of a clinical interview for behavioral emergencies). In addition, it should be understood that although the clinician should make every effort to be evidence based or evidence informed in the decision-making process, decisions about suicide risk or violence risk are ultimately based on clinical judgment.

BEHAVIORAL EMERGENCY CASE SCENARIOS

The cases that follow can be read and considered by the individual clinician. It can be more stimulating, however, if they are read and discussed in a group setting where different points of view can be presented.

Case 1: A Victim of Intimate Partner Violence

A psychotherapist in a group private practice has been seeing a recently married couple in their early 30s. The woman works for a small company and has just been promoted to a beginning level managerial position. Her husband is a construction worker who has a history of problems with anger and impulse control. He also drinks to intoxication episodically. They came to couples counseling because they have been having intense arguments that seem to revolve around the wife's desire to have some independent activities in her life. The arguments are also fueled by the husband's feeling that he is being left behind by his wife's success. She complains that her husband is too controlling and that he gets upset when she engages in activities, such as going out with her girlfriends, that don't include him. He feels that she is being neglectful of their life together at home.

After two or three sessions, it is revealed that there have been times when their arguments have led to physical abuse in which the husband has pushed and slapped his wife. It also becomes clear that the young woman now wants out of the marriage, but she is frightened of her husband's violent temper. Near the end of a session, she brings up the possibility of a trial separation. The husband is obviously upset and does not agree. The therapist suggests that they discuss the pros and the cons of such a suggestion during the next session. At the end of the meeting, he counsels them about how such a difficult and emotional topic could lead to an escalation of anger with the risk of further physical abuse. They both agree that they will not let anything like that happen.

Several days later, the therapist is working in his practice and seeing an older man who is grieving the recent loss of his wife of 50 years. He has become tearful about the loss for the first time, and the therapist feels that this is an important breakthrough.

At this point, the group practice secretary calls the therapist and informs him that there is an urgent phone call from one of his other patients. He is not happy about being interrupted and asks if the call can wait until the session is over in another 30 minutes. She is insistent that the patient sounds very tense and on edge. The therapist reluctantly apologizes to his current patient, says he will be back shortly, and goes to another room to take the call. The secretary informs him that the caller is the wife in the aforementioned couple.

The therapist takes the call, and the woman sounds distressed. She states that although they had said that they would not get into a confrontation at the end of their last session, they had, in fact, had a terrible argument, and her husband had threatened her with a knife, saying he would kill her if she left him. She has fled to her sister's house, where she has been staying, but she now believes that she has seen her husband sitting outside in his car watching the house. She fears that he is building up to further violence, and she is not sure what to do.

The therapist is concerned about having abandoned the bereaved patient whom he has in his office, but he talks further with the patient on the phone and asks if there are other people with her. She says that her sister and her brother-in-law are there. Her brother-in-law has had a good relationship with her husband, and he is inclined to go out to talk with him. She also says that she has thought of calling the police, but she is reluctant to do so because she fears that it will only aggravate her husband further and make things worse in the long run. She is still hoping that he will just leave and she can find somewhere else to stay until things calm down.

At this point, the patient's brother-in-law takes the initiative and goes out to talk with her husband. The therapist remains on the line and talks with the patient about calling the police if there is any sign of an altercation. He also asks his secretary to check in with the elderly patient in his office and to tell him that it will be a little longer than expected before he will be back with him. After about 10 to 15 minutes, the brother-in-law returns and the husband drives off. The brother-in-law tells the patient that her husband has been drinking and is both angry with her and remorseful about having threatened her. He claims that he wants her to return home so that they can try to work things out. The patient tells the therapist that she is going to think about whether to return home.

Author's Comment

This case has a number of the evidence-based acute risk markers for intimate partner violence. As Riggs, Caulfield, and Fair (2009) noted, relationship conflict, and particularly an increase in arguments and verbal aggression, typically precedes violent interactions between partners. In this case, the wife has suggested a trial separation, something that the husband seems to have seen as possibly leading to termination of the relationship. The termination of a relationship in which there has been violence has been found to be associated with an increased risk of further violence. The wife in this case sensed that her husband might be building up to further violence, and there is some evidence that women who have experienced intimate partner violence may be in a better position than anyone to predict their partner's future violent behavior. It has also been found that alcohol abuse during times of conflict increases the risk of partner violence, and the male partner in this case abuses alcohol. Finally, her husband's behavior in coming to her sister's house and waiting and watching could be the beginning of stalking behavior.

Although the husband leaves the scene and the immediate risk seems to have passed, the wife needs to understand that, at this point, the risk of future violence remains high. Given that her husband recently threatened her with a weapon, it may be in her interest to review and make plans for her physical and emotional safety. She is a competent adult, and she could choose to return to her husband. Were she to decide to do so, it would clearly be important to see if she can identify situations in which risk might be heightened in the immediate and longer term future. It would also be important to ask if there are particular people whom she can contact at any time or particular places where she can go for help. In the event of increasing risk, can she develop an action plan? If she is considering a return to the relationship with her husband, might she want to link that to his enrollment in a program for perpetrators of domestic abuse?

Given the level of risk, the clinician would, of course, also want to introduce the option of going to a safe house or shelter for abused women where staff might assist her in making plans for safety. Although she has been reluctant to involve the police or to obtain a restraining order, the clinician should discuss whether a call to the police might be indicated should her husband become more aggressive in pursuing her or threatening her.

Case 2: A Suicidal Adolescent

The therapist in this case is a clinical child psychologist working in a family practice. He has been seeing a depressed and angry 16-year-old Caucasian boy who comes from a single-parent family in a poor and crime-ridden neighborhood. When the patient was age 3, his father abandoned him and his mother. He has no memory of his father. His mother worries about him because he has seemed depressed and also because of the dangerous neighborhood in which they live—on two recent occasions, their apartment was burglarized. His mother has become concerned for their safety and has purchased a revolver for protection.

Because his mother has had to work as a waitress to support them, the patient's maternal grandparents provided considerable child care during his earlier years. In his teen years, however, he has preferred not to go to their home after school. In school, his grades have been low, and he has gotten into several fights with classmates; in one he became enraged and had to be pulled off of the boy he was fighting. He has a 15-year-old girlfriend, and their relationship has grown intense and, at times, tumultuous. He has wanted a very exclusive relationship, and they have argued about her tendency to flirt with other young men. As a couple, they have, on occasion, skipped school and engaged in shoplifting. They also smoke marijuana two or three times a week.

In treatment, the therapist has taken a cognitive–behavioral approach and has been working with the patient on his low self-esteem, his tendency to make negative statements about himself, his difficulty tolerating strong affect, and his impulsivity. His demeanor has remained somewhat sullen, but the clinician feels that he is starting to make some small progress. The patient is prescribed an antidepressant by a psychiatrist with whom the clinician works.

Several days after his last visit, the therapist is in his office reviewing some notes on a young couple that he is scheduled to see in 10 minutes. The secretary for the family practice contacts him and tells him that the mother of his adolescent patient is on the phone, and it sounds urgent. He takes the call, and the mother, who sounds very upset and anxious, tells him that her son came storming into the house saying that his girlfriend had cheated on him and dumped him. He has grabbed the gun that she kept in the drawer of her bedside stand, gone to his room, and locked the door. He refuses to come out and has been making comments about how he can't take much more of this miserable life that he has. His mother is fearful that he may shoot himself. She says that the relationship with his girlfriend has "meant everything to him." At this point, he has not made any threats toward the girlfriend. The therapist asks her to let him know that he is on the phone and to ask if he would talk with him. (He also lets the secretary know that she should tell the couple he was about to see that he will be late.) Initially, the patient refuses to leave his room, but eventually, and with considerable coaxing from his mother, he comes to the phone while still holding the gun.

Author's Comment

This patient is depressed, angry, and emotionally wounded by what has happened with his girlfriend. He seems to have many of the features of a conduct disorder, and his behavior has been impulse ridden. He has a mixture of acute risk factors (e.g., depressed and angry mood, loss of relationship, possibly absolutistic thinking about the loss) and chronic risk factors (e.g., impulsivity, conduct disorder). The situation seems volatile. Under such circumstances, it is probably good for the therapist to remind himself that the patient has not done anything while his mother contacted him and that he has come to the phone. These may be signs of ambivalence about suicide, and ambivalence is something that clinicians can work with.

There is clearly no known "right" way to deal with this type of an emergency situation that will guarantee a positive outcome. Because a lethal weapon is involved, some might advise immediately calling the police. There are times, however, when the arrival of the police may mean to the individual that an effort is being made to take away his or her perceived means of escape from intolerable pain, something that can escalate the situation. Some have attempted to write " a suicide prevention text" that might guide the clinician in a real-time emergency such as this one (Omer & Elitzur, 2001, p. 129); however, others have found the text too prescriptive and lacking in empathy with the individual's emotional pain (Orbach, 2001).

The challenge to the clinician at a time like this is to find a way to empathize with the patient's pain and to encourage him to discuss it.

Simple questions such as "Would you tell me in your own words what has happened?" and "Can you tell what you are feeling right now?" can indicate your interest in hearing the person's story. If the patient can put his pain into words, the clinician can begin to understand what he may be experiencing and find ways to intervene or help him problem solve (Miller & Emanuele, 2009). Thus, for example, if the patient sees the end of his relationship with his girlfriend as catastrophic, the clinician might ask if he has had other bad things happen and try to understand how he got through them. Can he let the therapist and perhaps his mother help him to find ways to get through this situation and reach a point where he might feel less pain? Might there be possible reasons for living?

If the patient has begun to agree that there may be some hope for his future, or if he realizes that his death by suicide would have very negative effects on others whom he cares about (such as his mother), it may be time to see if he is willing to put the gun aside or relinquish it. Might he also agree to a plan involving being seen by the therapist or at an emergency room? Would he be okay if the police arrived with an ambulance to take him to an ER? If his suicide risk increases before he can be seen, are there things he can do to decrease the risk? In short, can a plan of action be developed with him?

Of course, if the patient abruptly leaves or hangs up the phone, or becomes more agitated, or if others, like his girlfriend or his mother, appear to be at serious risk, the clinician should be prepared to involve the police or, if available, a crisis response team supported by the police.

Case 3: A Case of Potential Domestic Violence and/or Suicidal Behavior

The patient is a 41-year-old Hispanic man who comes to the urgent care clinic where a clinician is on call for the mental health service. He is accompanied by his girlfriend, with whom he is living, and by their 1-year-old daughter. The clinician interviews him while his girlfriend and daughter sit in the waiting room.

The patient appears depressed, and he reports that he has been having angry outbursts at home. He has thrown things around, but he denies that he has been violent toward his girlfriend or his daughter. He is fearful, however, that his anger could easily escalate to physical violence, especially when he is drinking. The clinician asks if he has ever been violent in the past, and he reports that he has spent some time in jail for assault and battery on a police officer when drinking.

The patient then reports that he has also had some recent thoughts of suicide, but he denies making a plan. He states that suicide would be an impulsive act for him. If an opportunity presented itself and he felt depressed, he might act on impulse. The clinician asks about any past attempts at suicide, and he states that he made two suicide attempts in the past. In one, he impulsively ran his car into a wall but did not sustain any serious injury. In another, he overdosed on pills, but some friends who were present kept him from taking more than a few.

The patient goes on to report that he has many stressors at present. He and his girlfriend are arguing frequently and generally not getting along. He feels that she is not supportive and that their relationship has turned negative. He loves his young daughter, but having an infant in the house is also stressful. She is awake frequently at night, and he has not been able to sleep well. He is working at an auto repair service, which does not pay very well, and he is also trying to go to a training program to become a car mechanic. All of this activity is stressful for him, and when stressed, he uses alcohol to relax. On most days, he will have three to five beers a day, but then he will have a day or two when he increases his drinking to six to seven 24-ounce beers plus a few shots of hard liquor. On some occasions, he snorts cocaine.

A nursing staff member interrupts the interview at this point and informs the clinician that another patient has arrived in the clinic who is depressed and agitated with suicidal ideation. The clinician goes back to her current patient knowing that she will not have much more time before she will need to attend to the new patient.

The clinician asks the patient about his personal history. He reports that his father left the family when he was a very small child and that he was raised by his mother. His mother worked and also had a number of short-lived relationships with men that preoccupied her. He spent a great deal of time with his grandfather while growing up. He had a history of being disciplined for getting into fights with other children at school. When he was old enough, the patient joined the army to get away from home. As an adolescent and young adult, he went through several relationships and actually has two sons from one of these relationships. He sees his sons only rarely, and he feels guilty about not being much of a father to them. Given the time pressure, the clinician asks about the patient's current mental state. His mood is depressed, but he also has poor sleep, decreased appetite, and decreased energy, and he is often irritable. There are few things that he currently enjoys. He denies any hallucinations or delusions. His thinking is linear and goal directed. He is alert and oriented, and his short-term memory is intact, but his concentration is impaired. He endorses having occasional panic attacks in which he gets short of breath and his heart pounds, but these events are infrequent.

The patient seems to need to stop drinking, not only to determine the nature of his depression but also to reduce his risk for violence. Given his depressed state, it may be unlikely that he has the resources to do so on his own. Moreover, his ability to adhere to a safety plan seems tenuous if he continues to feel depressed, experience the same stressors, and drink. For these reasons, a brief hospitalization seems to make sense so that he might get a detoxification from alcohol, start treatment for his depression, and be referred to both appropriate mental health and substance abuse follow-up care. The patient, however, is reluctant to be hospitalized and asks if he might be able to go home to take care of a few things and return tomorrow for admission to the hospital.

Author's Comment

This patient is depressed with vegetative symptoms (i.e., insomnia, poor appetite, low energy, anhedonia). There is a question of whether he has a major depressive episode or a substance-induced mood disorder. Regardless of the diagnosis, his mood is depressed, and he is abusing alcohol. This comorbidity is a risk factor for suicidal behavior, and the patient's irritability, trouble managing his anger, history of behavioral problems as a child, and history of violence when drinking all suggest that he is at risk for violence (see McNiel, 2009). His relationship with his partner is conflicted and not supportive. He is feeling stressed by needing to work, go for training, and deal with the demands of a young child. He is concerned about his ability to maintain self-control. His concern for his daughter is a protective factor, but the risk factors seem to outweigh the protective factors.

If the patient refuses hospitalization, the clinician would be faced with making a decision about whether the risk to self or others is sufficient to warrant involuntary hospitalization. From what is known of the patient, it would seem hard to say that the risk to self or others was clearly imminent. He is seeking help and denies current intent to harm himself or others. Nonetheless, it might be necessary to work with the patient on a safety plan for the night and agree to have him return the next day. Such a plan might entail going over warning signs for increased risk; discussing coping strategies that might help to reduce risk; encouraging contacts with friends for support; having him agree to limit his drinking overnight; and informing him that he can go to the nearest emergency room, call a crisis hotline, or call 911, if necessary.

If, however, the patient were to have difficulty entering into a firm agreement about a safety plan and/or agreeing in a convincing way to return the next day for voluntary hospitalization, it would suggest increased risk that might require an involuntary hospitalization. In such an event, the clinician must know the law about temporary involuntary commitment in the state or jurisdiction where she is practicing. In addition, because the patient could become agitated and angry about such a decision, it would also be wise for the clinician to alert the urgent care clinic staff and the medical center police before informing the patient that her opinion is that he will need to be hospitalized against his will. In this way, if he were to become threatening or attempt to leave, assistance would be readily available.

Case 4: A Suicidal Iraq War Combat Veteran

A psychologist at a Veteran's Outreach Center has been asked to see a young Caucasian army veteran who served in the Iraq War and who was brought to the center by two veteran buddies who have been encouraging him to seek help. He is 28 years old and married, and he has a 3-month-old son. The patient seems tense and impatient and tells the clinician that the only reason he's there is because his friends pressured him to come in after hearing that he had frightened his wife the night before last. At the time, he had had a war-related nightmare, and when his wife tried to wake him, he jumped up and aggressively pushed her. His reaction was reflexive, and he denied any intent to hurt her, but the incident frightened both of them. The patient then reported that he has had two deployments to Iraq and could be called up for a third tour to Afghanistan—so what's the point of seeking treatment? He's likely to be going back to war.

In Iraq, the patient was frequently involved in firefights during both tours. He also experienced mortar attacks and witnessed improvised explosive device (IED) detonations. There were times that he had to handle dead bodies. Sometime during his first deployment, he began to have nightmares almost every night, and they disrupted his sleep. He began drinking heavily as a way to calm himself. The heavy drinking continued on his return to civilian life after his second deployment. When his son was born 3 months ago, the patient decided to stop drinking and was able to do so on his own and without assistance.

Now that he is sober, however, other symptoms of PTSD have emerged. He has continued to have nightmares, but he has also had intrusive thoughts about Iraq during the day, as well as anxiety attacks and feelings of distress triggered by reminders of the war, such as the sound of a helicopter overhead. His wife tells him that he seems numb and lacking in affection. Two weeks ago, he apparently had a flashback while watching a football game on TV, and he ran out to a wooded area behind his house and began to dig a foxhole.

The clinician asks the veteran about his nightmares, and he states that he has one that recurs frequently. It is about an incident that occurred during his second tour. He was traveling in the back of a truck that was part of a convoy. The convoy suddenly came under fire, and the truck in front of the patient's truck was hit by a rocket-propelled grenade. The patient grabbed his gun and jumped up ready to shoot. He saw two young Iraqi boys (about age 12) running toward his truck, and he thought that they might have explosives strapped on. He yelled at them to stop, but they didn't. He shot and killed them both, only to learn later that they were unarmed and may have been seeking refuge.

The patient's recurrent nightmare is about this incident. He was told by fellow soldiers that he had no choice; they were being attacked and might have all been killed if these boys had explosives on them. Nonetheless, he continues to feel very guilty about having shot these unarmed children. He appears depressed and tearful, and the clinician empathizes with how he is suffering. He says that he doesn't feel that this event is something he can ever forgive or forget. The clinician asks if he has thoughts of wanting to punish or harm himself, and the patient states that he doesn't want to answer that question. He then abruptly says that he thinks that it's time for the interview to end. He feels that he should be strong enough to manage his own problems and gets up to leave.

Author's Comment

This situation is one in which the clinician needs to think and act quickly. The patient is obviously distressed and in emotional pain, but he has refused to allow an assessment of his suicide risk. He appears to have combat-related posttraumatic stress disorder (PTSD), a diagnosis that is a chronic risk factor for suicide (Bullman & Kang, 1994; Ilgen et al., 2010). Beyond that, however, he is having reexperiencing symptoms of PTSD, and he has guilt over combat actions. Both of these symptoms have been associated with increased risk of suicidal ideation and/or suicidal behavior (J. B. Bell & Nye, 2007; Hendin & Haas, 1991). In addition, he seems acutely depressed and distraught, and his reexperiencing symptoms are acutely exacerbated. The manner in which the patient terminated the interview when the question of suicide risk was raised only seems to increase concerns that he may, in fact, be thinking of suicide.

Of course, the clinician would initially attempt to convince the patient that she is trying to work with him and ask him to stay and complete the evaluation. It might also be possible to see if the veteran's buddies who brought him in might have some influence with him. If these efforts fail, however, it would be important, as noted in Case 3, for the clinician to know the law about temporary involuntary commitment in the state or jurisdiction where she is practicing. In Massachusetts, for example, the law governing these situations (Mass. Gen. Laws ch. 123, sec. 12[a] and 12[b]) states that, if an examination for risk to self and/or others is not possible because of the emergency nature of the case and because of the refusal of the person to consent to such an examination, the physician, qualified psychologist, qualified psychiatric nurse specialist, or licensed independent clinical social worker may determine that hospitalization may be necessary and have the individual held against his or her will. That, however, may not be the case in other jurisdictions, or there may be differences in what the clinician needs to do or how he or she is to proceed.

When a decision has been made to invoke a temporary involuntary commitment with a resistant patient, there still may be opportunities to pursue the least restrictive means of holding the patient for the evaluation. Under such conditions (and as also noted in Case 3), it is wise to have initiated the involvement of the center's crisis response team, security guards, or police so that they can be present and available. At times, such a so-called show of force may be sufficient to calm and convince the patient to stay and complete the evaluation. If not, and the patient is threatening or determined to leave, then physical restraint may be necessary as a humane response to a situation that could lead to life-threatening consequences for the patient.[1]

Case 5: A Psychotic Patient Who May Be Dangerous to Others

A psychologist in private practice has worked with seriously mentally ill (SMI) patients in a hospital setting in the past. She accepts a referral to her private practice of a 35-year-old man who has a history of recurrent hospitalizations but whom she has been told is currently at his baseline of functioning and is no longer acutely psychotic. In the past, he completed about 2 years of college before being forced to leave school because of a psychotic episode. It is hoped that an individual therapy relationship will provide some stability and interrupt the cycle of repeated hospitalizations. The patient has been somewhat of a diagnostic dilemma and at times has been diagnosed with a paranoid delusional disorder or with a schizoaffective disorder or with paranoid schizophrenia. He also has a history of alcohol abuse. He has been treated with a variety of psychotropic medications and is currently prescribed Risperidone and Zoloft by a psychiatrist who sees him every 3 months.

---

[1] Because it would take the reader far afield, I do not present a detailed description of the use of physical (and/ or chemical) restraint. Rather, the interested reader is referred to the description provided by Kleespies and Richmond (2009).

In the referral, the therapist was informed that the patient had a very traumatic childhood and that trust is an issue. As a very young child, he was reportedly burned over a stove on repeated occasions by his mother. His father abused alcohol and also physically abused the patient, his two siblings, and his mother. The father eventually abandoned the family. Beginning at the age of 13, the patient was sexually abused for 3 to 4 years by a police officer who lived in the neighborhood.

In the psychologist's initial session with the patient, she learns that he has stopped taking his medications and has started using alcohol on occasion. Given the severity of his problems, she presses him on the importance of taking his medication. In response, he becomes very agitated and paranoid and accuses her of attempting to control his mind by giving him mind-altering drugs. To her denials, he states that even if she isn't trying to control him, another force might be working to do so through her mind. He then states that he hates child molesters and he believes that God has appointed him as an "avenging angel" to kill such people. The therapist asks how he might know that someone is a child molester, and he replies that he will "just know." He goes on to state that there is a man named John Doe who lives across the street from him whom he believes has abused children in the neighborhood. The patient plans to beat him up and punish him. The therapist asks if he has ever hurt anyone in the past. He states that a number of years ago, he slashed a man in the face who allegedly made a pass at him. He always carries a knife for protection when he is out on the streets.

The psychologist says that he (the patient) seems very distressed about these issues and that it might be good if the patient returned to the hospital to get some relief from the stress. The patient, however, is very negative about such a possibility. He says that he's not distressed; there are evil people out there who need to be punished. He says that he's not going to be locked up again, and he quickly gets up and leaves her office. As an individual private practitioner, she does not work with other staff that are trained to detain such a patient and on whom she might call.

Author's Comment

This patient is obviously in an acute paranoid and psychotic state. He exhibits many of the risk factors for violence seen among the subset of

SMI patients who can become violent. Not only is he paranoid, but he is also easily agitated, and he perceives threat in the environment while denying any personal contribution to his problems. His delusional state seems consistent with what Link and Stueve (1994) referred to as a *threat/ control override* delusion; that is, he has psychotic symptoms that make him feel personally threatened and thoughts that can justify overriding self-control of his aggressive impulses to eliminate the threat. A large sample study by Teasdale, Silver, and Monahan (2006) supported the hypothesis that such beliefs predict violent behavior by male SMI patients in the community. In addition, the patient has a history of violence, something that is known to be the best single predictor of future violence.

Under the circumstances, it seems that the risk is high that this patient is a danger to others in the community. In many states, the mental health clinician has a legal duty to protect the reasonably identifiable victim or victims of his or her patient, whereas in other states the duty is to protect those who are foreseeably endangered (Packman, Andalibian, Eudy, Howard, & Bongar, 2009). In this case, it seems as though there is a threat to someone who is an identifiable victim *and* who is foreseeably at serious risk of being victimized. The clinician, therefore, needs to take steps to protect this individual. Some states provide guidance on what a clinician is to do to fulfill his or her duty to protect. If this case were in Massachusetts, for example, the clinician might complete a temporary involuntary commitment form, inform the local police of the threat to the individual in question, and ask them to search for the patient at his home and bring him to the nearest hospital emergency room for further evaluation. They could also attempt to obtain John Doe's contact information so that he might be warned of the threat to his safety.

Case 6: An Elderly Patient With Physical Illness and Suicidal Thoughts

A psychologist works in the primary care clinic at a large urban medical center. One of the primary care physicians asks him to see an 85-year-old Caucasian man who has multiple medical problems and who came in with chest pain that was not cardiac in origin. While being seen, he made the passing remark that he wished the doctor would just give him enough medication to end his life. The physician felt that the patient was probably only venting his frustration, but nonetheless he thought that it might be wise to have him evaluated for suicide risk.

The psychologist has a staff meeting in about 45 minutes at which he is to present on a complex case for which he is seeking some peer input. Although it disrupts his preparation for the presentation, he feels obliged to see this man who may be at risk for suicide. He asks him about the comment he made to his primary care doctor, and he tells the psychologist that he's had these thoughts about ending his life several times in the past weeks and months, but he has not thought about a plan other than his vague idea of an overdose of medication. He then proceeds to inform the clinician that he is an insulin-dependent diabetic who had a serious heart attack about 2 years ago. His heart attack led to a coronary artery bypass, and although the bypass helped, he does not feel that he has regained his former baseline of functioning. More significant to the patient, his vision is now very impaired as a result of cataracts, macular degeneration, and glaucoma. In addition, he has had a significant loss of hearing. He has had to give up driving and can no longer read. It is difficult for him to leave home. He feels dependent and despondent about his situation. He has no prior mental health or psychiatric history.

The patient lives with his 82-year-old wife, who depends on oxygen 24 hours a day because of emphysema. Although she is on oxygen, she can still drive, and she brings him to his appointments. Otherwise, he does not like to ask her for help because of her own poor health. The couple has a son and a daughter as well as three grandchildren. His son lives in the same town and typically visits his parents on the weekend. Yet, the patient has never had a close relationship with his children and grandchildren. The family relationships have been more important to his wife. The psychologist inquires about his early history and learns that the patient's father left the family when he was age 3. His mother had to go to work to support herself, the patient, and his two siblings. From ages 4 through 13, the patient spent time in 15 different foster homes. His mother was able to bring him home at age 13, and at age 17 she signed so that he could join the army.

After his military service, the patient worked as a car salesman, and over the course of 20 years he bought three small apartment buildings. He then left car sales and spent his time managing his apartment buildings. Last year, because of his age and poor health, he could no longer keep up the maintenance work and sold the buildings. Although he made a good profit on the sale, he also felt the loss of his work as a loss of purpose.

It seems clear that the psychologist will need to spend some additional time inquiring about risks with this patient. He calls and explains that he will be late for his presentation, but he hopes that it will be no more than 10 to 20 minutes.

The patient reports that he has had no history of suicide attempts. He also denies owning any weapons. The psychologist inquires about signs of depression. The patient states that since he has gotten older, he has slept less (about 5–6 hours per night) and his appetite and energy have diminished, but he ascribes these changes to aging. He denies any current suicidal ideation or intent, says that he isn't clear about why he had this evaluation, and states that he would like to be on his way home with his wife.

The psychologist sees the patient as having a difficult time adjusting to his decreased level of functioning and to his poor health. He does not appear to have a major depressive disorder. The clinician feels that his recent report of suicidal ideation is a reflection of demoralization and a request for help. He sees his level of immediate risk as mild. He recommends a referral to a geriatric mental health clinic where the staff work with older adults who have multiple physical illnesses. The patient agrees that this seems like a good idea. The psychologist contacts the clinic and learns that there is a waiting list and that it may be 6 weeks before he can be seen. He informs the patient about the situation. He is feeling pressure to get to his staff meeting, so he quickly makes a crisis plan with the patient for the intervening time. The psychologist asks what he might do to comfort himself if he becomes emotionally distressed. The patient states that he finds listening to sports events on the radio helps him to forget his troubles. The psychologist asks whom he would talk with if he began to feel like ending his life, and the patient states that he would talk with his son rather than burden his wife. The psychologist informs him and his wife that should an emotional crisis occur, he has options such as calling the psychologist and arranging a visit, calling a crisis hotline (and he gives the patient the number), going to the nearest emergency room, or calling 911. The psychologist then rushes to make his staff meeting.

Author's Comment

Although this patient does not appear to have a major mental illness (e.g., a major depressive disorder) that has an associated risk of suicide, there is increasing evidence that the presence of multiple physical illnesses can also constitute an independent risk factor for suicide, particularly in older people (see Kleespies, Hough, & Romeo, 2009, for a summary). The patient reports that he is unhappy about his need to depend on others and may feel that he is a burden to his family. His apparent sense of demoralization could be a sign of a deeper sense of hopelessness. Although he has support from his wife, he worries about asking too much of her, and he does not appear to have a strong bond with his children and grandchildren, something that may be the result of his own disrupted relationship with his parents as a child. Further, it has been noted that a high percentage of elderly people who actually commit suicide are likely to have visited their physician (rather than a mental health provider) in the month prior to their death (Conwell, 1997). The patient had planned to see only his primary care provider and was referred to the psychologist by a physician who had some awareness of suicide risk. One concern is that perhaps the psychologist should have exercised greater caution with this patient and arranged for either in-person or scheduled telephone contact with him until he was under the care of the geriatric mental health clinic. The psychologist considers giving him a call.

Case 7: A Potentially Violent Adolescent

A psychologist at a local high school is asked by an English teacher to take a look at a provocative essay submitted by a 17-year-old student who is in his senior year. The essay was to be about someone whom the student has admired. In his essay, the student in question portrays the two young men responsible for the shootings at Columbine high school in Colorado as heroic in that they sent a message to bullies everywhere that there could be retribution. The teacher states that this student has seemed angry, depressed, and withdrawn in class. He is of slight build and often wears dark glasses and a trench coat about the school. She has seen other students mocking the exaggerated way in which he presents himself as an angry and defiant young man. She has shown the essay to the school principal, and they have agreed that they would like to have him seen to determine if there is a need for and a possibility of mental health intervention.

Despite her heavy caseload, the psychologist rearranges her schedule to meet with him that afternoon. He appears sullen and defensive. The counselor notes that his English teacher was somewhat concerned about the essay that he had written and that she had brought it to the attention of the principal who had asked the psychologist to talk with him. She notes that she will keep what he tells her in confidence, but that there are limits to confidentiality in that if she felt that he was at imminent risk of harming others or taking his own life, she would need to report that to keep him and/or others safe.

The counselor asks him to tell her about his essay. He responds by saying that he believes that the Columbine shooters made people stop and think about bullying and how it can affect those who are their victims. She asks if he has ever felt bullied or harassed. He says, yes, many times. There are other students who make fun of him, but he'll manage it. He doesn't need a "shrink"; he'll handle his own problems. She asks how he might do that, and he says never mind, he'll take care of it if necessary. She asks if he has thoughts of doing something like the Columbine incident, and he replies that he doesn't know if he could actually do something like that. She continues and asks if he has access to weapons, and he states that his father is a Gulf War veteran who has guns at home. He lets him use them for target practice. Once when he had been taunted and harassed by several other students, he had started to bring a handgun with him to school for protection, but halfway there he decided to hide it in some bushes and later picked it up on his way home.

The counselor asks about his family, and he says that he lives with his father. His mother, who has a drug problem, abandoned them about a year ago. He's not sure where she is at this point. He has a younger sister who is 14 years old and a freshman at the high school. His father works long hours as a carpenter to support them. He admires his father and tries to watch out for his younger sister. The counselor asks if he misses his mother, and he says that he both misses her and is angry with her for leaving them. He begins to tear up, but then quickly asks if he can leave. The counselor empathizes with how hard it must be to have lost his mother in this way. She asks if he might want to return to talk more about it in a few days. He says that he might, and she makes an appointment for him. She inquires again if he has any plans to bring a gun to school or to harm anyone at school or otherwise. He states that he does not, and he also denies any thoughts of wanting to take his own life. He states that he feels some relief from having talked with someone about his situation. The counselor asks what he has done in the past to comfort himself when he has felt hurt and angry. He states that going on a run for several miles seems to help him feel calmer. He also likes to talk with his sister about how she is doing in school. The counselor encourages him to use some of these coping resources if he starts to feel agitated and angry; she also gives him her cell phone number and a National Crisis Line number, either of which he can call at any time, and she notes that he could also contact the nearest hospital emergency room if he is in a crisis.

Author's Comment

This high school student appears to be at some risk for violence. One way of estimating the risk is to use the heuristic device (remembered by the acronym ACTION) that Borum (2009) recommended for assessing risk of youth violence:

- "A" stands for Attitudes that support or facilitate violence. The student's essay and his comments to the psychologist sound supportive of violent action toward those who harass and bully others.
- "C" stands for the Capacity to carry out such a violent act. The student seems uncertain about whether he has that capacity.
- "T" is for Thresholds crossed and, with lethal weapons available at home, he crossed a threshold when he brought a handgun with him on his way to school. He fortunately hesitated and decided not to take it onto school property.

- "I" s for Intent and, at present, he does not seem to have clear intent to commit an act of violence. Rather, he seems ambivalent and uncertain.
- "O" is for Others' reactions and responses, and he has certainly gotten the attention of his teacher and the principal, both by his essay and by his behavior.
- "N" is for Noncompliance with efforts to reduce risk, and on this issue he again seems ambivalent and leaning toward seeking help rather than clearly being noncompliant; that is, he seems inclined to accept therapeutic intervention.

Given some of the dramatic and tragic school shootings in the past decade in the United States, some might feel that the safest course would be to hospitalize this student. It appears, however, that he has not developed clear intent and is ambivalent about acting on his impulses. Moreover, he seems willing to accept therapeutic intervention. The student appears to be struggling with the loss of his mother, an issue that may, in part, be driving his anger but also something that might be alleviated in therapy. As Borum (2009) pointed out, hospitalization may be necessary to incapacitate someone who is considered to be at imminent risk of violence, but for those who are not at that point, community-based interventions have been found to work better than inpatient treatment. Continued efforts to have the student engage in therapy or counseling seem to be indicated. If possible, his father could be involved in his treatment and might be enlisted in restricting his son's access to weapons. Of course, if the student decides to reject efforts to help, the estimate of risk would be increased, and his behavior would need to be closely monitored for any escalation toward violence.

Case 8: A Victim of Childhood Sexual Abuse and Military Sexual Trauma

A psychologist is working in a walk-in clinic at a VA community-based outpatient clinic. She is expected to spend no more than 20 to 30 minutes completing a screening type of evaluation and arranging a disposition for patients who are seen there. A 30-year-old woman presents to the clinic with a vague complaint of depression and anxiety following a breakup with a boyfriend of 6 months. She is an army veteran of the Iraq War. During her year in Iraq, she primarily did clerical work, but she also experienced mortar attacks and witnessed several IED explosions.

The patient explains that she has not had much success with relationships, and this recent breakup is one out of a number she has gone through. She has been feeling down and anxious, and she has not eaten in 2 days. She does not like being alone, but she is beginning to despair about ever finding a more enduring relationship. She started drinking heavily after the breakup, and although she is not a habitual drinker, she had about 10 gin and tonics yesterday.

The psychologist asks about her background, and she reports that she grew up in a large family with two brothers and four sisters. Her father was an alcoholic who was physically abusive when drinking. She had two uncles who harassed the girls in the family, and one of the uncles sexually abused the patient and her older sister when the patient was age 13 to age 15. He was eventually incarcerated when her sister brought sexual assault charges against him. The patient joined the U.S. Marines at age 18, in part to get away from her family situation.

The clinician inquires about the patient's experiences in Iraq. She responds by describing a mortar attack in which a trailer near to her own station was hit and blown up. She remembers that they found belongings, articles of clothing, and some body parts, but no one in the trailer survived. She was horrified and feared for her own life for the remainder of her time in Iraq. Since she returned from the war, she has had nightmares and intrusive thoughts about her experiences there. She has had interrupted sleep, is hypervigilant, and is easily irritated. It seems very likely that she has combat-related PTSD.

Given that the patient was a woman in such a male-dominated environment as the Marines, the clinician asks if she was ever sexually harassed. The patient reports that, on several occasions, she felt coerced into having sex. She explains that, at the time, she decided that it was less punishing to give in than to try to physically resist. She, however, felt violated and degraded. She did not register a complaint because she felt that her commanding officer would not be sympathetic and that she would be ostracized in her unit.

The limited time for the screening is running short and the clinician asks about her mood. She reiterates that she is feeling depressed and not sleeping or eating well. The clinician asks if she has hope that things will improve for her. The woman states that she has some hope or she would not be there, but she is not optimistic that things can change. She feels emotionally "used and abused" and as though she can never have an intimate partner whom she can trust. She acknowledges that she has had thoughts of suicide and that her plan would be to take an overdose. She attempted suicide in the past by taking an overdose of Tylenol when she was a teenager and when her uncle was abusing her. She did not tell anyone and apparently slept it off with no other known major consequences.

Author's Comment

Women are 3 or 4 times less likely than men to commit suicide, but they are 3 or 4 times more likely to make a nonfatal suicide attempt. Certain suicide attempts can have serious consequences—for example, a serious overdose with Tylenol can cause significant damage to the individual's liver. This patient has a history of a suicide attempt by Tylenol overdose.

Sexual abuse victims are at elevated lifetime risk of depression and of making suicide attempts (Berliner & Elliott, 2002). In some sense, the patient has been twice abused, as a young adolescent and as a young adult in the Marines. In addition to the military sexual trauma that she suffered, she also seems to be suffering from PTSD related to the mortar attack that she witnessed and its aftereffects. Beyond these chronic risk factors, she has the acute risk factors of depressed mood, poor sleep, abuse of alcohol, loss of a relationship, feelings of aloneness, a sense of hopelessness about the future, and likely low self-esteem. She has had recent thoughts of suicide, but they are not present now. She is seeking help.

The patient seems to be at moderately high risk of making a suicide attempt if she cannot resolve her current crisis. It is not clear that the risk is imminent; that is, it would occur in the next few hours, days, or weeks. Nonetheless, a brief voluntary hospitalization to alleviate some of her acute symptoms and assist her in connecting with longer term outpatient treatment would not be out of the question. Were she to refuse hospitalization, a carefully and collaboratively constructed safety plan would be needed as well as a referral to outpatient treatment in a setting such as a women's stress disorder treatment program. As noted in Case 3, a safety plan to reduce risk might consist of going over warning signs for increased risk; discussing coping strategies that might help to reduce risk; encouraging contacts with friends and family for support; and informing her that she can go to the nearest emergency room, call a crisis hotline, or call 911, if necessary. The clinician might also wish to schedule some telephone contacts with the patient to check on her condition and provide support until she has made contact with her treatment providers.

Case 9: An Employee at Risk of Workplace Violence

A psychologist at a large urban medical center is also a member of the medical center's committee to prevent workplace violence. The committee works with the Employee Assistance Program and the Employee Health Service, and occasionally the psychologist is asked to consult on instances when there is concern that an employee may be at risk of becoming violent at work.

Late one afternoon, the clinician is called and asked to see an employee on an urgent basis because he has reportedly made some threatening sounding remarks to the chief of the Medical Administration Service. He agrees to do a threat assessment with him through the Employee Health Service and in the emergency department. The employee is a 42-year-old divorced man who has worked as an administrative clerk for the past 5 years. During that time, he has had several poor performance ratings from his supervisor for being rude and abrasive with patients and for frequent instances of coming late to work. There have also been instances in which he was argumentative and angry with fellow employees, leading two or three of them to complain that he frightened them.

Recently, there was another incident in which he had intimidated a fellow administrative clerk by angrily shouting at her about a mistake that she had made. The chief of the Medical Administration Service and the clerk's immediate supervisor decided to meet with him to discuss his behavior. The meeting did not go well. The clerk said that he had not shouted but had spoken loudly. He saw the administrative clerk whom he had reportedly yelled at as incompetent and deserving of the way he had spoken to her. He didn't know why they were talking to him. They should be talking to her about her poor work performance.

The chief of the service pointed out that several other employees had complained that his behavior had at times frightened them. They didn't want to work in an environment where they felt frightened and he (the chief) didn't want that for them, either. At this point, the clerk became even more defensive and angry and said he knew where this was going. He accused the chief of the service and his supervisor of wanting to get rid of him. He resented the poor performance ratings that he had been given. He felt that they were totally unwarranted. He said that he hoped that they weren't going to try to take his job. If that happened, he would need to treat them as he would treat anyone who tried to take something from him on the street. The chief of the service then asked him if that was a threat. He said they could make of it what they wanted. He was fed up with how he was being treated.

At this point, the chief of the service said that he thought that they should bring the meeting to an end (because it didn't seem to be leading to anything positive), but that he wanted the employee to talk with a counselor in the Employee Health Service that same day. The clerk said that he'd talk with anyone they would like him to, but it wouldn't change how he felt.

The clinician meets with the employee in a cubicle in the emergency room. He seems tense, angry, and on edge. The clinician asks him to tell him what has led to his current situation. He proceeds to go on a rant about his supervisor and the chief of the service and the injustice with which they have treated him. He's worked for them for 5 years and he's never even been considered for promotion. He's often thought about how he'd like to just have it over with and punch them out when they disrespect him or harass him. The clinician asks if he's made any type of a plan to hurt them. He says no, these are thoughts that occur to him when he gets particularly angry. He's read some in the papers about people who brought weapons to work and shot people. He denies owning any weapons.

Author's Comment

This employee externalizes blame and, at present, has little insight into his contribution to his problems. He sounds as though he might be at risk of what White and Meloy (2007) referred to as *affective* (or *reactive*) *violence*—that is, violence that occurs in an emotionally charged situation in which the individual is and/or feels threatened. It is impulsive violence and occurs without a great deal of forethought. On the other hand, he has features that could lead to *planned* or *predatory violence*—that is, violence that is targeted at a particular individual or individuals and is carried out after considerable preparation. Thus, he has a profound sense of being a victim, and there are particular individuals whom he feels have treated him unjustly. There are times when it sounds as though he may dwell on violence as a way of resolving perceived injustice, and he has apparently taken some interest in incidents of workplace violence as described in the media. These factors could be signs of being in the early stages of a path that might possibly lead to more targeted or planned violence.

Again, as White and Meloy (2007) pointed out, there is a natural inclination to want to gain distance from potentially violent individuals. Hasty decisions to terminate such employees, however, may in fact be perceived as humiliating by the individual and provide the triggering event that galvanizes an individual to move further along a pathway to planned violence. In cases such as this one, it may be more productive to attempt to establish an ongoing therapeutic relationship and see if the person can gain perspective and explore new ways of understanding his problems and nonviolent means of dealing with them. Should this approach fail to bring about change, however, he may need to be monitored in his contacts with a counselor for any further progression along a pathway to targeted violence.

Case 10: A Suicidal Inpatient With Schizophrenia

A psychologist who works on an inpatient psychiatry unit has been asked to work with a 32-year-old, never-married, African American man who was diagnosed with paranoid schizophrenia in his early 20s. He was admitted after a suicide attempt in which he cut both wrists deeply with a box cutter and was sitting in a chair in the basement of the family home and bleeding profusely. His brother, who had been concerned about him, had come home unexpectedly to check on him. He called an emergency ambulance, and the patient was rushed to a local emergency room, where he reported that he felt that he was worthless and a failure and wanted to die. His wounds were treated and sutured at the emergency room and he was transferred to the hospital for psychiatric admission. He reluctantly signed a voluntary admission form. On admission, it was found that he had been taking his antipsychotic medication only sporadically and had begun to hear voices once again, something that distressed him greatly.

When the patient was first diagnosed, he was in college and taking courses in economics. He was bright and had a good grade point average. He began to hear voices, however, and became very paranoid that his roommates were plotting against him. He was hospitalized and diagnosed with schizophrenia, but he refused to accept his diagnosis and took medication only under pressure. His psychosis improved, however, and he attempted to return to college, but once out of the hospital he stopped the medication and quickly decompensated into a psychotic episode once again. He repeated this cycle of being hospitalized, improving, and attempting to return to school, but he again decompensated once he had stopped his medication. His academic advisors suggested that he take a leave of absence from his studies, and he never returned to school.

Over the next several years, the patient had a number of psychiatric hospitalizations. Some were for psychotic episodes, and others were also for suicide risk. A couple of them were after suicide attempts by overdose. His delusions and hallucinations became more intense. He was tried on a variety of antipsychotic, antidepressant, and mood-stabilizing medications, but it was always with resistance and poor compliance. When he was in a compensated state, he often spoke about what a disappointment his life had become and how he had failed to accomplish anything.

On this admission, the therapist meets with the clinical team on the unit, and it is decided that given the seriousness of the suicide attempt, the patient should be on one-on-one observation in the day room. One-on-one observation means that the patient is restricted to the day room and a nursing assistant is to be within arm's length of him at all times. The therapist talks with the patient and explains that staff concern for his safety is the reasoning for the decision to have him on close observation. She tells him that she will be back later to talk with him more. After she has left, the patient becomes restless and begins to pace about the day room. Despite having a nursing assistant at his side, he is able to go to a refrigerator in the day room, break off a light bulb in it, and stick the jagged end of the bulb into his neck. He attempts to jab himself again with the bulb, but the nursing assistant and other staff restrain him. He is put into four-point leather restraints and medicated. The wounds in his neck are superficial and attended to through a medical service consultation.

Within a day and a half, the patient is calmer and able to talk some about his condition. He states that he is still hearing voices but that he is able to ignore them at this point. He denies any suicidal ideation or intent, and he is released from restraints. Initially, he is kept on close observation for suicide risk, but he shows no signs of attempting to harm himself again. He takes his medication as prescribed, and the therapist meets with him daily. Although his mood is much improved and he appears less distressed, he seems to quickly seal over about the problems that led to his suicide attempt. The therapist asks about having his family come in for a family meeting, but he says that he does not want to burden his family with his problems. He acknowledges that he is disappointed that he has not finished his college degree, that he has not been able to enter into the business world, that he is still living in his parents' home, and that he has not been able to have a relationship with a partner. He sees these things, however, as due to his failings and not due to a mental disorder. He says that psychologists have "your pigeonholes for people," but he doesn't believe them. He wants to leave the hospital.

The therapist is concerned about the violence of his recent suicide attempt and the determination with which he injured himself in the hospital. The patient appears more composed, he is not acutely psychotic, and he does not seem profoundly depressed at present, but little has otherwise changed for him. Once out of the hospital, he has not been very compliant with follow-up care. The therapist attempts to convince him to stay in the hospital somewhat longer so that she and the staff might work with him further. He refuses, however, and submits a letter requesting a discharge against medical advice (AMA). In the state where this therapist is practicing, the patient can be held against his will for further evaluation for up to 3 days after submitting an AMA letter. After the 3 days are up, he must either be released from the hospital or the hospital must make application to an appropriate court of law for a longer term commitment. The therapist meets with the treatment team to decide about how to proceed.

Author's Comment

Among individuals with schizophrenia, suicide risk is greater among males, and it often arises earlier (i.e., before age 40) in the course of the disorder. Those at risk often have a negative attitude about treatment. Prospective studies have found that it is most frequently associated with feelings of hopelessness, depression, obsessive–compulsive features, paranoid ideation, and subjective distress. The schizophrenic suicide victim is often brighter and more aware of how his or her life has deteriorated. He or she gets demoralized and depressed, and depression can be an acute risk factor for suicide (L. J. Cohen, Test, & Brown, 1990; Peuskens et al., 1997).

The patient in question seems to have many of these features. He has regained his equilibrium very quickly, perhaps too quickly to indicate that it is a reliable improvement. Nonetheless, he is denying current suicidal ideation or intent. If the therapist holds him for 3 days on the basis of her assessment of his suicide risk, she may have time to talk with him further about her concerns, and there could be some positive shift in his attitude toward treatment. If nothing changes, however, she will need to decide whether the patient seems to be at great enough risk in the immediate future for her to pursue a court-ordered commitment.

CONCLUDING REMARKS

The cases presented in this chapter represent a range of people of differing ages, genders, races/ethnicities, and socioeconomic levels who are at risk to self and/or others. The cases involved a variety of clinical settings, as most practicing psychologists, regardless of the setting in which they work or the population they serve, will, on occasion, encounter patients or clients who are at risk of suicide or violence to others (Kleespies & Ponce, 2009).

5

The Use of Decision-Support Tools in Behavioral Emergencies

The limitations of clinical judgment in assessing the risk of suicide and violence are well known (McNiel, Lam, & Binder, 2000; Way, Allen, Mumpower, Stewart, & Banks, 1998). In the often high-demand and high-stress situations involving behavioral emergencies, the clinician needs any reliable aids that he or she can access. As discussed earlier in this book, these emergency situations require that the psychologist make decisions quickly, and he or she cannot be expected to interrupt the flow of events to have the patient undergo psychological testing or complete an assessment instrument. Nor would a highly agitated or distraught patient be likely to tolerate doing so.

In this chapter, I discuss tools that may be of aid to the clinician who needs to make decisions about short-term risk to self and others in a relatively brief time frame. First, I discuss the commonly used clinical method of considering significant risk and protective factors and arriving

http://dx.doi.org/10.1037/14337-006
Decision Making in Behavioral Emergencies: Acquiring Skill in Evaluating and Managing High-Risk Patients, by P. M. Kleespies

at a judgment about risk. This section is followed by a brief discussion of more strictly actuarial methods of risk assessment. Finally, I consider decision-support tools that have been developed from a framework known as *structured professional judgment*. This framework attempts to synthesize clinical and actuarial methods in assessing risk of violence and/or suicide.

RISK AND PROTECTIVE FACTORS AS A BASIS FOR ASSESSING BEHAVIORAL EMERGENCIES

Clinicians who work with patients at risk to self or others should have a working knowledge of the literature on suicide risk and violence risk (see, e.g., Webster, Bloom, & Augimeri, 2009). Frequently, they use known risk factors and protective factors as an aid in decision making about level of risk. Risk factors for suicide and violence can be demographic, biological, psychological, social, and cultural. They can also be characterized as chronic (lifetime) and acute, or distal and proximal. Many chronic or distal risk factors are static or unchangeable. If a patient has made a suicide attempt in the past, or if he or she has been violent in the past, these events are a part of the patient's history, and they will remain as chronic risk factors for the foreseeable future. Acute or proximal risk factors are often dynamic or modifiable. If a patient is at risk because of limited resources for coping with problems or stresses, his or her coping abilities can be improved with intervention. An example of a listing of suicide risk and protective factors is presented in Table 5.1.

In using risk and protective factors in decision making, clinicians should remember that a risk factor is merely a variable that is associated with an increased risk of morbidity or mortality; that is, the relationship between the factor and suicide or violence risk is correlational and not necessarily causal. Likewise, a protective factor is merely a variable that is associated with a decreased risk of morbidity or mortality. The relationship is also correlational and not necessarily causal. Protective factors, such as a strong social support network, are often viewed as providing a counterweight to risk factors. Little data exist, however, on how risk factors and protective factors may interact. It is also not

Table 5.1

Risk and Protective Factors for Suicide

Category of risk/ protective factors	Specific risk/protective factors
I. Chronic/distal risk factors	
A. Demographic factors	Male gender
	White or Native American race/ethnicity
	Divorced, widowed, separated, single
	Ages (36–64; 75–85+; 2009 official data)
B. Past self-injurious/ suicidal behavior	Past suicidal ideation/plans[a]
	Past suicide attempts[a]
	Past self-injurious behavior
C. Past impulsive or violent behavior	Past impulsive behavior
	Past reckless and self-endangering behavior
	Past violent behavior
D. Cognitive/ psychological features as traits	Absolutistic thinking
	Tunnel vision
	Limited coping/problem-solving ability
	Limited capacity for self-soothing
	Perfectionism
E. Family/peer group factors	History of sexual or physical abuse/trauma as child/adolescent
	Family history of suicide or suicide attempts
	Family history of violence, substance abuse, psychiatric disorders needing hospitalization
	Family/self-rejection of sexual orientation
	Parental divorce as a young child
F. Socioeconomic factors	Barriers to accessing mental health care
	Stigma related to accessing mental health care
G. Easy access to lethal methods (esp. firearms)	Guns in the home
	Hoarding of medications
H. Mental disorders	Mood disorders (including major depressive disorder and bipolar disorder, depressed)
	Substance use disorder (esp. alcohol abuse/dependence, cocaine abuse, nicotine dependence)

(continued)

Table 5.1
Risk and Protective Factors for Suicide (*Continued*)

Category of risk/ protective factors	Specific risk/protective factors
	Schizophrenia
	PTSD (esp. combat-related PTSD)
	Anxiety disorder
	Personality disorder (esp. borderline and antisocial)
	Eating disorders
	Body dysmorphic disorder
	Conduct disorder (in adolescents)
	Comorbid disorders (e.g., depression and anxiety, alcohol abuse and depression.
	schizophrenia and depression, PTSD and alcohol abuse)
I. Medical illness	Cancer (risk greater in first year)
	HIV/AIDS (risk greater with progression of disease)
	End-stage renal disease (risk greater—age >60)
	Spinal cord injury/disease (risk greater in first 2–5 years)
	Traumatic brain injury (risk greater with cerebral contusions)
	Epilepsy (risk greater for women)
	Stroke (risk greater when age <50)
	Multiple sclerosis (risk greater in first year)
	Huntington's disease (risk greater just prior to diagnosis and with decreased functioning)
	Comorbid Axis III and Axis I disorders (e.g., Axis III disorder and depression or alcohol abuse)
II. Acute/proximal risk factors	Current suicidal ideation[b]
A. Suicide ideation/ behavior	Current suicidal plan[b]
	Current suicidal plan includes very lethal means
	Preparation for suicide (e.g., giving away valued possessions)
	Recent suicide attempt (with no wish to be saved)
B. Acute symptoms of mental disorder	Acute depression
	Active abuse of alcohol (esp. increased use relative to historical pattern)
	Depression following cocaine use

Table 5.1

Risk and Protective Factors for Suicide (*Continued*)

Category of risk/ protective factors	Specific risk/protective factors
	Rapid mood cycling in bipolar disorder
	Command hallucinations (to commit suicide)
	Insomnia
	Persistent nightmares
C. Acute comorbid mental disorders	Acute depression and anxiety or panic symptoms
	Acute depression and agitation
	Alcohol abuse and acute depression
	Schizophrenia and depressed mood
	PTSD and active alcohol abuse
	Borderline personality disorder and depression
D. Physical illness and acute emotional distress	Physical illness and depression
	Burdensomeness of multiple physical illnesses
	Unremitting and disabling pain
E. Cognitive/ psychological features	Feelings of hopelessness
	Severe anhedonia and depressed mood
	Global insomnia and depressed mood
	Decreased self-esteem
	Feelings of shame or humiliation
	Feelings of intolerable aloneness
	Few or no reasons for living
	Feeling loss of purpose or meaning
	Feelings of being trapped
F. Behavioral features	Increased impulsive behavior or recklessness
	Increased anger and/or aggression
	Recent violent behavior
	Final act behaviors (e.g., making last will; giving possessions away)
	Evidence of stalking or preparation for murder/suicide
	Nonsuicidal self-injury

(continued)

Table 5.1

Risk and Protective Factors for Suicide (*Continued*)

Category of risk/ protective factors	Specific risk/protective factors
G. Psychosocial issues	Recent loss or disruption of relationship
	Lack of social support
	Recent discharge from psychiatric hospital
	Unemployment
	Financial strain
	Loss of socioeconomic status
	Suicide cluster (contagion; esp. with adolescents)
	Exposure to suicide of a peer or of someone admired
	Dramatic media coverage of a suicide
	Victim of bullying (esp. with children and adolescents)
	Pending legal charges or criminal charges
III. Protective factors	Good social support
	Family cohesion and involvement (for adolescents)
	Involvement in school activities
	Easy access to mental health care and substance abuse treatment
	Good problem-solving skills/ability to consider options
	Children under 18 in the home
	Pregnancy
	Multiple reasons for living
	Cultural/religious beliefs that provide meaning and discourage suicide
	Restriction of access to highly lethal weapons/methods of suicide

Note. I thank the following members of the Section on Clinical Emergencies and Crises (Section VII of APA Division 12), Alan Berman, PhD, David Drummond, PhD, Lisa Firestone, PhD, and Marc Hillbrand, PhD, for their assistance and contributions in the development of this list of risk and protective factors for suicide. Reprinted with permission of the Society for Clinical Psychology (Division 12 of the American Psychological Association).

[a]The absence of past suicidal ideation/attempts cannot be taken as an indicator of lower risk. It is estimated that more than 60% of suicides occur on the first attempt.

[b]An individual's denial of current suicide ideation or plan should not be taken to mean that there is no suicide risk. Also, both active suicide ideation and passive suicide ideation (e.g., wishes to die without thoughts of killing oneself) confer increased risk.

always clear how much weight to assign to any given risk or protective factor or any given combination of risk or protective factors. The co-occurrence of certain risk factors might be additive (i.e., equal to the sum of the risk associated with each factor) or subadditive (i.e., equal to a risk greater than that of one factor but not equal to the sum of the two). Risk factors might also interact synergistically, and the combined risk could be greater than the simple sum of the risk associated with each factor.

Familiarity with risk and protective factors (such as those in Table 5.1) can provide the clinician with guidance as he or she attempts to arrive at a formulation or judgment about the level or degree of suicide risk for the individual in question. The list of factors in Table 5.1 is by no means exhaustive, given that there are hundreds of identified risk factors for suicide. As noted previously, such a list should be regarded as an aid for the clinician, but a review of risk and protective factors should never be mistaken for a *risk assessment,* which is something that entails a more complete evaluation and case formulation. The presence of risk factors for suicide or violence should alert the clinician to the possibility that an individual is at risk, particularly if the factors appear to be very serious risk factors (e.g., a recent, near-fatal suicide attempt with strong intent to die). It should be borne in mind, however, that in general, the presence of one or more risk factors does not necessarily mean that a patient or client is currently suicidal or potentially violent. Again, that judgment should ideally be made after an evidence-informed evaluation and a carefully considered case formulation that includes a consideration of risk and protective factors.

There are clearly limitations to the use of risk and protective factors for determining suicide risk or violence risk. In 2003, the American Association of Suicidology convened a working group that took the position that risk factors (particularly those that are long-standing risk factors) are insufficient to assess suicide risk (Rudd et al., 2006). This working group argued that the current state of the individual must also be taken into account. Thus, they attempted to contrast the concept of suicide risk with that of a *suicide crisis* (i.e., a time-limited emotional state in which there is imminent risk of suicide).[1] They also posited that there are warning signs in the suicide crisis state that suggest near-term risk (i.e., risk within the next few hours to days) of suicidal behavior.

By expert consensus within the working group, Rudd et al. (2006) suggested a two-tier model of warning signs for suicide. The first tier consists of three warning signs that should direct the individual to call 911 or seek immediate professional help:

- (a) someone threatening to hurt or kill themselves;
- (b) someone looking for ways to kill themselves; and
- (c) someone talking or writing about death, dying, or suicide.

The second tier consists of nine warning signs that should direct the individual to seek help without specifying the need to get immediate assistance:

- (a) hopelessness;
- (b) rage, anger, seeking revenge;
- (c) acting reckless or engaging in risky activities seemingly without thinking;
- (d) feeling trapped—like there's no way out;
- (e) increasing alcohol or drug use;
- (f) withdrawing from friends, family, or society;
- (g) anxiety, agitation, unable to sleep, or sleeping all the time;
- (h) dramatic changes in mood; and
- (i) no reason for living or no sense of purpose in life.

Van Orden et al. (2006) examined whether reading the warning signs would increase awareness of identifiable signs of a suicidal crisis and prompt individuals to engage in helping behaviors. They recruited 275 introductory psychology students to read two sets of warning signs. The experimental group first read a list of warning signs for diabetes and then the list of warning signs for suicide. The control group first read a list

---

[1] As used here, the term *suicide crisis* appears to be similar to what I have referred to as a *behavioral emergency* or, more specifically, a *suicidal emergency* (Kleespies, 1998a, 2009).

of warning signs for diabetes and then a list of warning signs for heart attack. Both groups then completed a measure of mood and a health beliefs questionnaire designed to measure attitudes, beliefs, and expectancies related to the three health conditions—that is, diabetes, heart attacks, and suicide. The findings indicated that those participants who read the list of warning signs reported a greater ability to recognize when someone was suicidal. The researchers, however, did not find that reading the warning signs for suicide increased awareness of the seriousness of the signs for suicide or of the preventable and treatable nature of suicidality. They hypothesized that a brief exposure to the suicide warning signs may not have been sufficient to produce changes in knowledge or beliefs about suicide risk.

ACTUARIAL METHODS FOR ASSESSING RISK

Since Meehl (1954) published his classic book *Clinical Versus Statistical Prediction,* it has been known that actuarial risk prediction methods frequently achieve a higher level of accuracy than unaided clinical judgment. Douglas, Ogloff, and Hart (2003) reiterated this point in reference to the prediction of violence to others. There are clearly those who strongly support the use and further development of actuarial methods (Hilton, Harris, & Rice, 2010). Others (e.g., Douglas et al., 2003, and Meehl himself) have pointed out that there are shortcomings associated with strict actuarial models of risk prediction. Thus, for example, Douglas et al. (2003) stated that the application of a formula or actuarial table to arrive at the probability of a particular outcome can be a rigid process that overlooks or excludes clinical nuances and is often insensitive to dynamic changes in the individual and the circumstances. The evaluator is forced to consider a fixed set of static factors to the exclusion of unique or context-specific variables that might have a significant impact on the assessment. In addition, others have argued that risk assessment should drive risk management and that the historical and static risk factors that comprise actuarial models have little to offer in terms of management, direction for reduction in risk, and violence prevention (Haggard-Grann, 2007).

In the remainder of this section, I briefly review two of the actuarial instruments that have been widely discussed in the literature on violence risk assessment. I then discuss the approach to risk assessment known as *structured professional judgment* and some of the risk assessment tools associated with it.

The Psychopathy Checklist

The Hare Psychopathy Checklist–Revised (PCL-R; Hare, 1991) was not originally devised as a violence risk assessment instrument. It was intended as a measure of the clinical construct of psychopathy, which is defined by a cluster of affective and behavioral personality traits including superficiality, egocentricity, deceitful or manipulative behavior, shallow emotions, lack of empathy and/or remorse, early behavioral problems, impulsivity, and irresponsible and/or criminal behavior. Research, however, began to indicate that psychopathy as measured with the PCL-R was also correlated with violent and criminal behavior, particularly in correctional and forensic psychiatric populations (Fabian, 2006). The findings seemed sufficiently impressive that violence risk assessment instruments such as the Historical-Clinical-Risk Management-20 (HCR-20; Webster, Douglas, Eaves, & Hart, 1997) and the Violence Risk Appraisal Guide (VRAG; Rice & Harris, 1995) included the administration of the entire PCL-R as an item on their checklists.

Given that the administration of the PCL-R is time consuming, a shorter version, the Psychopathy Checklist: Screening Version (PCL:SV), was developed (Hart, Cox, & Hare, 1995). As a screening tool, it is considered appropriate for use with civil psychiatric populations, and a working familiarity with its administration and content could be helpful when a clinician is under time pressure to make a decision about violence risk. It consists of 12 items (as opposed to the 20 items on the PCL-R), and it assesses most of the traits and behaviors noted in the previous paragraph. Recent review articles, however, have pointed out that the psychopathy checklist has a high false positive rate and explains only a small percentage of the violent behaviors that it seeks to predict (Fabian, 2006). In addition, Singh, Grann, and Fazel (2011), in a comparative study of nine of the most commonly used structured violence risk assessment instruments, found that the PCL-R produced the lowest rates of predictive validity of any of the nine instruments.[2]

The Violence Risk Appraisal Guide

The VRAG is an actuarial instrument originally designed to predict violent recidivism for offenders being considered for release to the community or to other minimum security settings. It consists of 12 historical variables that include living with both biological parents to age 16, elementary school maladjustment, history of alcohol problems, marital status, criminal history for nonviolent offenses, failure on prior conditional release, age at index offense, victim injury, any female victim, diagnosis of personality disorder, diagnosis of schizophrenia, and psychopathy as measured by the PCL-R. It is scored with both positive and negative ratings and thus assesses for both risk and protective factors. Its ability to predict violent recidivism for mentally disordered and convicted offenders has been extensively studied, and it has been found to have good reliability and predictive validity not only with violent offenders but also, in modified form, with sexual offenders (Quinsey, Harris, Rice, & Cormier, 1998).

There has been an effort to modify the VRAG to predict the risk of interpersonal violence posed by nonforensic psychiatric patients. Harris, Rice, and Camilleri (2004) used archival data from the MacArthur Violence Risk Assessment Study (Monahan et al., 2001). The participants were voluntary and civilly committed inpatients from three public hospitals in different regions of the country. Two of the original VRAG items (e.g., failure on prior conditional release) were dropped, and there were other minor modifications. Over a 20-week follow-up period, the modified and shortened VRAG yielded a large effect size in predicting the occurrence of subsequent serious violence. The authors felt that their findings supported those of other studies indicating that the clinical problems of forensic and

---

[2] In a separate meta-analytic comparison of violence risk assessment tools, Yang, Wong, and Coid (2010) found that the PCL-R, the PCL:SV, the HCR-20, and the VRAG all had about the same moderate level of predictive accuracy. The comparative study by Yang et al. did not include assessment tools such as the Structured Assessment of Violence Risk in Youth (SAVRY) or the Spousal Assault Risk Assessment Guide (SARA), both of which are discussed later in this chapter.

nonforensic patients are similar and that the predictors of violence are quite general rather than specific to particular populations.

As noted previously, the VRAG requires the administration of another instrument, the PCL-R. The PCL-R requires a relatively extensive and time-consuming interview. This requirement greatly reduces the VRAG's utility in emergency situations in which there are time constraints on decision making. Moreover, in the meta-analytic review by Singh et al. (2011), there was no evidence that the VRAG or any of the other actuarial instruments in that review produced better levels of predictive validity than decision-support tools developed in the structured professional judgment framework, as discussed in the next section.

STRUCTURED PROFESSIONAL JUDGMENT AND DECISION-SUPPORT TOOLS

An emerging and promising alternative to either solely clinical or strictly actuarial assessment is an approach that has been referred to as *structured professional judgment*.[3] The structured professional judgment model attempts to draw on the strengths of both the clinical and actuarial approaches to decision making (Borum, Lodewijks, Bartel, & Forth, 2010). As a model, it is in keeping with the effort of Westen and Weinberger (2004) to reframe the clinical versus statistical prediction debate. These authors proposed that, in this debate, psychologists have largely overlooked or failed to focus on the value of crossing clinical observation with statistical aggregation (or actuarial methods) in risk prediction. Thus, in structured professional judgment, the clinician typically uses a set of key evidence-based risk factors to guide his or her judgment. The evaluator reviews all relevant clinical data, and his or her clinical impression is taken as an appropriate and potentially valuable part of the assessment process. The evidence-based set of risk factors, however, constitutes a guide to the exercise of the clinician's judgment. Such

---

[3] A great many decision-support tools have been developed in the past 20 years. The discussion of decision-support tools in this section is not intended to be an exhaustive review. Rather, it is a presentation of a few examples of such instruments that have established reliability and predictive validity.

a set of risk factors has typically been referred to as a *decision-support tool* and is usually available in manual form. Decision-support tools are not standardized psychological test instruments. Many of them have been assessed for their reliability and predictive validity, but they have been viewed as more of an *aide memoir* for the clinician. Some authors of these tools (e.g., Borum, Bartel, & Forth, 2006, the authors of the Structured Assessment of Violence Risk in Youth [SAVRY]) instruct the clinician to rate risk factors as low, moderate, or high but do not call for assigning numerical values to the factors. This approach explicitly avoids attempting to derive standardized scores or norms as one would in developing a psychometric instrument.

As noted previously, Singh et al. (2011) conducted a comparative study of nine of the most commonly used structured violence risk assessment instruments. Their review included 68 studies, 88 independent samples, and 25,980 participants. In their meta-analysis, they found substantial differences in the predictive validity of these nine tools. In the remainder of this chapter, I discuss three of the structured professional judgment tools that Singh et al. found to have the highest predictive validity (i.e., the HCR-20, the SAVRY, and the Spousal Assault Risk Assessment [SARA]) and that have been used with civil rather than strictly forensic populations.[4] Although it was not included in the study by Singh et al., I also discuss the Short-Term Assessment of Risk and Treatability (START), a relatively new instrument that attempts to aid in the assessment of both risk of violence and risk of suicide. Although most of the structured professional judgment instruments noted previously were developed to attempt to detect acute or short-term risk, they were not necessarily designed for use in an emergency situation. Nonetheless, a working familiarity with a select few of them can help to inform the judgment of the clinician who must deal with a behavioral emergency.

---

[4]A recent systematic review and meta-analysis of the most commonly used actuarial instruments and the most commonly used structured clinical judgment tools for violence risk assessment (including 73 samples and 24,827 participants) found that these instruments had higher negative predictive values than positive predictive values (Fazel, Singh, Doll, & Grann, 2012). In other words, the instruments or tools identified those who were less likely to be violent with high levels of accuracy (specificity) but (with one notable exception—the SAVRY) had low to moderate levels of accuracy in identifying those who were likely to actually become violent (sensitivity).

The Historical-Clinical-Risk Management-20 (Version 2)

One of the decision-support tools in the review by Singh et al. (2011) has generated a great deal of research and clinical interest in recent years. The HCR-20 (Webster et al., 1997) involves coding 20 variables that the support tool's authors have determined to be evidence based in the research literature on estimating violence risk. There are

- 10 Historical items (i.e., previous violence, young age at first violent incident, relationship instability, employment problems, substance use problems, major mental illness, psychopathy, early maladjustment, personality disorder, and prior supervision failure),
- five Clinical items (i.e., lack of insight, negative attitudes, active symptoms of major mental illness, impulsivity, and unresponsiveness to treatment), and
- five Risk Management items (i.e., plans lack feasibility, exposure to destabilizers, lack of personal support, noncompliance with remediation attempts, and stress).

Each item is coded on a 3-point scale, with 0 indicating that the item is *not present,* 1 indicating the *possible* or *partial presence* of the item, and 2 indicating that the item is *clearly present.*

A number of studies have provided evidence for the utility of the HCR-20 in assessing the short-term risk of violence in both civil and forensic settings. In fact, there is an extensive and annotated bibliography (Douglas, Blanchard, Guy, Reeves, & Weir, 2010) documenting the empirical support for the HCR-20 that can be obtained at http://kdouglas. wordpress.com. I cite several selected studies here to give the reader a perspective on the type of support that has been accumulating for the HCR-20.

McNiel, Gregory, Lam, Sullivan, and Binder (2003) used a retrospective case control method of sampling in evaluating the HCR-20 and two other decision-support tools, the PCL:SV and the McNiel-Binder Violence Screening Checklist (VSC). They selected 50 cases of individuals who had become violent after admission to a locked psychiatric inpatient unit. They then used a random numbers table to select 50 patients who had been admitted to the same unit in the same year and had not become violent after admission. Two doctoral students who had been trained in the use of the decision-support tools and who were blind to whether the patients had subsequently become violent rated the cases on the basis of the medical record at the time of admission. They found that the HCR-20 total score was significantly correlated with the likelihood of violence, but the finding was primarily due to the Clinical items on the scale. The VSC also showed a significant association with the likelihood of later violence. In a subsequent multivariate logistic regression analysis in which violence was predicted on the basis of subscales of the HCR-20, subscales of the PCL:SV, and the VSC, only the Clinical subscale of the HCR-20 and the VSC made independent contributions to violence prediction.

The investigators concluded that in their study of short-term risk, the Clinical items of the HCR-20 were predictive of violence. They pointed out, however, that other studies (e.g., Douglas, Ogloff, Nicholls, & Grant, 1999) have found the Historical items more predictive of long-term risk. Taken together, they commented that the findings suggest that the HCR-20 has good flexibility and that elevations of its subscales seem to vary as a function of the phase of the individual's mental illness.

In a prospective study, Douglas et al. (2003) selected 100 forensic psychiatric patients who were found not guilty by reason of a mental disorder and who, during a 1-year period (1996–1997), were subsequently released to the community. Of this group, 92% had a previous charge of violence, 79% had a current violent index offense, and 96% had previously received psychiatric treatment. One objective of the study was to test the reliability and validity of the structured final risk judgment of potential for violence made under the structured professional judgment model. They used the HCR-20 as the guide for structured professional judgment. Raters reviewed the clinical information, completed the HCR-20, and then made structured final risk judgments of 1 = *low risk*, 2 = *moderate risk*, or 3 = *high risk*.

Using receiver operating characteristic analysis and bivariate survival analysis, they found that when any violence, or any physical violence, was used as the dependent measure, structured final risk judgments emerged as a significant predictor of violence in the community. Using Cox regression analyses and entering the HCR-20 scale scores into the model, they found that only the Clinical scale of the HCR-20 was a significant predictor of violence. When the structured final risk judgments were added to the model, however, they produced a significant improvement in the prediction of violence. The investigators concluded that the structured final risk judgments were strongly related to the prediction of violence beyond the actuarial scores in the HCR-20 scales. The study was taken as validation for the use of the HCR-20 in arriving at a structured professional judgment about risk while also demonstrating the value of clinical judgment as a part of the decision-making process.

In a previously cited study (see Chapter 3 of this volume), Teo, Holly, Leary, and McNiel (2012) examined first whether unstructured violence risk assessments completed by experienced attending psychiatrists were more accurate than those completed by psychiatric residents, and second whether the addition of information from the HCR-20 would improve the accuracy of the risk assessments by the residents. Using a retrospective case-control design, the research team selected 151 patients from four locked psychiatric units of a county hospital who had physically assaulted staff during the years 2003 through 2008. They also selected an equal number of nonviolent patients matched for psychiatric inpatient unit and month of admission. Physicians, on admission to these units, rated each patient on a 4-point assault precaution checklist that ranged from 0 (*no clinical indication for violence precautions*) to 3 (*strong intent is present or unable to control impulses*). Two psychiatric nurses who had been trained in the use of the measure rated the HCR-20 on the basis of information in the medical record at the time of admission. The nurses were blind in regard to whether the patients later became violent.

As stated in Chapter 3, it was found that the unstructured clinical assessments by attending psychiatrists had a moderate degree of predictive validity, whereas those completed by residents were no better than chance. The violence risk assessments by the attending psychiatrists were significantly more accurate than the risk assessments by residents. In addition, however, incremental validity analyses showed that the addition of information from the HCR-20 Clinical scale had the potential to improve the accuracy of risk assessments by residents to a level close to that of the attending psychiatrists. The investigators concluded that less training and experience is associated with less accurate violence risk assessment;

however, the use of structured methods such as the HCR-20 holds promise for improving the risk assessments of those who are less experienced.

As noted earlier, a requirement of the HCR-20 in its present form (Version 2) is that the clinician base his or her rating of Historical item 7 (psychopathy) on scores obtained from the PCL:SV or PCL-R (Hart et al., 1995). This requirement introduces the need to complete a second and more time-consuming assessment, something that seems to make the HCR-20, in its present form, less potentially useful as an *aide memoir* when there is time pressure to make a decision about how to manage a particular case. Questions, however, were raised in the meta-analytic review by L. S. Guy, Douglas, and Hendry (2010) about whether the PCL-R adds anything to the predictive validity of the HCR-20.[5]

Interestingly, the research group that created the HCR-20 has attempted to move beyond the assessment process to the task of preventing violence. They developed the *HCR-20 Violence Risk Management Companion Guide* (Douglas, Webster, Hart, Eaves, & Ogloff, 2001), the purpose of which is to assist the clinician, on the basis of an assessment using the HCR-20, in considering how best to reduce the risk of aggression and violence. The Historical factors on the HCR-20 are taken as static, but the Clinical factors and the Risk Management factors are dynamic or changeable variables. In the companion guide, these 10 dynamic factors are discussed, and strategies for changing them in a positive direction are suggested. Thus, for example, if an individual is positive for the Clinical factor of impulsivity, the companion guide suggests an approach based on dialectical behavior therapy (Linehan, 1993). This approach stresses a behavioral analysis of impulsive behavior and learning distress tolerance skills and emotion regulation strategies.

The Structured Assessment of Violence Risk in Youth

The SAVRY (Borum, Bartel, & Forth, 2006) is modeled after existing structured professional judgment instruments like the HCR-20, but it is specifically designed for assessing violence risk in adolescents (ages 12–18).

---

[5] As noted, the discussion presented above was based on the HCR-20 (Version 2). While this book was in production, Version 3 of the HCR-20 was published. In Version 3, the clinician may use the PCL-R of PCL-SV in rating item 7 (psychopathy), but he or she is not required to do so.

The authors of the SAVRY designed the protocol with the understanding that youth are actively developing and changing. Relative to adulthood, certain personality characteristics and behaviors in childhood and adolescence are much less stable across time and context. These characteristics and behaviors can vary in presentation at different stages of psychosocial and emotional development.

The SAVRY has 24 risk factors that are divided into three sections: (a) Historical risk factors, (b) Social/Contextual risk factors, and (c) Individual/Clinical risk factors. It also has six items that are considered Protective factors, and a section for additional risk factors that may emerge from the individual case and can be added to the protocol. Each risk factor is rated on a three-level scale—that is, low, moderate, or high. As noted earlier in this chapter, a numerical rating is typically not assigned to avoid the implication that a score would have scientific significance.

- The 10 Historical risk factors are history of violence, history of nonviolent offending, early initiation of violence, past supervision/intervention failures, history of self-harm or suicide attempts, exposure to violence in the home, childhood history of maltreatment, parental/caregiver criminality, early caregiver disruption, and poor school achievement.
- The six Social/Contextual risk factors are peer delinquency, peer rejection, stress and poor coping, poor parental management, lack of personal/social support, and community disorganization.
- The eight Individual/Clinical risk factors are negative attitudes, risk taking/impulsivity, substance use difficulties, anger management problems, low empathy/remorse, attention-deficit/hyperactivity difficulties, poor compliance, and low interest/commitment to school.
- The six Protective factors are noted as present or absent; these are prosocial involvement, strong social support, strong attachments and bonds, positive attitude toward intervention and authority, strong commitment to school, and resilient personality traits.

After converting the SAVRY risk ratings to numerical scores (*low* = 0, *moderate* = 1, *high* = 2), Dolan and Rennie (2006) found good internal consistency for the SAVRY risk total with an alpha coefficient of .83. In terms of interrater reliability, Vincent, Guy, Fusco, and Gershenson (2012) conducted two complimentary studies of the SAVRY, one under laboratory-like conditions and one under field conditions. In the former, the researchers had 408 juvenile probation officers and social workers rate four standardized case vignettes with the SAVRY. The juvenile probation officers had a high level of agreement with expert consensus on the rating of overall risk and total scores. In the field study, the SAVRY was used with 80 young offender cases that were rated by juvenile probation officers and trained research assistants. The intraclass correlation coefficients were excellent for the SAVRY total score (.86) and for most domain scores (ranging from .81 to .86, with the exception of the Social/Contextual domain, which was .67). They were also good (.71) for overall risk ratings. The authors concluded that the SAVRY and the method of structured professional judgment can be used reliably in the field by juvenile probation officers and has reliability indices comparable to those reported under more lab-like conditions.

In the review by Singh et al. (2011), the SAVRY, among the nine violence risk instruments examined, was found to have the highest rates of predictive validity across four outcome measures—that is, the area under the receiver operating characteristic curve, the positive predictive value, the negative predictive value, and the diagnostic odds ratio. In addition, there have been studies examining the link between summary risk ratings on the SAVRY and actual violent recidivism. Thus, Catchpole and Gretton (2003) found that youth classified as High Risk on the SAVRY had a 40% violent recidivism rate, whereas those classified as Moderate Risk and Low Risk had recidivism rates of 14% and 6%, respectively. In a second study of SAVRY-assessed youth (Gammelgard, Weitzman-Henelius, & Kaltiala-Heino, 2008), those adolescents in Finland who were rated at High Risk for violent recidivism had a 67% rate of recidivism, whereas those assessed as Moderate Risk had a 29% rate, and those assessed as Low Risk had only a 4% rate. Logistic regression analysis adjusted for gender, age, diagnosis, service level, and time of follow-up showed that the odds of violent recidivism increased according to risk level. In fact, the High Risk group was found to be nearly 28 times more likely to reoffend violently than the Low Risk group, whereas the Moderate Risk group was nearly 4 times more likely to reoffend than the Low Risk group.

For those interested, a more extensive listing and description of studies on the predictive validity of the SAVRY can be found in the recent book chapter by Borum, Lodewijks, Bartel, and Forth (2010).

The Spousal Assault Risk Assessment Guide

The SARA (Kropp, Hart, Webster, & Eaves, 2008) is a clinical checklist of risk factors for spousal assault. It consists of 20 individual items identified by a review of the empirical literature and by an examination of articles written by clinicians with extensive experience in evaluating men who abuse their spouses or partners. The relevant studies present risk factors that have discriminated those who were violent toward spouses and those who were not, as well as risk factors associated with recidivistic violence among known spousal assaulters. The risk items are grouped into five content areas: (a) criminal history, (b) psychosocial adjustment, (c) spousal assault history, (d) index offense (i.e., current or most recent incident of assault), and (e) a final section that allows the examiner to note risk factors not included in the SARA.

The items grouped under criminal history include

- (a) past assault of family members,
- (b) past assault of strangers or acquaintances, and
- (c) past violation of conditional release or community supervision.

Those grouped under psychosocial adjustment include

- (a) recent relationship problems;
- (b) recent employment problems;
- (c) victim of and/or witness to family violence as a child or adolescent;
- (d) recent substance abuse/dependence;
- (e) recent suicidal or homicidal ideation/intent;
- (f) recent psychotic and/or manic symptoms; and
- (g) personality disorder with features such as anger, impulsivity, or behavioral instability.

Those included under spousal assault history are

- (a) past physical assault,
- (b) past sexual assault/sexual jealousy,
- (c) past use of weapons and/or credible threats of death,
- (d) recent escalation in frequency or severity of assault,
- (e) past violations of "no contact" orders,
- (f) extreme minimization or denial of spousal assault history, and
- (g) attitudes that support or condone spousal assault.

Those grouped under index (current or most recent) offense include

- (a) severe and/or sexual assault,
- (b) use of weapons and/or credible threats of death, and
- (c) violation of "no contact" order.

As noted previously, there is a final section that allows the clinician to include important risk factors that may be particular to the individual case and not included as an item in the SARA—for example, a current emotional crisis, a history of torturing sexual partners, or easy access to firearms. The evaluator is also to indicate whether any item or factor is considered critical (i.e., particularly relevant to decisions about risk).

As with the HCR-20, each item on the SARA is coded on a 3-point scale with N indicating that the item is *not present,* P indicating the *possible* or *partial presence* of the item, and Y indicating that the item is *clearly present.* By converting these scale points to a numerical scale ($N = 0, P = 1, Y = 2$), a total risk score can be obtained for research purposes, but the SARA (like the HCR-20 and the SAVRY) was not designed to be a psychological test with standardized scores. Rather, it is a guide for clinicians to use in arriving at an estimated level of risk (low, moderate, or high).

The reliability and predictive validity of judgments made with the SARA were initially evaluated by Kropp and Hart (2000), who based their ratings on interviews with a sample of adult male offenders that included a total of 2,681 men. The subjects comprised two large groups: (a) men serving terms of probation for offenses related to spousal assault and (b) inmates serving custodial terms for violent offenses, most of which (65%) were not spousal assaults. SARA ratings were made by correctional mental health staff and research staff. They also rated participants on the PCL:SV and the VRAG. The investigators found that interrater reliability for the SARA was high for judgments of the presence of individual risk factors and for overall perceived risk. In terms of discriminant validity, SARA ratings were found to significantly discriminate between offenders with and without a history of spousal violence, and between recidivistic and nonrecidivistic spousal assaulters. In addition, SARA ratings for both general violence and for spousal assault showed moderate convergent validity with the PCL:SV, whereas general violence risk items on the SARA had moderate correlations with the VRAG. Further, using hierarchical logistic regression, the authors found that their summary risk estimates significantly differentiated between recidivists and nonrecidivists even after controlling for actuarial scores on the SARA. They concluded that decisions made using structured professional judgment outperformed decisions made using a more strictly actuarial method.

There is evidence that not only psychologists and psychiatrists but also police officers and other criminal justice professionals can be trained in the structured professional judgment approach and in the use of instruments like the SARA. Storey, Gibas, Reeves, and Hart (2011) trained police and criminal justice professionals in the administration of the SARA. In pre- and postevaluations using multiple-choice testing and assessment of responses to case vignettes, they found significant improvements in knowledge about spousal assault, identification of risk factors for spousal assault, identification of risk level, and identification of management strategies to reduce risk. The authors felt that their findings supported the use of the SARA by appropriately trained police officers.

For those clinicians who may need to make decisions about short-term risk under time pressure, it should be mentioned that work is being done on a briefer support tool based on the SARA—that is, the Brief Spousal Assault Form for the Evaluation of Risk or the B-SAFER (Au et al., 2008).

The Short-Term Assessment of Risk and Treatability

The START (Webster, Martin, Brink, Nicholls, & Desmarais, 2009) is a more recently developed decision-support tool with the same lead author as the HCR-20, Christopher Webster. It is an ambitious effort to construct a relatively brief clinical guide for the assessment of seven defined risks: (a) risk of violence to others, (b) risk of self-harm, (c) risk of suicide, (d) risk of taking unauthorized leave, (e) risk of substance use, (f) risk of self-neglect, and (g) risk of being victimized by others. To those of us who have advocated for a more integrated approach to behavioral emergencies (e.g., Kleespies & Hill, 2011), it is of interest in that it assumes that violence directed at others and violence directed at the self are, at least in certain respects, interrelated and have certain risk factors, if not causes, in common.

The START is not independent of the HCR-20, but it has significant differences, is more complex, and is somewhat more complicated to administer. Building on research (e.g., Chu, Thomas, Ogloff, & Daffern, 2011) that suggests that dynamic factors have independent and incremental validity over static factors in assessing for acute violence risk, the START is focused far more on present factors and less than the HCR-20 on historical factors. Nonetheless, it is noted in the START manual that it should be supplemented by a careful assessment of historical factors (Webster, Martin, et al., 2009).

The START requires the clinician to rate its 20 factors as present or not present on two scales: a scale that assesses whether the particular factor is *minimally present* (0), *moderately present* (1), or *maximally present* (2) as a strength; and a scale that assesses whether the particular factor is *minimally present* (0), *moderately present* (1), or *maximally present* (2) as a vulnerability. With this type of rating, the authors attempted to assess not only risk factors but also protective factors. Because the scales for strengths and for vulnerabilities are separate, it is possible that certain factors may be rated as both a strength and a vulnerability. The 20 START factors are social skills, relationships, occupational (participation in work), recreational (participation in recreational activities), self-care, mental state, emotional state, substance use, impulse control, external triggers, social support, material resources (adequate financial means), attitudes, medication adherence, rule adherence, conduct, insight, plans, coping, and treatability. Those using the START are also encouraged to insert and rate one or two write-in items, which may not be covered by the factors noted previously but which may be risk or protective factors in the individual case.

Although research investigating the validity of the START is in its early stages, there are studies that address the issue of validity. Nicholls, Brink, Desmarais, Webster, and Martin (2006) conducted the original prospective validation study. These investigators recruited 137 patients from a forensic psychiatric hospital in Canada who had all been deemed not criminally responsible for a violent crime by virtue of a mental disorder. The patients were typically men who suffered from schizophrenia and comorbid substance abuse. They all also had to appear before an annual review board to have their progress and status reviewed. Prior to appearing before the review board, treatment team members were asked to complete the START with each patient. Of the 137 patients, 51 were retained in the hospital for the 1-year follow-up period of the study. These 51 patients constituted the validation sample. Data were collected on each of these patients using the Overt Aggression Scale (OAS; Yudofsky, Silver, Jackson, Endicott, & Williams, 1986), which assesses observable aggressive or violent behavior. The data were obtained by trained research assistants from the patients' clinical–legal records.

Analyses of the follow-up data found that there was good internal consistency for the instrument as well as good interrater reliability. Also, the mean START scores of patients who aggressed against others were significantly higher than for those patients who remained incident free during the follow-up period. This finding held true across multiple types and severity of aggressive behaviors. In addition, mean START scores differed significantly between those patients who aggressed against themselves and those who did not. Of the patients who committed acts of self-harm, 77.8% were also found to have been physically aggressive to others. Moreover, patients who were physically aggressive to others were also found to be at greater risk of being victimized themselves.

In a more recent study, Desmarais, Nicholls, Wilson, and Brink (2012) examined the reliability and validity of START assessments in predicting inpatient aggression in comparison with the Historical subscale scores of the HCR-20 and the PCL-SV total scores. As in the study by Nicholls et al. (2006), these investigators randomly selected 120 male patients in a secure forensic psychiatric hospital in Canada. Most of the participants had a schizophrenic spectrum disorder, and over 50% had a comorbid substance use disorder. Most had had an index offense that was violent in nature, and most had been found not criminally responsible by virtue of a mental disorder. The OAS had been used to collect data on incidents of inpatient aggression during a preceding 12-month period. Trained research assistants, who were blind to which patients had had incidents of inpatient aggression, completed the START, the HCR-20, and the PCL-SV with each patient.

The interrater reliability was high for the START Strength and Vulnerability total scores. Strength and Vulnerability total scores were found to have strong correlations with violence risk estimates. In particular, as Strength total scores increased, estimates of violence decreased; as Vulnerability total scores increased, estimates of violence also increased. In terms of validity, the predictive capacity of the START violence risk estimates exceeded those of the HCR-20 and the PCL-SV. The researchers also assessed the incremental validity of START assessments over historical risk factors. Using direct entry hierarchical logistic regression analyses, it was found that, in all models with the Historical scale scores of the HCR-20 and with the PCL-SV, the addition of the START violence risk estimates produced increases in predictive capacity and revealed unique contributions to the violence risk estimates originally made with these instruments.

Desmarais et al. (2012) concluded that their findings suggested that the START may be useful in distinguishing between patients who are more or less likely to engage in aggressive behaviors. They also noted that their findings add to the body of literature supporting the importance of dynamic factors in risk assessment. They cautioned, however, that historical variables should provide the foundation on which dynamic factors can build in making risk assessments. They also pointed out that the START is intended to guide assessors in determining risk across several domains, but their study only addressed risk of violence to others. Moreover, in the violence domain, the study did not speak to the ability of START assessments to predict violence in the very short term (i.e., over days and weeks rather than a year).

The START has primarily been tested on a rather narrow population— that is, male patients in a forensic psychiatric hospital who are predominantly schizophrenic, have a history of violence, and have been found to be not criminally responsible for their violent acts by virtue of mental disorder. There is clearly a need to test its predictive capability with civil psychiatric and outpatient populations. Although it is designed for the short-term assessment of risk, like the HCR-20, it is not necessarily amenable to the rapid assessment and decision making about short-term risk that is needed in emergency situations. Nonetheless, familiarity with the evidence-based dynamic risk and protective factors in the START would seem to be useful to the clinician when such rapid decisions need to be made.

CONCLUDING REMARKS

In this chapter, I have discussed an interesting direction in the assessment of short-term risk, a direction that has been most actively pursued by researchers in violence risk assessment. As mentioned, actuarial methods of violence risk assessment have long been known to be better than clinical methods; however, the structured professional judgment approach has led to the development of several decision-support tools that integrate actuarial and clinical methods and have shown good promise in terms of their predictive validity. Each of these decision-support tools calls for a focused interview to complete, and they may therefore not be easily used in high pressure, time-limited, mental health emergency situations. I contend, however, that a working familiarity with these instruments can serve as a so-called *aide memoir* that keeps the clinician focused on key evidence-based risk and protective factors when he or she is under pressure to quickly arrive at a decision about level of risk and appropriate management.

6

Training for Decision Making With *Experience Near* or Actual Behavioral Emergencies

Some time ago, Bongar, Lomax, and Harmatz (1992) pointed out in regard to the assessment of suicide risk that "knowledge of risk factors and the capacity to respond in an effective way to those patients who present as an imminent risk of suicide may be independent areas of clinical competence" (pp. 262–263). These areas of knowledge and skill may be separate competencies or perhaps the separate components of a competency, but the statement by Bongar et al. highlights my position that making good decisions in high-stakes situations in which the patient is at risk of suicide or violence to others, and in which there are many associated stressors, is something that is more fully learned only under real-life conditions. This position is not one that, in any way, denies the value of lectures, courses, workshops, discussions of past cases, or discussions of hypothetical case vignettes. These are all clearly important methods by which mental health professionals gain knowledge and learn about

http://dx.doi.org/10.1037/14337-007
Decision Making in Behavioral Emergencies: Acquiring Skill in Evaluating and Managing High-Risk Patients, by P. M. Kleespies

the assessment and management of behavioral emergencies. They are all methods, however, that provide education and training in a calm and controlled setting. Although there might be an effort to recreate or simulate the pressure and tension of an emergency situation, at the end of day there are no real consequences or potential for a bad outcome in real time. Moreover, they are often discrete episodes of learning rather than a more extended series of learning experiences that might be more likely to lead to recognition priming and allow for achieving greater mastery.

The APA Task Force on the Assessment of Competence in Professional Psychology (2006) attempted to provide a conceptual framework for thinking about competence in the practice of psychology. They seemed to embrace a definition of professional competence that had been proposed for the medical profession but that they felt was also relevant for professional psychology. With this definition, *competence* is "the habitual and judicious use of communication, knowledge, technical skills, clinical reasoning, emotions, values, and reflection in daily practice for the benefit of the individual and community being served" (R. M. Epstein & Hundert, 2002, p. 227). In this definition, there is an emphasis on the *habitual judicious use of knowledge, skills, and abilities in daily practice* as integral to achieving competence in professional functioning.

The APA Task Force went on to state that there are *competencies* that are elements of *competence*. Competencies are conceptualized as clusters of integrated knowledge, skills, and abilities that enable an individual to fully perform a task. They are divided into *foundational* competencies and *functional* competencies. Foundational competencies have to do with scientific knowledge, scientific methods, knowledge of ethical and legal standards, and so forth. They form the building blocks of what psychologists do. Functional competencies, on the other hand, have to do with assessment, diagnosis, intervention, consultation, and so forth. They reflect the knowledge, skills, and attitudes needed to actually perform the work of a professional psychologist. It seems to me that the assessment and management of behavioral emergencies is a functional competency that is important (I would argue *essential*) to the development of overall competence for practicing psychologists.

The APA Task Force report, while recommending that there be a culture shift in psychology toward placing a high value on the assessment of competence, also indicated that there have been many problems with arriving at a consensus about what constitutes competence and how to assess competence and competencies. It emphasized, however, that assessment should reflect fidelity to actual practice; that is, the assessment method should evaluate, as closely as possible, the actual behaviors that the clinician performs in practice. Thus, in assessing functional competencies, the APA Task Force suggested the development of reliable methods that use case vignettes, videotapes, or audiotapes of patient–practitioner interactions, written work samples, and/ or live patient–client situations. It is acknowledged that these methods are time intensive, labor intensive, and can be costly. Nonetheless, the APA Task Force's emphasis is on devising assessment methods that are *experience near.*

Experience near is a term used by the APA Task Force to describe the degree to which a task or measure reflects the actual behaviors the clinician must perform in practice. Thus, an assessment or training technique that involves the evaluation of a clinician while assessing a simulated patient is more experience near (i.e., closer to actual experience with a patient) than having the clinician take a multiple-choice exam assessing his or her knowledge of a particular clinical condition. Although a multiple-choice exam may be a good way to assess someone's knowledge base, evaluating a clinician while he or she assesses a simulated patient is a way to assess the individual's clinical skills.

In regard to training to become competent in the assessment and management of behavioral emergencies (i.e., in assessing and managing patients or clients who are at high risk of suicide or violence or both), I contend that the training itself, let alone the assessment of competence, is best accomplished in real-life encounters with actual patients/clients at risk in which the practitioner not only receives training but also experiences the stress training discussed in Chapter 3 of this volume. In the current chapter, I present a model for such a training program for behavioral emergencies.

TRAINING IN EVALUATING AND MANAGING BEHAVIORAL EMERGENCIES

As discussed in Chapter 3, training to evaluate and manage behavioral emergencies can be carried out using the three categories recommended in the report of the APA Task Force on the Assessment of Competence in Professional Psychology (2006)—that is, knowledge, skills, and attitudes. Such training is also compatible with the stress exposure training (SET) model. In the sections that follow, I discuss the content of a knowledge base that can be used to help the clinician-in-training learn about the major behavioral emergencies and associated conditions and situations. Then I discuss a supervisory model for teaching the skills and attitudes needed to do this work.[1] Further, I discuss the settings in which this training can best be accomplished. Next, I describe a model training program for teaching the evaluation and management of behavioral emergencies. Finally I review issues related to the assessment of competence in this area of clinical service.

A Knowledge Base in Behavioral Emergencies

As noted in Chapter 1 of this volume, the book *Behavioral Emergencies: An Evidence-Based Resource for Evaluating and Managing Risk of Suicide, Violence, and Victimization* (Kleespies, 2009) was structured as a proposed curriculum for teaching a knowledge base for behavioral emergencies. This curriculum is outlined in Table 6.1. It begins with a section on foundational knowledge (Section I: Foundations) that includes an overview of the definition and domain of behavioral emergencies and draws a distinction between behavioral emergencies and crises. Because crises frequently precipitate emergency situations, however, instruction in crisis theory and crisis intervention as applied in emergencies is important. Therefore, an integrated model of crisis intervention and emergency intervention that provides guidance in responding to both situations is

---

[1]As noted in Chapter 3, the knowledge, skills, and attitudes for evaluating and managing behavioral emergencies are presented in a sequential manner here, but they are likely to have considerable overlap in the learning process.

Table 6.1

A Proposed Curriculum for a Knowledge Base in Behavioral Emergencies

Section	Content
I. Foundations	A. Emergency intervention and crisis intervention
	B. Evaluating behavioral emergencies: The clinical interview
II. Evaluation and management of suicide risk	C. Evaluating and managing suicide risk in the adult patient
	D. Evaluating and managing suicide risk in children and adolescents
	E. Evaluating and managing suicide risk in people with medical and terminal illness
III. Evaluation and management of risk of violence	F. Evaluating and managing risk of violence in the adult patient
	G. Evaluating and managing risk of violence in children and adolescents
IV. Evaluation and management of interpersonal victimization	H. Evaluation and intervention with victims of violence
	I. Evaluating and managing risk of intimate partner violence
V. Emergency-related crises and conditions	J. Evaluating and managing nonsuicidal self injury
	K. Evaluating and managing alcohol- and drug-related crises
VI. Medical conditions presenting as behavioral emergencies	L. Psychological and behavioral symptoms in neurological disorders
	M. Psychological and behavioral symptoms in endocrine disorders
VII. Follow-up treatment of patients at risk of recurrent emergencies	N. Psychological–behavioral treatment of the suicidal patient
	O. Psychological–behavioral treatment of the patient at risk of violence
	P. Psychological–behavioral treatment with victims of interpersonal violence
VIII. Legal and psychological risks in work with behavioral emergencies	Q. Legal and ethical risk management with behavioral emergencies
	R. The emotional impact of clinical work with the patient at risk

Note. Adapted from *Emergencies in Mental Health Practice: Evaluation and Management* (p. 13), by P. M. Kleespies (Ed.), 1998, New York, NY: Guilford Press. Copyright 1998 by Phillip M. Kleespies.

recommended. This section also includes a description of a model of a clinical interview for evaluating behavioral emergencies. The presentation of this model includes a discussion of the difficult task of containing the patient's emotional turmoil so that his or her problem(s) can be clearly defined. It concludes with guidance on how to decide whether the patient can be managed and treated as an outpatient or may require emergency intervention such as voluntary or involuntary hospitalization. The subject matter of the current book (i.e., training for decision making under stress) might also be considered foundational learning.

Sections II, III, and IV are concerned with educating the clinician about the core behavioral emergencies (i.e., suicide risk, risk of violence, and risk of interpersonal victimization) and how to evaluate and manage them. There are differences in risk and protective factors as well as developmental differences for children and adolescents as opposed to adults. The evaluation and management of suicide risk and violence risk with children and adolescents warrant discussion in their own right. In addition, recent studies have found that the burden of multiple medical illnesses, and certain individual medical illnesses themselves, can be independent risk factors for suicide. It is important to make psychology practitioners aware of how medical illness can have an influence on suicide risk. In terms of interpersonal victimization, the clinician needs to have knowledge of the impact and management of such events in general as well as knowledge more specific to intimate partner or domestic violence and victimization.

It is very important that the clinician know of certain emergency-related crises or conditions that are not behavioral emergencies per se but that may contribute to the risk of suicidal or violent behavior or, for diagnostic purposes, may need to be differentiated from behavioral emergencies (Section V). Thus, nonsuicidal self-injuries are often mistakenly seen as suicidal behaviors or suicide attempts. The clinician needs to have an understanding of such behaviors so that he or she can improve his or her ability to discriminate self-injuries with suicidal intent from those without such intent. In addition, alcohol- and drug-related crises are frequently present during behavioral emergencies and can increase the risk of suicidal behavior or violence. It is clearly important to have information about the effects of alcohol and drug abuse on the individual and on his or her suicidal or violent inclinations.

As noted in Section VI, there are certain medical conditions (e.g., hypothyroidism, multiple sclerosis) that can present with psychological or behavioral symptomatology much like a mood disorder. The patient who is suffering from them may appear to be in an emotional or behavioral emergency state. Practitioners need to be aware of such possibilities so that appropriate recommendations can be made for a medical evaluation.

After a behavioral emergency has been evaluated and immediate management has reduced or eliminated imminent risk to self or others, the patient or client is not necessarily free of longer term risk. The clinician needs to be aware that there are treatments available that have empirical support for reducing longer term risks of suicidal or violent behavior (Section VII). If the patient or client sees a need and is motivated, an appropriate referral can be made.

In working with patients who present with behavioral emergencies, the practitioner needs to be aware of the ethical and legal issues involved in such high-risk situations. He or she also needs to know about the emotional and personal toll that such work can take. The final section of the curriculum (Section VIII) addresses such issues as ethical and legal risk management as well as the emotional impact of working with patients who are at risk and how the clinician might cope with that impact.

A Supervisory Model for Teaching Skills and Attitudes

As noted by Kleespies (1998b, 2009), applying a knowledge base in practice with good supervision leads to skill development and clinical competency. When a patient or client is thought to be on the verge of suicide or violence, the situation can be stressful for the seasoned professional, let alone for those who are in training and less confident in their clinical abilities and status. When it comes to stressful clinical events, some in the past have felt that clinicians-in-training have a protective advantage over professionals in that they work under the direction of a supervisor and can process events in an organized program (Brown, 1987). Rodolfa, Kraft, and Reilley (1988), however, found that patient suicidal statements, patient suicide attempts, and patient attacks on the therapist were all rated as moderately to highly stressful by both professional psychologists and psychologists-in-training. Kleespies, Penk, and Forsyth (1993) also found evidence that the negative emotional impact of patient suicidal behavior on psychologists-in-training may be as great or greater than that on professional-level psychologists. It seems clear that those who are first learning to cope with such difficult emergency situations need considerable instruction and support to reduce their level of stress.

A mentor model for learning under such conditions seems advisable. In this model, an experienced clinician and an intern or trainee are paired in settings in which patients or clients at risk are evaluated. The intern or trainee has the opportunity to observe and work closely with a more seasoned professional who has been successfully engaged in this type of clinical work. The pressure of more complete clinical responsibility is only gradually assumed by the trainee, and anxiety is kept at manageable levels. In this model, it is important for the supervisor to be aware of the balance between support and intern responsibility and to shift the balance appropriately over time to promote the more independent functioning of the clinician-in-training.

As recommended in the SET approach, the clinician-in-training, in working with a mentor, has the opportunity to begin applying and practicing the skills that he or she has acquired through lectures, workshops, mental practice with case vignettes, and observation. With this gradated approach, the stress inoculation discussed by Meichenbaum (2007) can begin to occur. As Meichenbaum noted, stress in these situations is never completely eliminated, but the objective of stress training is to assist the clinician in viewing these scenarios as problems that he or she has the skills to solve. Constructive attitudes develop from these experiences of mastery.

Clearly, there have been instances in which relatively inexperienced trainees have been placed on the front lines of dealing with behavioral emergencies with little direct supervisory support. Under such circumstances, emergency and crisis work is often seen as trying and burdensome.

Good support and supervision, however, can go a long way toward preventing a negative viewpoint and aiding in the development of a sense of competence in dealing with emotionally charged cases. Long ago, Barlow (1974) observed that psychology interns responded initially to emergency department duty with moderate to severe anxiety. He further observed that within approximately 3 months, a second response of increased clinical confidence began to emerge. This sense of competence was described by interns as one of the more important developments in their training.

Settings for Training in Behavioral Emergencies

Hospital-based internship sites usually have an emergency room (ER) where patients with mental health emergencies are seen. This setting can be an excellent one for systematic training and experience in assessing and managing crises and potentially emergent situations. Zimet and Weissberg (1979) suggested that one of the reasons that psychologists seem to have avoided work in an ER is that it is a very medical setting, and medical factors can complicate the behavioral or psychological presentation. Covino (1989), however, found that the majority of psychiatric patients seen in a hospital ER had complaints that fell well within the competence of psychologists to manage. Moreover, with good collaboration from the nursing and medical staff, complications can be minimized. Brasch, Glick, Cobb, and Richmond (2004), as well as Kleespies (1998a), commented on the unique nature of the ER setting and the training opportunities it affords. In this regard, they have pointed to the unplanned nature of the visits, the urgency and the severity of the presenting problems, the time limitations for assessments, the disruptiveness of certain patient behaviors, the intensity of interactions, and the legal and ethical aspects of decisions about dangerousness to self or others as aspects of the ER with which the clinician-in-training (with close supervision) must learn to cope. If interns or trainees can develop the skills needed to deal with these conditions, it will prepare them for managing behavioral emergencies in their future practice.

A hospital or medical center ER, however, is not the only setting in which training in emergency services can occur. Many outpatient clinics now have urgent care clinics (UCCs) where patients with mental health emergencies are often seen. Outpatient mental health or psychiatric clinics also have such patients who apply for care. Asnis, Kaplan, van Praag, and Sanderson (1994), for example, reported that 26% of a sample of patients seeking treatment at the outpatient psychiatry department of a private medical center in New York had a history of homicidal ideation or of violence. Nearly a third of the group with past homicidal ideation reported having had such ideation within the past week. Eighty-six percent of the group with homicidal ideation or a history of violence also had a history of suicidal ideation, and 39% had a history of suicide attempts. Clearly, such outpatient departments deal with a subpopulation that is at risk and will, at times, present with emergencies. In medical inpatient settings, there is typically a psychiatric consultation/liaison team that is called on to work with either (a) patients who have a known mental disorder but are being treated for a medical condition or (b) patients with no known mental disorder but with a medical illness that has an associated risk for suicide or violence. Behavioral emergencies frequently occur in the inpatient setting with these patients (Kelly, Mufson, & Rogers, 1999; Kleespies, Hughes, Weintraub, & Hart, in press). Psychologists and psychology interns can become members of these teams, and interns can receive training in evaluating and responding to patients who are at risk for suicide or violence.

In small clinics and counseling centers in which resources for dealing with behavioral emergencies are relatively scarce, the clinic or center staff may need to develop a resource network. Such a network might include a consultant with expertise in evaluating and managing behavioral emergencies. Such a consultant might be available not only to consult on cases but also to provide lectures on emergency-related topics. In addition, the staff might develop plans for what they might need to do and how they might coordinate with the local police in the event that a patient at risk needs to be held on a temporary involuntary commitment and transported to a local ER. Further, it would be good in such settings to identify local legal counsel with experience in mental health–related legal matters who might be available for consultation. In addition to exposing trainees to these resources and plans, it might be necessary to develop an externship or part-time placement at another clinical site where they might gain supervised experience in emergency services.

A Model Training Program for Emergency Psychological Services

In the psychology internship program described here, interns may have three 4-month major rotations or two 6-month major rotations.[2] During one of their major rotations (e.g., a rotation in a general mental health clinic or in a substance abuse treatment program), each intern participates in consulting on cases in the ER or in a UCC where patients present with mental health or psychiatric problems or crises. The intern(s) may be on call to consult on cases in the ER or UCC on a morning or afternoon shift one day a week. These consultations and evaluations take place under the supervision of a staff member (or mentor) who is experienced in this work and who coordinates the training experience.

Given that it is important to prepare interns for the experience and to help them develop a knowledge base, the experience should have a weekly lecture series that begins with a good orientation to the setting and the types of patients and conditions that are likely to be encountered. Different staff or faculty with expertise on particular topics may be asked to provide lectures. The series might include such topics as the emergency interview; evaluating and managing suicide risk; evaluating and managing the risk of violence, alcohol, and drug abuse problems; neurological disorders that may present as behavioral or psychological problems; or other topics noted in Table 6.1.

Concurrent with the orientation and lectures, the participating interns can begin their experience in the ER or UCC by sitting in and observing the supervising psychologist as he or she does at least two evaluations. The patient is, of course, asked for his or her verbal consent to having the

---

[2]The model training program described here is based on training that I provided to psychology interns and psychology postdoctoral fellows in both an ER setting and a UCC setting.

intern observe for training purposes.[3] After the intern has observed two or three evaluations and has had the opportunity to read his or her mentor's written reports, the intern is usually ready to begin doing one or two evaluations with his or her mentor observing and contributing to the evaluation as appropriate. Subsequently, the intern is typically ready to become more autonomous in doing evaluations, but the mentoring psychologist is always present in the ER or UCC for consultation or assistance with difficult situations or decisions. Moreover, each case is discussed with the supervisor before a final decision is made about the disposition or plan for management and follow-up. Two to three days after the intern has been on call, there is a wrap-up and supervision meeting at which each of the cases seen that week are reviewed with the supervising psychologist. If two or three interns have been on call, this supervision can be held in a group session. Through this process of close supervision and increasing autonomy, interns develop a sense of being able to master the stresses and problems presented by work with patients who are at acute risk to self or others. They also begin to acquire a reservoir of experiences that they will be able to call on in the future.

Assessing Competence in Evaluating and Managing Behavioral Emergencies

When a clinician-in-training has completed training in an area of practice such as behavioral emergencies, assessing whether the individual is competent to practice independently is not a simple matter. As the APA Task Force on the Assessment of Competence in Professional Psychology (2006) indicated, assessment models for competence should have *validity, feasibility,* and *fidelity* to actual practice. Validity, of course, refers to whether the assessment measures the competency it purports to measure. Feasibility refers to practical issues such as the resources, cost, expertise,

---

[3] In medical-teaching facilities, patients, when they initially enter the health care system, are typically informed that teaching is an integral function of the particular health care system and that care may be provided by clinicians-in-training under the supervision of a staff member. If they object to treatment, or to involvement in treatment, by a clinician-in-training, treatment is provided only by a fully credentialed staff member.

and time needed to develop and maintain the assessment. Finally, fidelity refers to the degree to which the assessment reflects the actual behaviors that the clinician performs in practice.

The APA Task Force grouped assessment models used to measure professional development in the health care professions into four categories: (a) measures of knowledge; (b) measures of professional decision making; (c) measures of practice performance, including professional attributes; and (d) integrated assessments of practice-based skills and tasks. If we are interested in measuring knowledge that a trainee has acquired, we typically look to multiple-choice, essay, and short-answer questions as measurements. Multiple-choice tests are considered efficient and cost-effective ways of measuring knowledge, provided that they have been subjected to psychometric scrutiny and are standardized. If they are instructor made, they may include vague, confusing, and poor-quality questions that do not provide a reliable measure of the individual's knowledge base. Essay and short-answer questions present a problem or scenario and ask for a response that answers or addresses the problem or situation. They need to be selected to reflect specific areas of knowledge. There is a need for guidance on the elements of a good response for those who score these types of exams, and training of the examiners to establish scoring accuracy is clearly desirable. If well designed, such tests can provide a good measure of factual knowledge and conceptual understanding.

If we are interested in measuring professional decision making, the APA Task Force seemed to support the use of case-based oral examinations. This type of exam has been used extensively in specialty certification programs such as with the American Board of Professional Psychology certification. Case materials are presented in the form of written vignettes, videotapes, audiotapes, the clinician's own reports, or live patient/clinician interactions. The clinician must explain his or her actions and decisions about assessment, diagnosis, treatment, and/or case management. Examiners then question the clinician about his or her decisions. This approach to assessment requires standardization of case materials (e.g., the videotape or audiotape of an interaction that replicates a professional interaction) in addition to guidance for and training of the examiners if there is to be interrater reliability.

The APA Task Force indicated that what it refers to as *measures of performance* include ratings or judgments, at specified intervals in a training program, regarding competency in various areas of professional functioning. The ratings may be based on information obtained from multiple sources. There are often qualitative statements that accompany these ratings. This type of rating is used in virtually all health care education and training, and typically clinical supervisors make the ratings. A variation of this type of measure requires the individual in training to submit a portfolio or collection of encounters that provide evidence of learning, achievement, or accomplishment related to the competency that is being assessed. The encounters might include video and audio recordings or self-reflections on ethical issues or on the use of empirical evidence in making professional judgments.

The category of integrated assessments of practice-based skills and tasks involves the use of clinical case situations that attempt to portray the actual realities of practice. In this regard, approaches can include role playing by individuals who are trained to simulate patient conditions or situations, or computer simulations of clinical encounters, or tasks that require assessment or interpretation. Those who rate the clinician's performance are trained to observe certain criteria that indicate adequate or good responses or interactions. Another form of this sort of assessment is the Objective Structured Clinical Examination (OSCE; Harden, Stevenson, Downie, & Wilson, 1975). In the OSCE, the clinicians-in-training move through a series of stations, and at each station they may be presented with a simulated patient encounter or a task requiring the interpretation of clinical information. The individual's performance is evaluated against predefined competencies by a trained observer. The APA Task Force considers this methodology as useful for cross-sectional assessments of competencies but has noted that it is not as useful for measuring continuity of care across time.

Certainly there is a knowledge base in behavioral emergencies (Kleespies, 2009) that might be assessed using the multiple-choice, short-answer, or essay question methodology discussed previously. To assess competence in responding effectively to patients who are at imminent risk of suicide or violence, however, seems to require assessment more in keeping with what the APA Task Force termed *measures of professional decision making* and *integrated assessments of practice-based skills and tasks*. These measures or assessments use case vignettes, work samples, audiotapes, videotapes, role playing, computer simulations, and possibly even live patient/clinician interactions to present the clinician with significant clinical issues and problems that must be addressed. The clinician needs to respond and provide his or her thinking, case or problem formulation, and rationale for decisions under conditions that attempt to approach real life.

In this regard, one approach to both teaching and evaluating skills and attitudes that has been used in medical education is a methodology referred to as *problem-based learning* (Evensen & Hmelo, 2000). The APA Task Force cited this methodology as one that could be easily adapted to assessing competence in professional psychology. Thus, several vignettes of individuals with emotional and/or behavioral difficulties could be presented to those in training, who would then be asked to reflect on what they know or don't know about the person's problems, develop questions and hypotheses about what might facilitate problem solving, and state what they might do to address the person's difficulties. This sort of approach could be easily adapted to scenarios involving behavioral emergencies, and supervisors could assess performance on the basis of predetermined guidelines. In fact, some of the vignettes described in Chapter 4 of this volume could be adapted for this purpose.

In terms of behavioral emergencies, McNiel and his colleagues (Hung, Binder, Fordwood, Hall, Cramer, & McNiel, 2012; McNiel, Hung, Cramer, Hall, & Binder, 2011) have made strides toward developing an approach to evaluating competence in assessing and managing violence risk and suicide risk. Working within an OSCE framework, the investigators trained advanced psychiatry residents (3rd- and 4th-year residents) and psychology postdoctoral fellows to be standardized (simulated) patients and had them follow a script based on a clinical vignette of a young adult patient presenting to an ER. The script included the patient's chief complaint; history of present illness; psychiatric, medical, and psychosocial histories; and mental status examination findings. The subjects (or clinicians-in-training) were less advanced psychiatry residents (1st- and 2nd-year residents) and psychology predoctoral interns who initially had a 5-hour workshop on risk assessment for violence and suicide. Faculty members were trained as observers. Each OSCE team consisted of a clinician-in-training, a standardized patient, and a faculty member.

After receiving a brief description of the presenting problem, the clinician-in-training was asked to perform a violence risk assessment or a suicide risk assessment of the standardized patient. He or she interviewed the simulated patient and was asked to discuss what additional information he or she might seek if this were a real situation. The clinician-in-training was also asked to write a progress note and give an oral summary of the assessment and plan regarding the patient's risk.

To assess competence, the investigators developed two instruments: the Competency Assessment Instrument for Violence (CAI-V) and the Competency Assessment Instrument for Suicide Risk (CAI-S). These instruments were created on the basis of literature reviews and input from focus groups with mental health faculty from multiple sites in a large academic psychiatry department. The CAI-V and CAI-S consisted of a checklist of 31 and 30 components, respectively, on violence risk assessment and suicide risk assessment, including areas such as interviewing and data collection, case formulation and presentation, treatment planning, and documentation. In separate studies, the CAI-V and the CAI-S were found to have good internal consistency reliability ($a = .93$ and $a = .94$, respectively) and good interrater reliability (intraclass correlation coefficient [ICC] $= .93$ and ICC $= .94$, respectively).

After the clinician-in-training interviewed the standardized patient and discussed the case, the faculty observer rated the competence of the clinician's performance using the CAI-V or CAI-S as the case might be. For purposes of data analysis, the clinicians-in-training were divided into those at a senior level (2nd-year residents who had 6 months of supervised inpatient psychiatry experience) and those at a junior level (1st-year residents). The mean scores on the CAI-V and on the CAI-S were significantly higher for the senior-level clinicians-in-training. In addition, the global ratings of the overall quality of the violence risk assessments and the suicide risk assessments were significantly higher for the senior-level learners. The risk assessments by senior learners were also significantly more likely than those by junior learners to be rated as competent by the faculty examiners.

The investigators in these two studies noted that the CAI-V and the CAI-S had concurrent validity in that senior learners performed better than junior learners in the context of an OSCE. They further found that both learners and faculty expressed satisfaction with the method of assessment and how the CAI-V, the CAI-S, and the OSCE provided helpful structure for feedback and supervision concerning violence risk and suicide risk assessment and management.

In terms of limitations to these assessment methods, the researchers mentioned the cost of having faculty serve as examiners in an OSCE. In that regard, they suggested the possibility of having the simulated patient also be the person rating the clinician-in-training. They noted that a second limitation is that simulated patients may not show the range of problems that is comparable to the actual patients encountered in high-risk, clinical situations. They commented that future research could investigate the applicability of these measures in clinical supervision with actual cases.

I concur that it is unlikely that simulated patients will show the range of problems that an actual patient in a state of crisis might present. The limitations of cost and of having a simulated patient mentioned by McNiel and his colleagues might be addressed in a setting such as an ER or a UCC using the mentor model of supervision discussed earlier in this chapter. The supervisor (again with the patient's permission) could be an observer of an actual evaluation with a patient who presents with a question of suicide risk or risk of violence. Immediately following the evaluation, he or she could evaluate the competence of the clinician-in-training by completing an instrument such as the CAI-S or the CAI-V.

CONCLUDING REMARKS

In this chapter, an approach to training for evaluating and managing behavioral emergencies that emphasizes stress training using an SET model was described. A close-working relationship with a mentor or supervisor allows the clinician-in-training to model his or her supervisor, manage the anxiety that can attend these high-stakes clinical situations, and gradually attain greater autonomy and mastery. The objective is not to eliminate all stress in dealing with suicidal or potentially violent patients but to assist the clinician in approaching these scenarios as problems that they have the ability to manage. In addition, a proposed curriculum for teaching a knowledge base for behavioral emergencies was presented, potential settings in which such training might occur were discussed, and a model training program was described. Further, issues related to assessing the competence of those in training for evaluating and managing patients who are potentially suicidal or potentially violent were discussed.

I concur with the APA Task Force on the Assessment of Competence in Professional Psychology (2006) that clinical competence, and particularly (from my perspective) competence in dealing with high-stakes behavioral emergency situations, is best assessed during actual clinician–patient interactions or, if that is not possible, through experience near clinician–simulated patient interactions. In this way, we can aspire to Principle 6 of the guiding principles articulated in the APA Task Force report: "The assessment of competence must reflect fidelity to practice and must incorporate reliable, valid, and practical methodologies" (p. 104).

7

The Stress of Legal and Ethical Issues in High-Risk Cases

In previous chapters in this volume, I have emphasized the stress that the clinician often experiences in dealing directly with the behavior of patients or clients who are at serious risk of killing themselves or others, or of being the victims of violence. The stresses in such situations often seem self-evident and account for much of the apprehension that clinicians may have in working with suicidal or violence-prone individuals. As Packman, Andalibian, Eudy, Howard, and Bongar (2009) pointed out, however, another stressor for clinicians who work with patients who are at risk has to do with the fact that these are often cases in which a negative outcome can have legal, ethical, and professional consequences for the clinician. Thus, cases in which there is a suicide or others are killed or seriously injured can result in malpractice suits, complaints to licensing boards, and/or complaints to ethics committees about the competence

http://dx.doi.org/10.1037/14337-008
Decision Making in Behavioral Emergencies: Acquiring Skill in Evaluating and Managing High-Risk Patients, by P. M. Kleespies

of the clinician to evaluate and manage patients who are at risk of these behaviors.

In general, clinicians can manage these stressors provided they have a working knowledge of the legal and ethical issues and make risk management procedures a part of their routine clinical practice. The goal of this chapter is to heighten mental health clinicians' awareness of the major legal and ethical issues involved in work with high-risk patients so that they will be able to provide patient care in ways that are consistent with the ethical and legal standards that govern their practice. Initially, I discuss the legal definition of negligence in relation to malpractice claims. Then, I note some of the more common malpractice claims in cases of patient suicide and present them as caveats for one's clinical practice. Finally, I discuss clinicians' concerns in regard to patient violence and the so-called duty to protect third parties.

In regard to the clinician's approach to risk management, I believe that there is a need for a cautionary note. It is possible to err in two directions; that is, the clinician can ignore the potential legal problems that can occur with high-risk cases and be too lax about observing risk management procedures (possibly to his or her own eventual chagrin), or he or she can become overly concerned about legal issues and engage in *defensive practice.*

In defensive practice, the clinician either over- or underresponds to a patient who may be at risk (albeit perhaps mild–moderate risk), not out of concern for the patient's well-being or the well-being of others but primarily to protect himself or herself from future possible legal action. An example of overresponse might be to reflexively hospitalize a patient who makes mention of suicidal or violent thoughts (without engaging in a thorough evaluation of the individual's risk level) because hospitalization affords better protection from any legal claim of failure to manage the risk. In such a case, a more thorough assessment of the level of risk might indicate that the patient could derive greater benefit from working on his or her issues as an outpatient. An example of underresponse might involve the clinician ignoring a patient's mention of passing suicidal or violent thoughts as a way of avoiding involvement in any clinical or legal issues regarding suicidality or harm to others. In any event, it should be borne in mind that the American Psychological Association's (APA's) *Ethical Principles of Psychologists and Code of Conduct* places great value on clinicians working for the benefit of the patient (see Principle A: Beneficence and Nonmaleficence and Principle B: Fidelity and Responsibility; APA, 2010).

In terms of legal issues of concern to those who make decisions about the evaluation and management of patients who are at high risk of harm to self or others, clearly the fear or threat of a malpractice claim against the mental health treatment provider looms large (Bongar, Greaney, & Peruzzi, 1998; Bongar & Sullivan, 2013; Eddy & Harris, 1998). Therefore, it is important to remember that the rate of malpractice suits against psychologists and psychiatrists is relatively low; for example, fewer than 1.0% of psychologists insured by the APA Insurance Trust have had a malpractice claim brought against them, as reported by Bongar and Sullivan (2013). Nonetheless, it is important to gain an understanding of the legal issues involved and to develop a reasonable approach to dealing with them. Typically, the major issue in such malpractice claims has to do with negligence.

NEGLIGENCE AND MALPRACTICE

Malpractice claims are typically brought against mental health providers on the basis of negligence (Packman et al., 2009). *Negligence* has been described as either a commission on the part of the provider (i.e., doing something that the provider should not have done) or an omission (i.e., omitting something that the provider should have done; Bongar, Greaney, & Peruzzi, 1998). It has also been described as a failure to exercise the standard of care that a reasonable and prudent clinician would have exercised under similar circumstances (Packman et al., 2009). This standard of care is not necessarily an ideal or optimal standard of care, but the standard of care provided by the average practitioner operating in a reasonable manner (Silverman, Berman, Bongar, Litman, & Maris, 1998). Negligence law is subsumed under what is known as *tort law*. A tort action is concerned with a civil (rather than a criminal) wrong done by one party that has caused some injury to another party. If the basis of the claim is negligence, there is no requirement that there be any intent to harm the injured person. The individual (or defendant) may have had the best of intentions but still be held liable.

As Bongar, Greaney, and Peruzzi (1998) noted, four essential legal elements must be demonstrated by a preponderance of the evidence to establish a claim of negligence. First, there must have been a relationship between the clinician and the patient that created a duty of care. Second, the clinician must have breached the duty of care owed to his or her patient. Third, the patient must have suffered damage. Fourth, and finally, the negligence of the clinician must have been the proximate cause of the damage.

With behavioral emergencies, the fact that the clinician was evaluating the patient for risk of suicide or violence is typically sufficient to create a professional relationship between the two and a duty of care on the part of the clinician. If the patient commits suicide or suffers emotional and/or physical harm in a suicide attempt or becomes violent and harms or kills others, there are damages. Whether a clinician did or did not breach his or her duty of care is determined in a court of law according to the profession's average standard of care in such cases (Bongar, Greaney, & Peruzzi, 1998). This standard is established by examining legal decisions rendered in prior malpractice cases and through the testimony of expert witnesses.

As Packman et al. (2009) pointed out, whether the clinician's negligence was the proximate cause of the damage often hinges on, for example, whether the patient's suicidal behavior was considered reasonably foreseeable. If the court decides that the patient's behavior was foreseeable, then the clinician who did not make an adequate assessment of the level of risk, and institute preventive measures commensurate with that level of risk, is potentially liable. Generally, it is understood that clinicians cannot predict such low base rate events as suicide or homicide (Kleespies & Hill, 2011). What the courts attempt to determine, however, is whether the clinician's assessment of risk met the standard of care of the average and prudent practitioner under similar circumstances. If it did not, the court may decide that the practitioner, if he or she had met the standard of care, could have foreseen and prevented the death. The clinician is typically not judged on the fact that a suicide or a violent act occurred but on whether his or her assessment of the risk of suicide or violence met the proverbial standard of care.

CAVEATS FOR THE CLINICIAN IN REGARD TO MALPRACTICE CLAIMS ABOUT PATIENT SUICIDE

In their book *Risk Management With Suicidal Patients,* Bongar, Maris, Berman, and Litman (1998) provided some common duty-of-care failure scenarios. These scenarios can be taken as caveats for the clinician about situations in which malpractice claims have been, or in the opinion of the authors could have been, successfully made. They are helpful in that they alert us to particular areas of practice in which it may be wise to observe caution in working with the suicidal patient. At times, the same cautionary notes seem to apply to work with the potentially violent patient. In the sections that follow, I discuss a number of these outpatient failure scenarios (i.e., those considered most relevant to decisions about emergency situations) cited in the chapter by Bongar, Maris, et al. (1998), as well as several of the inpatient failure scenarios cited in the chapter by Silverman, Berman, Bongar, Litman, and Maris (1998).

Outpatient Areas of Concern

The areas of concern that follow are presented as outpatient areas of concern. It should be borne in mind, however, that they are, for the most part, also areas of concern for the inpatient clinician dealing with high-risk patients.

Evaluating for Suicide Risk at Intake

One-time evaluations to determine a patient's needs, arrive at a diagnostic impression, and make a decision about referral and disposition can occur in an emergency room (ER), an urgent care clinic (UCC), a walk-in clinic, or a private practice. As mentioned earlier in this book, some of these settings (e.g., an ER or an UCC) can require rapid-paced evaluations in which it is not possible to obtain full information about the patient. The evaluator is also not likely to have a prior relationship with the patient on which to build. Given the time pressure involved, the clinician can be at risk of not giving full attention to a risk assessment. In these situations, Bongar, Maris, et al. (1998) noted that special care should be taken to assess for risk to self and others (see Kleespies & Richmond, 2009, for an example of an emergency interview that includes an assessment for risk to self and others).

Securing Records of Prior Treatment and Taking a History

As noted in Chapter 2 of this book, when under pressure to make a decision (as when dealing with a behavioral emergency), we are often prone to use our intuitive thinking and jump to conclusions. Kahneman (2011) coined a saying for such situations: "What you see is all there is" (p. 86). When working with a high-pressure and potentially high-risk situation, it is easy to slip into believing that what you see in your observations and examination of a patient is all there is. Failure to take into account what other professionals have thought and the history that they may have collected in prior contacts with a patient, however, can be a serious oversight. Thus, for example, a patient may fail to report that 2 years ago, he or she put a gun to his or her head but decided to come to the ER seeking help rather than pulling the trigger. If the clinician did not check the medical record, this information about the patient's history of contemplating the use of a very lethal means of death would not have been included in an estimate of the current level of risk.

As health care systems have adopted the computerized medical record, it has become easier to obtain past treatment records, at least for treatment within the particular health care system. In the Veterans Health Administration, for example, it is possible to obtain a patient's medical and mental health records from any VA Medical Center health care facility in the United States simply by accessing remote data from the VA computer at the facility where the patient is being seen.

Conducting a Mental Status Exam

The *mental status exam* is a clinical method for systematically obtaining information on a patient's current mental state and functioning (see Kleespies & Richmond, 2009, for a description of the elements of a mental status exam). In crisis or emergency situations, it goes hand-in-hand with gathering essential historical information and forming a more complete evaluation of the patient's condition and level of risk. As Bongar, Maris, et al. (1998) pointed out, the mental status exam is routinely done in inpatient evaluations but often seems to be overlooked in outpatient settings in which the patient has been functioning in the community. When questions of risk arise with outpatients, however, it is important to the evaluation and to the decision-making process to have engaged in a clinical assessment of the areas of functioning covered by a mental status exam. By way of example, it can be very informative in terms of risk assessment to see how impaired a depressed patient's concentration is when asked to perform serial 7s (i.e., subtract 7 from 100 and keep subtracting 7 from each new total). Likewise, it can be helpful to learn whether a patient displays concrete thinking and limited cognitive resources when asked to interpret several proverbs.

Making a Diagnosis

A diagnosis is essential to formulating a treatment plan. In one-time evaluations under crisis or emergency conditions, the diagnosis or diagnoses may be provisional because, given the constraints of such evaluations, more complete information about the patient may not be immediately obtainable. Given that certain diagnoses (e.g., major depressive disorder, alcohol dependence, schizophrenia, posttraumatic stress disorder, borderline personality disorder) are associated with a higher risk of suicidal or violent behavior, the diagnosis is clearly important to the risk assessment, and the risk assessment drives decisions about management (e.g., outpatient management vs. hospitalization). Moreover, dual or multiple diagnoses (e.g., depressive disorder with anxiety, alcohol abuse with depression) can further heighten risk and impact decisions about what care may be needed. A failure to arrive at a diagnosis, or a failure to appreciate the importance of dual diagnoses, can be seen as negatively affecting appropriate management and care.

Arriving at a Formal Treatment Plan

Once there is a diagnosis or diagnoses, there needs to be a treatment plan that addresses how the condition(s) will be treated. There are currently some empirically supported cognitive–behavioral treatments that specifically target suicidal behavior and associated symptoms (Rudd, Joiner, Trotter, Williams, & Cordero, 2009). It would seem to be wise to make such evidence-based treatments a part of an outpatient treatment plan for patients who have mild to moderate risk of suicide. In a one-time crisis or emergency evaluation, however, immediate attention needs to be given to outpatient management (as opposed to a longer term treatment plan). Such management might include a safety plan for the patient (see, e.g., Stanley & Brown, 2012) that includes a prioritized list of coping strategies and sources of support. It might also include increased monitoring and support on the part of the clinician via frequent visits or phone contacts, as well as access to a 24-hour crisis hotline or encouragement to use a local ER in the event of increased risk.

Safeguarding the Outpatient Environment

Most obviously, the clinician needs to inquire about whether the patient at risk for either suicide or violence (or both) possesses guns. Firearms are the method of death in over 50% of suicides in the United States (McIntosh, 2012) and in over two thirds of the homicides (Centers for Disease Control and Prevention, 2009). Given the frequency with which such weapons are used, a clinician's failure to assess for their presence can be viewed as a major oversight. If the patient possesses such highly lethal means, efforts need to be made through *means restriction counseling* to reorient him or her toward reducing mental anguish through treatment rather than by suicide (Bryan, Stone, & Rudd, 2011). Having weapons in the home increases the possibility of a bad outcome. It is best to remove them or have them held safely by a third party either permanently or at least during the period of increased risk. There is also a need to inquire about other means such as stockpiling of pills or access to poisons. Although there are still other methods that might be used, if favored or highly lethal methods are not immediately available, it can delay action and provide time for reconsideration.

Evaluating the Need for Psychopharmacological Intervention

Psychologists who work in clinics and medical centers typically work within mental health services with psychiatrists. They can refer a patient for a psychopharmacological evaluation with relative ease. For those in private practice, the logistics of making a referral may be more cumbersome, but there are usually psychiatrists in private practice with whom one can establish a professional relationship for the purpose of referring patients who may be in need of an evaluation for psychopharmacological intervention. A patient at risk who is not improving with psychological intervention may benefit from the use of psychoactive medication. These medications need to be carefully monitored for side effects, particularly in patients who are at risk because, if accumulated in sufficient amounts, they can become the means of suicide attempts and suicide. If there is concern about a particular patient or the patient has a history of attempted overdose, medications should be dispensed in small quantities, and the treatment providers (both psychologist and psychiatrist) should frequently check on whether the patient is in compliance with taking the medication as prescribed. If the patient is in agreement, a family member might be enlisted to assist in observing the patient's use of his or her medication. In crisis or emergency situations, medications to reduce anxiety levels or to diminish insomnia can be helpful, but again, they should typically be prescribed in small quantities to assist a patient through a period of transition and until he or she can be seen in ongoing treatment.

Specifying Criteria for and Implementing Hospitalization

Bongar, Maris, et al. (1998) recommended using levels of risk as criteria for a decision about whether to hospitalize a patient or to treat him or her on an outpatient basis. Thus, those evaluated as at high risk should be hospitalized. Those at moderate risk might either be hospitalized or treated intensively as outpatients. Intensive outpatient treatment might include more frequent outpatient visits (e.g., visits twice a week rather than once a week), a phone check-in between regularly scheduled visits, frequent reevaluation of the treatment plan, and 24-hour safety plans such as going to an ER or calling a crisis hotline if risk increases. Low- or mild-risk patients might only require monitoring of the risk level and continuing with a treatment plan as usual. If hospitalization is needed, efforts should be made to collaborate with the patient to effect a voluntary admission. If the patient is at high risk, however, and he or she is unwilling to be hospitalized on a voluntary basis, the clinician should be familiar with the law in his or her state or jurisdiction that governs temporary involuntary commitments. He or she should also be familiar with the procedures in his or her treatment setting that are necessary to bring about an involuntary hospitalization. Although hospitalizations may not ultimately prevent suicide or violence, they do provide a relatively safe haven for a time.

Documenting Clinical Judgments, Rationales, and Observations

The success or failure of a malpractice suit can hinge on the documentation of the clinician's reasoning about the patient's condition and his or her management. Particularly with one-time evaluations involving decisions about behavioral crises and emergencies, it is important to document that attention was given to an evaluation of risk and to the thinking that went into arriving at an estimated level of risk. If feasible, it is wise to consult with a colleague about how he or she might evaluate and manage the particular case. Such a consultation can be a clear demonstration of efforts to meet the standard of care set by the average practitioner. The plan for management of the risk should then be stated in the record, along with how the plan is consistent with the estimated level of risk. The results of consultation with a colleague should also be noted in the record. Should there be a negative outcome and a malpractice suit is filed, contemporaneous progress notes explaining the clinician's decisions and actions can be a clear demonstration that he or she weighed the risks and benefits and met the standard of care of the average and prudent practitioner. In this regard, Packman et al. (2009) expressed the opinion that the importance of maintaining adequate records cannot be overstated.

Inpatient Areas of Concern

Among patients who are under mental health care, outpatients are more likely than inpatients to attempt or commit suicide. Nonetheless, as Bongar (2002) noted, the courts have tended to impose much stricter standards on inpatient care than on outpatient care. The courts may assume that inpatient psychiatric facilities have greater control over the patient's behavior and the care environment and that, therefore, they have a greater duty of care. For those clinicians who practice in an inpatient psychiatric facility, some of the caveats to attend to are discussed below. In selecting them, an effort has been made not to duplicate caveats already mentioned in regard to outpatient care.

Foreseeing Future Behavioral Problems

As mentioned by Silverman et al. (1998), foreseeing future behavioral problems does not refer to predicting suicide or violence. Rather, it is meant to refer to the clinician's attention to risk assessment and his or her awareness that suicidal and violent behaviors are potential issues. Once a patient at risk is admitted to an inpatient psychiatric unit, the clinician may feel that she or he is now in a safe environment and the risk is diminished. Although this is true to some degree, inpatient suicidal behavior (and suicide itself), or violent behavior, occurs on inpatient units. In fact, inpatient suicide has been among the five most frequent sentinel events reported to the Joint Commission in recent years (Joint Commission, 2013), and inadequate assessment has been reported as the root cause in over 80% of the reported suicides (Joint Commission, 2011). Not only must the inpatient clinician assess for life-threatening behaviors, he or she must also reassess regularly. In addition, there also needs to be good communication with other staff (e.g., nursing and social work staff) and a sharing of information about the patient's behavior and functioning. A treatment plan needs to be developed that includes attention to ways to reduce the patient's suicidality or potential for violence.

Observing and Supervising

Patients are frequently admitted to inpatient psychiatry units because they are considered to be at high risk for harm to self or others. In addition to the initiation of psychotherapeutic, psychosocial, and psychopharmacological interventions, these patients may need various degrees of observation and supervision to prevent suicidal or violent behavior (i.e., until they are more emotionally stable). The clinical staff needs to make decisions about how to keep the patient safe in the least restrictive way. Most units have a gradated system by which they can vary the degree of observation and supervision to fit the estimated level of risk. These measures can go, for example, from routine unit checks on patients during each shift to checks on an individual patient every 15 minutes or every 5 minutes to confinement in an area where the patient can be continuously observed (e.g., a dayroom) to having a staff member one-on-one with the patient at all times to confinement to a single room with a staff sitter in the doorway.

Although typically all efforts are made to have a restraint-free environment, there are occasions with patients who are actively attempting to harm themselves or others when leather restraints may be necessary. Restraint procedures, of course, can involve risk to the patient and to the staff. They are used when all other less restrictive efforts have failed or are not feasible. For a more detailed discussion of procedures for physical restraint and the use of psychoactive medication in an emergency, see Kleespies and Richmond (2009).

As a patient improves and is found to be at low risk for suicidal or violent behavior, psychiatric units usually have a system of privileges that involves increasing freedom and autonomy for the patient. These privileges can include time off the unit without supervision or passes off the hospital grounds or passes for a weekend at home. Decisions about increased freedom and decreased observation/supervision require careful clinical consideration. It is important for the patient to become increasingly autonomous, but there can also be times when a recently suicidal or aggressive patient can have a reemergence of emotional distress. It is important to develop a plan with the patient for what he or she can do should a crisis arise while away from the unit.

Communicating With the Treatment Team

On an inpatient psychiatry unit, good communication among the members of the patient's treatment team is essential, particularly with patients who are at risk of harm to self or others. Staff from different mental health disciplines (psychology, psychiatry, social work, nursing) interact with the patient and have different observations to share. Members of the treatment team need to feel free to offer their perspective on the patient's condition. Otherwise, vital information about risk and changes in risk status may be lost. Different staff may also have differing opinions about the patient's level of risk or how best to manage the risk. Treatment team meetings need to offer a forum for resolving these differences of opinion. Since the classic study by Stanton and Schwartz (1954), it has been known that poor staff communication and unresolved staff conflicts over how to treat or manage patients in a psychiatric hospital can have negative consequences for patient care.

Providing a Safe, Secure, and Protective Environment

Although observation, supervision, and coordinated care are essential to keeping high-risk patients safe, it is also important to carefully scrutinize the actual physical environment of the psychiatric unit for means by which a patient might harm himself or herself or others. Many facilities have an environment-of-care committee that periodically inspects the unit for physical aspects of the environment that may be safety risks. Thus, for example, hooks for clothing, wall fixtures, or showerheads should be break-away objects and not able to sustain the weight of a body. Storage or linen closets where a patient might conceal himself or herself should never be left unlocked. Housekeeping staff should closely watch cleaning solutions and never leave them unattended on the unit. Medical or other equipment that could be used for self-harm or harm to others should also never be left unattended. Windows should not be fully openable, and they should be nonbreakable. Staff offices where patients are seen should be free of objects or materials that might be used for harm to self or others. Although such measures make the environment less human, the safety of the patients must be made the priority. For a more extensive discussion of environmental safeguards on psychiatric units, see the article by Cardell, Bratcher, and Quinnett (2009).

Collaborating on Postdischarge Plans

When a patient seems to be emotionally stable and no longer reports suicidal ideation, it is generally assumed that he or she is ready for discharge from inpatient care and for the resumption of life in the community. In the majority of cases, this is true; however, a number of studies have highlighted the period of transition from inpatient to outpatient status as a time of increased risk for suicide. In this regard, Fawcett, Clark, and Busch (1993) found in their long-term prospective study that most of the affective disorder patients who completed suicide during the first year of follow-up had been inpatients rather than outpatients on entry into the study. Roy (1982) studied former inpatients who subsequently took their own lives and found that 44% of the suicides occurred within 1 month of hospital discharge, 70% within 4 months of discharge, and 89% within 1 year of discharge. In addition, the findings about completed suicides in the study by Kleespies, Ahnallen, et al. (2011) are also supportive of the need for concern about risk during this transitional period.

The data in the previous paragraph indicate that some patients may have a lingering wish to die that is no longer being verbalized or that some patients' suicidal intent can reoccur or fluctuate rapidly. It is therefore important to collaborate with the patient in making plans for outpatient treatment following hospital discharge. Ideally, appointments for follow-up care should be in place at discharge, and there should be a method of monitoring whether the initial outpatient appointments are kept. Moreover, the outpatient providers who will assume the care of the patient should be advised that hospitalization has not necessarily eliminated the risk to the patient. Close monitoring for suicidal ideation and intent must continue in the postdischarge period (Kleespies & Dettmer, 2000a).

MALPRACTICE CLAIMS AND PATIENT VIOLENCE

Clinicians' legal and ethical concerns about patient violence have most often revolved around what has been referred to as the *duty to protect* (i.e., the duty of the clinician to protect others from the violence of his or her patient) as set forth by the California Supreme Court in *Tarasoff v. Regents of the University of California* (1976). As briefly noted in Chapter 1 of this volume, what has been confusing for many is that the original *Tarasoff* case was decided in 1974 (*Tarasoff v. Regents of the University of California*, 1974), and the court ruled that the therapist or clinician had a *duty to warn* those who were at risk of violence perpetrated by his or her patient. This ruling, however, was vacated when the court revisited the case in *Tarasoff v. Regents of the University of California* (1976).

The duty to warn meant that the mental health provider had a duty to warn an identifiable person to avert danger if his or her patient intended to physically harm that person (Welfel, Werth, & Benjamin, 2009). This ruling raised great concern in the mental health community because it meant that the practitioner had to break the patient's confidentiality to warn the intended victim. In reviewing the case, however, and changing the duty to warn to a duty to protect, the *Tarasoff* court actually expanded the duty to warn. It expanded it in the sense that the court ruled that simply warning the intended victim might not be sufficient and what the clinician needed to do was to take the necessary steps to protect the intended victim from harm. Although this second ruling was an expansion, it also implied that there could be more than one way (i.e., other than warning the intended victim) to protect the individual (e.g., the clinician might afford the intended victim more protection by having the patient hospitalized).

The *Tarasoff* ruling originally only applied as case or common law in California. It was taken, however, as applying far more widely, and this too has led to confusion at times. California passed legislation that both changed the common law in some ways and codified the duty to protect into statutory law. Such a mandatory duty law creates a legal obligation for the mental health provider to protect third parties from his or her patients' threatened violence. Not every state, however, has followed suit. Benjamin, Kent, and Sirikantraporn (2009) investigated the status of duty to protect in all of the United States plus the District of Columbia as well as in the 12 provinces of Canada. They found that 24 states have a mandatory duty to protect created by statute, while nine states have a common law duty established by court decisions. Ten other states and eight Canadian provinces have statutes or rules establishing a so-called permissive duty to protect—that is, a law that allows the practitioner to breach patient confidentiality to protect third parties from patient violence but does not require him or her to do so. These laws allow the practitioner more discretion in how to act under the particular circumstances of an individual case. The law in the remaining 13 states and provinces is silent about whether a duty to protect (or a duty to warn) exists.

Not only are there differences in which states have a mandatory or permissive duty-to-protect law, but there are also differences in how each state's law is written. Thus, there can be differences in what may trigger a duty to protect in different states or what conditions must be met for the clinician to have fulfilled his or her obligation under the law. To trigger the law in Massachusetts, for example, the patient must communicate to the mental health professional an explicit threat to kill or inflict serious bodily injury on a reasonably identified victim or victims, or the patient must have a history of physical violence that is known to the practitioner, and the practitioner must have a reasonable basis for believing that there is a clear and present danger that the patient will attempt to kill or seriously injure a reasonably identified victim or victims (Mass. Gen. Laws ch. 123, sec. 36B). This law uses the *reasonably identified victim* standard. As Packman et al. (2009) pointed out, however, the duty-to-protect law in the state of Nebraska has been interpreted as being triggered by the *foreseeable victim* standard; that is, it is triggered when the mental health practitioner knows or should know that his or her patient presents a danger to others. In such a circumstance, the law has been said to impose a duty to protect the public at large.

In terms of fulfilling one's obligation under a duty-to-protect mandate, again in Massachusetts the law (Mass. Gen. Laws ch. 112, sec. 129A) states that the practitioner shall be deemed to have taken reasonable precautions if he or she has made reasonable efforts to take one or more of the following actions: (a) communicate the threat to the reasonably identified person; (b) notify an appropriate law enforcement agency near where the patient or any potential victim resides; (c) arrange for the patient to be hospitalized voluntarily; and/or (d) initiate proceedings for the involuntary hospitalization of the patient. This law indicates that the clinician can meet his or her obligation by warning the intended victim, but it allows for some discretion in meeting the obligation by other means. However, as Welfel et al. (2009) pointed out, state statutes and case law are continuously evolving, and the mental health practitioner cannot assume that how he or she might meet the duty to protect in one state will necessarily be the same in another.

Mental health clinicians have ethical as well as legal concerns related to the duty to protect. As Sommers-Flanagan, Sommers-Flanagan, and Welfel (2009) noted, the APA's Ethics Code has identified the protection of patient privacy as a core value of the profession. The code, however, grants exceptions to confidentiality without patient consent in circumstances in which other ethical values carry greater weight (APA, 2010). Protecting third parties from serious harm or death at the hands of a patient or protecting children or elders or the handicapped from abuse and neglect are also values of the profession. If the need to protect others from serious harm conflicts with confidentiality, then the ethics code permits breaching confidentiality. Nothing in the code, however, mandates a breach of confidentiality. It acknowledges that there are legal limits to confidentiality in certain jurisdictions and otherwise allows the practitioner to breach confidentiality to protect the patient, the psychologist, and others from harm. As Sommers-Flanagan et al. stated, in jurisdictions where there is no legal requirement, psychologists can use their professional judgment about how advisable it may be to break confidentiality with the patient, even when the patient constitutes a danger to others.

In addition to the legal and ethical issues surrounding duty-to-protect situations, Borum (2009) cautioned that there can be psychosocial repercussions to warning a potential victim as well. Warnings that someone has threatened to seriously harm or kill you can be very frightening. They can provoke a very fearful, or a very aggressive, response. If a clinician, by law or because other means of protecting the individual are not feasible, must warn an intended victim, he or she should do so with care. The warning should specify the nature and seriousness of the threat, discuss potential signs of increased danger, and include a plan that describes safety measures and offers resources to contact.

CONCLUDING REMARKS

With an awareness of the caveats and issues noted in this chapter, the mental health practitioner should be better prepared to manage the stresses of the legal and ethical aspects of behavioral emergency cases. Many problems with suicidal or potentially violent patients can be avoided if there is full disclosure about the limits of confidentiality before any suicidal or violent ideation is expressed (Benjamin et al., 2009). Such disclosure can avoid having the patient feel surprised and betrayed if confidentiality must be broken to provide safety for him, her, or others. It can also become a base from which to collaborate with the patient in determining what risks to self or others may exist. This transparency on the part of the treatment provider can also set the tone for a more honest and open working alliance with the patient, and a good working alliance is clearly a key to the appropriate and safe management of high-risk cases.

One of the best ways to manage legal and ethical concerns when dealing with behavioral emergencies is to do a good evaluation of risk that should lead to an appropriate safety and management plan. Unfortunately, as discussed in Chapter 1 of this volume, psychologists and other mental health providers are often not well trained in this area of practice despite the serious clinical, ethical, professional, and legal consequences that can occur if there is a negative outcome (Kleespies & Ponce, 2009). Speaking of training in the assessment and management of suicide risk, Schmitz et al. (2012) argued that this is a problem in systems-level ethics: "The system of training mental health professionals has, generally, not prepared them to function in the best interests of their patients in regard to the crucial issue of assessing and managing patient suicidality" (pp. 297–298). In my opinion, the same can be said in terms of training mental health professionals for the assessment and management of patient violence. This lack of preparation, of course, also applies to many, if not most, psychologists-in-training at the present time.

At the level of the individual clinician, Bongar (2002) noted that psychologists must each evaluate their own professional competence to evaluate and treat suicidal patients. They must also evaluate their competence to supervise trainees who must work with patients at risk to self or others. The psychology supervisor (as the licensed professional) is, after all, ultimately responsible for the management of the case. Moreover, the APA Ethics Code states that a psychologist provides only those services that are within his or her area of competence (see Ethical Standard 2: Competence in APA, 2010).

The so-called twin pillars of risk management for the practitioner are consultation and documentation. If a clinician has doubts about his or her evaluation of risk or plan for managing risk, a consultation with a colleague or peer is indicated. Not only can a consultation yield the benefit of another perspective, it can also demonstrate that the clinician has made an effort to determine the community standard and to abide by the thinking of the proverbial *reasonable and prudent practitioner.* Consultations should be documented in the patient's record as an integral part of the process undertaken to evaluate and manage risk to self or others. Should there be a negative outcome, it is clearly important for the practitioner to have entered into the record his or her thinking about the risks and benefits of the course of action that was taken. After the fact, there can always be doubt about the subjective, verbal report of the treatment provider. The written record bears witness to the clinician's thinking prior to the outcome and before the outcome may have made for a more defensive rendering of events.

8

Coping With the Emotional Aftermath of Negative Events

Although good training can lead to improved competence in managing behavioral emergencies, there still can be negative outcomes in working with high-risk patients. Despite improvements in the prediction of violence with decision-support tools, for example, we are still not particularly near to being able to predict and prevent most patient violence. As noted in Chapter 1 of this book, both patient suicide and patient violence are statistically low base rate events that we do not have the clinical sensitivity or instruments to predict. We, however, continue to work at improving our ability to estimate risk and prevent such tragic events.

Given this state of affairs, it is important to think about the potential emotional impact of patient suicide or patient violence on the clinician himself or herself and how he or she might be assisted in coping with that impact. Although the stress of dealing with these behavioral emergencies was briefly discussed in Chapter 3, in this chapter I discuss what is known

http://dx.doi.org/10.1037/14337-009
Decision Making in Behavioral Emergencies: Acquiring Skill in Evaluating and Managing High-Risk Patients, by P. M. Kleespies

about the impact these negative events, when they actually occur, have on clinicians. I also discuss how clinicians might cope with that impact.

PATIENT SUICIDE, VIOLENCE, AND VICTIMIZATION

Because each of these events (i.e., patient suicide, patient violence, and patient victimization) can affect practitioners in different ways, each is discussed individually.

The Impact of Patient Suicide

There is now considerable, albeit retrospectively gathered, evidence that clinicians from virtually all of the mental health disciplines (e.g., psychologists, psychiatrists, social workers) often report feelings of shock, disbelief, failure, self-blame, guilt, shame, helplessness, anxiety, and/or depression when confronted with the suicide of one of their patients (Brown, 1987; Chemtob, Hamada, Bauer, Kinney, & Torigoe, 1988; Chemtob, Hamada, Bauer, Torigoe, & Kinney, 1988; Darden & Rutter, 2011; Grad, Zavasnik, & Groleger, 1997; Hendin, Haas, Maltsberger, Szanto, & Rabinowicz, 2004; Jacobson et al., 2004; Kleespies, Penk, & Forsyth, 1993; Kleespies, Smith, & Becker, 1990; Ruskin, Sakinofsky, Bagby, Dickens, & Sousa, 2004; Sanders, Jacobson, & Ting, 2005; Ting, Sanders, Jacobson, & Power, 2006). Some investigators have administered the Impact of Event Scale (Horowitz, Wilner, & Alvarez, 1979) and found retrospectively rated elevations on the Intrusion and Avoidance scales, suggesting that clinicians who have a patient suicide often struggle with intrusive thoughts about the event or make efforts to avoid reminders of it (Chemtob, Hamada, Bauer, Kinney, & Torigoe, 1988; Chemtob, Hamada, Bauer, Torigoe, & Kinney, 1988; Jacobson et al., 2004; Kleespies et al., 1990, 1993; Ruskin et al., 2004). Brown (1987) and Kleespies et al. (1993) found that these reactions usually diminished substantially over a period of weeks or months, but some effects (e.g., anxiety when evaluating suicidal patients) can apparently remain for years for some clinicians.

Hendin et al. (2004) conducted in-depth personal interviews with 34 therapists who had experienced a patient suicide. About one third of these therapists reported severe distress in the aftermath. The sources of distress that were most frequently mentioned were (a) failure to hospitalize a patient who then committed suicide, (b) having made a treatment decision that may have contributed to a patient's suicide, (c) negative reactions from the therapist's clinic or medical center administration after a patient suicide, and (d) fear of a lawsuit by relatives who blamed the therapist. Those therapists who were less distressed, compared with those who were very distressed, appeared to have the ability to view the situation as a learning experience rather than as an occasion for self-reproach.

It has been suggested that clinicians-in-training who have experienced a patient suicide may be shielded from negative emotional effects because they are under supervision and do not bear the ultimate ethical and legal responsibility (Brown, 1987). Alternatively, the opposite has been suggested; that is, that those in training are more likely to assume responsibility for "fixing the client" (Rodolfa, Kraft, & Reilley, 1988, p. 47) and have stronger feelings of inadequacy if treatment interventions fail. There is some evidence that those in training tend to be more distressed than those at the professional level (Ruskin et al., 2004). In addition, Kleespies et al. (1993) found a negative relationship between intrusive thoughts and images and the year in training in which a patient suicide was experienced (i.e., the earlier in training the suicide occurred, the greater the impact of intrusive thoughts). One hypothesis is that trainees who are less experienced may feel less prepared, less secure in their roles, or more shocked by patient suicide than more experienced trainees and professionals.

The Impact of Patient Violence

Because of the apparent impact of patient violence on mental health staff in a public mental health care system in Massachusetts, Flannery, Fulton, Tausch, and DeLoffi (1991) started an Assaulted Staff Action Program (ASAP). ASAP was a voluntary, systemwide, peer-help program to assist staff in coping with the psychological sequelae of patient violence. In terms of psychological effects, those involved with ASAP noted that a significant number of staff victims of violence reported a disruption in a sense of mastery of their work, a disruption of their caring attachments to patients, and distress about the meaning of the event (Flannery, Stone, Rego, & Walker, 2001).

The findings of Flannery et al. (2001) seem consistent with those of J. Guy, Brown, and Poelstra (1991) as well as with the findings in studies of patients/clients who stalk clinicians as noted in Chapter 1 of this volume (Gentile, Asamen, Harmell, & Weathers, 2002; Purcell, Powell, & Mullen, 2005). J. Guy et al., in a national survey of patient violence directed at psychotherapists, found that 40% of those who reported one or more instances of patient violence had a dramatically increased sense of vulnerability in the aftermath. Not surprisingly, the greater the extent of any physical injury, the greater the sense of fear and vulnerability that followed. Some of the clinician victims reportedly experienced a decrease in overall emotional well-being and in a sense of professional competency.

Some episodes of patient violence reported in the survey by J. Guy et al. (1991) required that the clinician be active in his or her own defense or have the patient physically restrained. As J. Guy and Brady (1998) pointed out, these practitioners sometimes have fears about possible litigation or malpractice claims.

Most therapists in the survey by J. Guy et al. (1991) did not reduce their caseload after an episode of patient violence, but many engaged in other protective measures. The most frequent protective measure was to refuse to accept patients whom they perceived as having a potential for violence. Their tendency was to refer such patients to other clinicians. They also reported being more active about setting limits on patient disruptive and aggressive behavior and about formulating contingency plans for obtaining assistance in the event another incident occurred. Some reported having relocated to a safer office or building or having their home phone number unlisted. Others avoided working alone in the office, hired a secretary, or installed an alarm system.

The Impact of Working With Victims of Violence

Although therapy can be very important to the recovery of individuals who have been traumatized by interpersonal violence, research and clinical knowledge inform us that therapists who provide this treatment can be at risk of experiencing a range of personal reactions. Working with individuals in crisis after being the victims of violence can lead therapists to develop anxiety, intrusive thoughts about the patient's experiences, and emotional numbing. They may find themselves using avoidance strategies to keep away from traumatic material in session (McCann & Pearlman, 1990).

These reactions in therapists occur frequently enough to have become identified, as noted in Chapter 3, by at least two terms: *vicarious trauma* (VT) and *secondary traumatic stress* (STS). These terms are often used interchangeably, but there are some conceptual differences. VT emphasizes cognitive disruptions for the therapist such as disturbances in beliefs or cognitive schemas related to intimacy, trust, safety, control, and self-esteem (Saakvitne & Pearlman, 1996). STS, on the other hand, focuses on emotional or social disturbances that are similar to the symptoms of posttraumatic stress disorder (PTSD)—for example, reexperiencing the patient's trauma event, avoidance or numbing in response to reminders of the event, and arousal symptoms such as irritability (Figley, 1995).

There is some evidence in the literature for VT. Using five subscales of the Traumatic Stress Institute Belief Scale (McCann & Pearlman, 1990), Schauben and Frazier (1995) found that counselors who worked with a higher percentage of sexual assault survivors in their caseloads had more disrupted beliefs (particularly about the goodness of other people) than counselors who saw a lower percentage of sexual assault survivors. Similar findings have been reported by Bober and Regehr (2006) and VanDeusen and Way (2006), who respectively found an increase in cognitive disruptions for rape counselors and counselors who work with sexual abuse survivors.

Raquepaw and Miller (1989) reported that VT could lead to lower quality of care and that psychotherapy itself could be compromised. Saakvitne and Pearlman (1996) outlined specific examples of how VT can affect the clinician. They indicated that those affected by VT may have trouble accessing emotions, often experience guilt, and may find it difficult to be intimate with their partners because of intrusive thoughts about a client's or patient's abuse. In terms of symptoms of STS, Munroe (1990) reported that therapists who worked with veterans with combat-related PTSD could become more irritable, less able to attend to trauma stimuli, and more prone to misdiagnosis.

COPING WITH THE STRESS OF PATIENT SUICIDE, VIOLENCE, AND VICTIMIZATION

In the sections that follow, some of the issues confronted by clinicians who need to cope with negative clinical events (e.g., patient suicide, violence, victimization) are discussed. Although there are some commonalities, these differing events can evoke different reactions and concerns.

Coping With Patient Suicide

Efforts to cope with the impact of patient suicide can be complicated by the nature of the clinician's relationship with the patient. As both Farberow (1993) and Jones (1987) have suggested, patient suicide can bring about both a personal crisis and a professional crisis for the clinician. On a personal level, mental health professionals often come to know the most intimate feelings of their patients and therefore can have intense reactions to a patient's self-destructiveness. On the professional level, however, the clinician who has a patient suicide may have concerns about responsibility, possible malpractice suits, censure from colleagues, damage to reputation, and so forth. Furthermore, the professional concerns can complicate and inhibit the clinician's personal reactions and potential grief. They can cause the therapist to withdraw from colleagues and to distance himself or herself from possible sources of support.

Kleespies (1998c) suggested that a way to learn to cope with patient suicide was to have preparatory training for suicide risk assessment in which such an eventuality would be discussed. On the basis of a similar assumption, Lerner, Brooks, McNiel, Cramer, and Haller (2012) developed a curriculum on coping with patient suicide for psychiatric residents. The curriculum consisted of two distinct components: a biennial half-day workshop on medical–legal issues and coping skills and an as-needed module for individual clinicians should they have a patient who commits suicide. The workshop included a large-group lecture, small-group discussions led by faculty members who had experienced a patient suicide, and a reconvening of the large group with a guest speaker who had experienced the loss of a relative by suicide. The lecture covered topics such as discoverability and confidentiality, risk management, malpractice insurance, whether to contact the family, what to do with unpaid bills, documentation, relevant institutional policies, and common emotional reactions of clinicians and their colleagues. The small-group discussions were an opportunity for participants to reflect on and discuss their emotional reactions to the topic. The guest speaker then talked about the effects of suicide on family members. The as-needed module was developed as a postvention effort for a clinician who has a patient suicide. The focus of this module (when used) was on emotional support, institutional processes, and learning.

Forty-two psychiatry residents from all levels participated in the half-day workshop. In a pretest, they completed a questionnaire about their perceived competence in coping with a patient suicide. They also read a fictional vignette about a patient who committed suicide and responded to open-ended questions assessing their knowledge of pertinent emotional and medical–legal issues related to the case. A similar posttest followed the workshop, and a different case vignette was read. The responses to the questions were rated by two psychiatrists who were blind to whether they were pretests or posttests. The results of the study showed large and significant increases in knowledge on the posttest. They also showed substantial increases in self-perceptions of confidence in addressing the emotional, clinical, and medical–legal aspects of coping with patient suicide. The investigators concluded that specific training about this topic can yield measurable improvements, but further research is needed to see if these positive outcomes are maintained over time.

There have been a number of single-case or small-sample reports of what proved helpful to clinicians in coping with the aftermath of a patient suicide (e.g., see Alexander, 1991; Berman, 1995; Darden & Rutter, 2011;

Spiegelman & Werth, 2005). Kleespies et al. (1993) sought a somewhat larger sample and found that former psychology interns who had patient suicides while in training reported coping primarily by the use of support systems and case reviews. The greatest percentage reported turning to their case supervisors for emotional support, followed by seeking out peers, other staff members, and finally family or significant others. They also found discussions of the case with their supervisor to be very beneficial.

Talking with a colleague who knew the patient or who had had a similar experience with a patient has been reported as beneficial in reducing isolation in single case studies (Alexander, 1991; Berman, 1995; Spiegelman & Werth, 2005). At times, this sort of discussion has happened in a group format. Thus, Kolodny, Binder, Bronstein, and Friend (1979) reported how meaningful it was for four therapists to meet over the course of a year to discuss their reactions to patient suicides that each had recently experienced. In addition, Jones (1987) described a successful self-help group for therapist survivors. The group provided a nonjudgmental atmosphere in which therapists could share their feelings and issues related to patient suicide.

It should be noted that Bongar (2002) and Ruben (1990) have sounded a cautionary note about intern discussions with a supervisor or post-mortem case reviews in the wake of a patient suicide. They have contended that such discussions may be open to the legal discovery process in the event of a malpractice suit. As a protective measure, Bongar (2002) suggested that such discussions "be confined to the context of psychotherapeutic or legal consultation" (p. 250). This is a legally conservative position, but it would seem to deter student therapists from accessing sources of support and professional development. As noted previously in the study by Kleespies et al. (1993), the greatest percentage of psychology graduate students and interns, in the wake of a patient suicide, sought support from case supervisors and found discussions of the case with their supervisors to be the most beneficial form of case review as they attempted to understand the patient's decision to commit suicide and their own functioning in the patient's treatment.

As noted by Kleespies and Ponce (2009), Ellis and Dickey (1998) sought legal consultation on this issue, and although caution was advised, they reported that there seemed to be no legal precedent for a supervisor being required by a court to divulge information from a postsuicide debriefing or case review in a malpractice proceeding. They also noted that programs might be at equal or greater risk if they failed to try to examine and understand what led up to a patient's suicide. From an ethical perspective, Behnke (2005) reminded us that when the therapist is a trainee, the legal responsibility for the patient's or client's treatment resides with the supervisor. It would seem as though the supervisor would have a need to know what had occurred in the therapy sessions. Behnke also informed us that the supervisor not only protects the client's welfare but also helps the trainee to attain competence as a treatment provider, something that might be difficult for the supervisor to do if he or she could not review what occurred in the treatment sessions with the trainee therapist.

From my perspective, the issue seems similar to what I referred to earlier in this volume as *defensive practice*. In this situation, however, a more appropriate term might be *defensive supervision* in which the processing and review of critical clinical events is discouraged or suppressed because of a very uncertain legal risk. If such an approach were adopted, the clinician-in-training would likely be deprived of the learning that can come from the opportunity to share his or her thinking about the case with those who are in the best position to make it a learning experience. Trainees and interns clearly need their supervisor's input to deal with and learn from such sad and unsettling events.

Coping With Patient Violence

As noted earlier in this chapter, Flannery et al. (1991) developed a voluntary program in a state mental health care system (i.e., the ASAP) in an effort to assist staff members who experienced an assault by a patient. Initially, this program included *critical incident stress debriefing* (CISD; Mitchell, 1983) as one of its services. CISD was developed as a debriefing for the military and other first responders (e.g., firefighters, police officers) who were exposed to potentially traumatizing events. There has been great controversy, however, about whether such intense debriefings shortly after a traumatizing event are helpful or harmful (Tuckey, 2007). Moreover, it has been found that many people have their own coping resources and are resilient in the aftermath of potentially traumatizing events (Bonanno, 2004). As a result of these issues, the ASAP adjusted its emphasis to a more supportive, or so-called psychological first aid, approach (Flannery, Juliano, Cronin, & Walker, 2006). If a patient assault occurs, an ASAP team member responds to the individual staff member to offer support and see whether any needed medical care is being provided. The team member discusses whether the victim feels able to manage his or her feelings and continue to work. If desired, the staff victim can be referred to a weekly support group for assaulted staff members or can be seen individually for support. The team member offers to recontact the staff member in 3 days and 10 days to see how the victim is doing.

Most clinicians, of course, do not have access to a program like ASAP. If they have feelings of, for example, guilt or responsibility for the patient's violent behavior, J. Guy and Brady (1998) suggested that they find a trusted colleague with whom to discuss these issues. As reported by J. Guy et al. (1991), it was not unusual for clinicians in their national survey to report that they entered or reentered personal therapy following an event in which a patient assaulted them. Clearly, issues regarding personal vulnerability and safety can be activated under such circumstances. A therapist can assist the clinician victim in dealing with his or her concerns and in reducing the possibility that these concerns can affect the individual's work with other patients.

Coping With Patient Victimization

In a survey of female psychologists and counselors who worked with victims of sexual violence, Schauben and Frazier (1995) found that some treatment providers (often those with greater levels of distress) reported disengaging from the patient. Most psychologists and counselors, however, reported using active coping strategies such as redoubling efforts to help the patient solve problems related to the trauma. In discussing work with trauma survivors, Deiter, Nicholls, and Pearlman (2000) as well as Trippany, White Kress, and Wilcoxin (2004) emphasized that therapists should care for themselves by attending to professional needs such as obtaining continuing education, having ongoing supervision, and seeking consultation with trauma-sensitive colleagues. They recommended balancing trauma work with other types of work as well as with rest and recreation. In discussing the stress of hearing about and dealing with the trauma experienced by combat veterans, Munroe (1990) suggested that therapists may need to learn to use supervision and consultation to address potential secondary traumatization. He felt that therapist responses and reactions to trauma material should be regularly reviewed with a supervisor or consultant. He also recommended that trauma therapists do their work as part of a team in which team members have an awareness of the potential stress involved in trauma work and are supportive of each other.

Although intuitively it seems that coping strategies such as those just mentioned would clearly be helpful, Bober and Regehr (2006) did not find an association between secondary trauma scores and time devoted to leisure, self-car, or supervision. Rather, as H. Bell, Kulkarni, and Dalton (2003) had also suggested, they recommended a focus on structural changes to assist trauma therapists. A structural change, for example, might include distributing or redistributing workloads in a manner that limits the amount of exposure of any individual therapist to traumatized patients.

CONCLUDING REMARKS

In this chapter, we have discussed how working with patients who are at risk of suicide or violence or interpersonal victimization can be stressful, but when there is a negative outcome (e.g., the patient commits suicide or becomes violent or is assaulted), the impact on the clinician can be considerable. We noted efforts to cope with such events through preparatory training and individual coping strategies. Efforts to cope, however, can be supported or made difficult by the environment or system within which one works. Kleespies and Dettmer (2000b) asserted that clinical sites and training programs need to be sensitive to clinicians who undertake the potentially stressful task of evaluating and treating patients who are at high risk of life-threatening behavior. Clinics and hospitals can try to foster a health-promoting environment (Stokols, 1992) in which clinicians and clinicians-in-training feel supported and protected in their efforts to work with and discuss difficult cases, or they can be primarily focused on defending institutional interests narrowly defined. It is my contention that those who take the former approach will ultimately reap the benefit of having clinicians who are less stressed and better able to function to their fullest capacities.

Afterword

In this volume, I have described a model for acquiring skill and attaining competence in evaluating and managing behavioral emergencies. The model involves having a knowledge base as described in the book by Kleespies (2009), but beyond that it requires considerably more. Thus, it involves learning a decision-making strategy that is suited to intense, high-pressure, time-limited conditions such as those that can occur when patients may be at imminent risk of life-threatening behavior. It involves a gradated type of stress training (SET or stress exposure training) that enables the clinician-in-training to avoid becoming overwhelmed and allows him or her to gain key emergency-related experiences. These experiences prime the clinician to be able to quickly "size up" future crises and emergencies and respond to them more rapidly and effectively. The gradated approach to training further allows the clinician to begin to see these high-pressure situations as challenges that can be managed rather than as anxiety-provoking situations that seem beyond his or her capability.

The model described in this book promotes attaining competence that is in keeping with the report of the APA Task Force on the Assessment of Competence in Professional Psychology (2006). The APA Task Force recommended that the assessment of competence in the provision of psychological services demonstrate fidelity to practice. They recommended using experience near or actual patient–clinician interactions in determining competence. By extension, I have recommended that we train to competence in evaluating and managing behavioral emergencies through the gradated use of experience near and actual patient–clinician interactions with close supervision or mentoring. As noted earlier in this volume, learning about behavioral emergencies (e.g., patient suicide risk and patient violence risk) through lectures, courses, workshops, and case discussions can be very valuable and should undoubtedly be encouraged; however, this is learning carried out in a controlled setting without the pressure, tension, and potential consequences of real clinical interactions with patients at serious risk. There is a cost, in terms of staff or faculty time, to the close supervision needed for this type of skill acquisition. In Chapter 6, however, I have provided a model training program that has been used in a psychology internship and postdoctoral setting and could potentially be implemented in other such settings.

As noted in various places in this volume, behavioral emergencies force clinicians to confront what can be life-and-death decisions. If there is a negative outcome, serious clinical, ethical, legal, and professional questions can be raised about the management of the case. As pointed out, there have been numerous calls to action to improve the training of mental health clinicians in suicide risk assessment and intervention. These calls have largely gone unheeded (Schmitz et al., 2012). There is little reason to think that training in the evaluation and management of potential patient violence is appreciably better. Although individual clinicians, at times, obtain this type of training, the gap in training is at a systems level. The APA Task Force on the Assessment of Competence in Professional Psychology (2006) urged professional psychology to embrace a culture of competence as well as a culture of the assessment of competence. In this vein, is it not time for professional psychology to embrace training and competence in such a critical area of practice as the assessment and management of patient life-threatening behaviors?

References

Alexander, V. (1991). *Words I never thought to speak: Stories of life in the wake of suicide.* New York, NY: Lexington Books.

Alpert, J., & Paulson, A. (1990). Graduate-level education and training in child sexual abuse. *Professional Psychology: Research and Practice, 21,* 366–371. doi:10.1037/0735-7028.21.5.366

American Association of Suicidology. (2011). *Recognizing and responding to suicide risk.* Retrieved from http://www.suicidology.org/web/guest/education-and-training/rrsr

American Psychological Association. (2010). *Ethical principles of psychologists and code of conduct* (2002, Amended June 1, 2010). Retrieved from http://www.apa.org/ethics/code/index.aspx

APA Task Force on the Assessment of Competence in Professional Psychology. (2006, October). *APA Task Force on the Assessment of Competence in Professional Psychology: Final report.* Washington, DC: American Psychological Association.

Apter, A., Gothelf, D., Orbach, I., Weizman, R., Ratzoni, G., Har-Even, D., & Tyano, S. (1995). Correlation of suicidal and violent behavior in different diagnostic categories in hospitalized adolescent patients. *Journal of the Academy of Child and Adolescent Psychiatry, 34,* 912–918. doi:10.1097/00004583-199507000-00015

Arthur, G. L., Brende, J. O., & Quiroz, S. E. (2003). Violence: Incidence and frequency of physical and psychological assaults affecting mental health providers in Georgia. *Journal of General Psychology, 130,* 22–45. doi:10.1080/00221300309601272

Asnis, G., Kaplan, M., van Praag, H., & Sanderson, W. (1994). Homicidal behaviors among psychiatric outpatients. *Hospital and Community Psychiatry, 45,* 127–132.

Au, A., Cheung, G., Kropp, R., Yuk-chung, C., Lam, G., & Sung, P. (2008). A preliminary validation of the Brief Spousal Assault Form for the Evaluation of Risk (B-SAFER) in Hong Kong. *Journal of Family Violence, 23,* 727–735. doi:10.1007/s10896-008-9198-z

Barlow, D. (1974). Psychologists in the emergency room. *Professional Psychology, 5,* 251–256. doi:10.1037/h0037278

Basile, K. C., Chen, J., Black, M., & Saltzman, L. (2007). Prevalence and characteristics of sexual violence victimization among U.S. adults, 2001–2003. *Violence and Victims, 22,* 437–448. doi:10.1891/088667007781553955

Behnke, S. (2005, May). The supervisor as gatekeeper: Reflections on ethical standards 7.02, 7.04, 7.05, 7.06, and 10.01. *Monitor on Psychology, 36*(5), 90–91.

Bell, H., Kulkarni, S., & Dalton, L. (2003). Organizational prevention of vicarious trauma. *Families in Society: The Journal of Contemporary Human Services, 84,* 463–470. doi:10.1606/1044-3894.131

Bell, J. B., & Nye, E. (2007). Specific symptoms predict suicidal ideation in Vietnam combat veterans with chronic post-traumatic stress disorder. *Military Medicine, 172,* 1144–1147.

Benjamin, G. A., Kent, L., & Sirikantraporn, S. (2009). A review of duty-to-protect statutes, cases, and procedures for positive practice. In J. Werth, Jr., E. Welfel, & G. A. Benjamin (Eds.), *The duty to protect: Ethical, legal, and professional considerations for mental health professionals* (pp. 9–28). Washington, DC: American Psychological Association.

Berliner, L., & Elliott, D. (2002). Sexual abuse of children. In J. Myers, L. Berliner, J. Briere, C. Hendrix, C. Jenny, & T. Reid (Eds.), *The APSAC handbook on child maltreatment* (2nd ed.; pp. 55–78). Thousand Oaks, CA: Sage.

Berman, A. (1983). *Training committee report.* Washington, DC: American Association of Suicidology. Unpublished manuscript.

Berman, A. (1995). "To engrave herself on all our memories; to force her body into our lives": The impact of suicide on psychotherapists. In B. Mishara (Ed.), *The impact of suicide* (pp. 85–99). New York, NY: Springer.

Berman, A. (2011, August). *On reforming formulations of suicide risk.* Paper presented at the Section on Clinical Emergencies and Crises (Section VII of APA Division 12) Career Achievement Award ceremony at the convention of the American Psychological Association, Washington, DC.

Bober, T., & Regehr, C. (2006). Strategies for reducing secondary or vicarious trauma: Do they work? *Brief Treatment and Crisis Intervention, 6,* 1–9. doi:10.1093/brief-treatment/mhj001

Bonanno, G. A. (2004). Loss, trauma, and human resilience: Have we underestimated the human capacity to thrive after extremely aversive events? *American Psychologist, 59,* 20–28. doi:10.1037/0003-066X.59.1.20

Bongar, B. (2002). *The suicidal patient: Clinical and legal standards of care* (2nd ed.). Washington, DC: American Psychological Association. doi:10.1037/10424-000

Bongar, B., Berman, A., Maris, R., Silverman, M., Harris, E., & Packman, W. (Eds.). (1998). *Risk management with suicidal patients.* New York, NY: Guilford Press.

Bongar, B., Greaney, S., & Peruzzi, N. (1998). Risk management with the suicidal patient. In P. M. Kleespies (Ed.), *Emergencies in mental health practice: Evaluation and management* (pp. 199–216). New York, NY: Guilford Press.

Bongar, B., & Harmatz, M. (1991). Clinical psychology graduate education in the study of suicide: Availability, resources, and importance. *Suicide and Life-Threatening Behavior, 21,* 231–244.

Bongar, B., Lomax, J., & Harmatz, M. (1992). Training and supervisory issues in the assessment and management of the suicidal patient. In B. Bongar (Ed.), *Suicide: Guidelines for assessment, management, and treatment* (pp. 253–267). New York, NY: Oxford University Press.

Bongar, B., Maris, R., Berman, A., & Litman, R. (1998). Outpatient standards of care and the suicidal patient. In B. Bongar, A. Berman, R. Maris, M. Silverman, E. Harris, & W. Packman (Eds.), *Risk management with suicidal patients* (pp. 4–33). New York, NY: Guilford Press.

Bongar, B., & Sullivan, G. (2013). *The suicidal patient: Clinical and legal standards of care* (3rd ed.). Washington, DC: American Psychological Association. doi:10.1037/14184-000

Borum, R. (2009). Children and adolescents at risk of violence. In P. M. Kleespies (Ed.), *Behavioral emergencies: An evidence-based resource for evaluating and managing risk of suicide, violence, and victimization* (pp. 147–163). Washington, DC: American Psychological Association. doi:10.1037/11865-007

Borum, R., Bartel, P., & Forth, A. (2006). *Structured Assessment of Violence Risk in Youth: Professional manual.* Lutz, FL: PAR.

Borum, R., Lodewijks, H., Bartel, P., & Forth, A. (2010). Structured Assessment of Violence Risk in Youth (SAVRY). In R. Otto & K. Douglas (Eds.), *Handbook of violence risk assessment* (pp. 63–80). New York, NY: Routledge.

Brasch, J., Glick, R., Cobb, T., & Richmond, J. (2004). Residency training in emergency psychiatry: A model curriculum developed by the Education Committee of the American Association for Emergency Psychiatry. *Academic Psychiatry, 28,* 95–103. doi:10.1176/appi.ap.28.2.95

Brown, H. (1987). Patient suicide during residency training: 1. Incidence, implications, and program response. *Journal of Psychiatric Education, 11,* 201–216.

Bryan, C., Stone, S., & Rudd, M. D. (2011). A practical, evidence-based approach for means-restriction counseling with suicidal patients. *Professional Psychology: Research and Practice, 42,* 339–346. doi:10.1037/a0025051

Bullman, T. A., & Kang, H. (1994). Posttraumatic stress disorder and the risk of traumatic deaths among Vietnam veterans. *Journal of Nervous and Mental Disease, 182,* 604–610. doi:10.1097/00005053-199411000-00002

Calderwood, R., Klein, G., & Crandall, B. (1988). Time pressure, skill, and move quality in chess. *The American Journal of Psychology, 101,* 481–493. doi:10.2307/1423226

Callahan, J. (1998). Crisis theory and crisis intervention in emergencies. In P. M. Kleespies (Ed.), *Emergencies in mental health practice: Evaluation and management* (pp. 22–40). New York, NY: Guilford Press.

Callahan, J. (2009). Emergency intervention and crisis intervention. In P. M. Kleespies (Ed.), *Behavioral emergencies: An evidence-based resource for evaluating and managing risk of suicide, violence, and victimization* (pp. 13–32). Washington, DC: American Psychological Association. doi:10.1037/11865-001

Cardell, R., Bratcher, K., & Quinnett, P. (2009). Revisiting "suicide proofing" an inpatient unit through environmental safeguards: A review. *Perspectives in Psychiatric Care, 45,* 36–44. doi:10.1111/j.1744-6163.2009.00198.x

Catchpole, R., & Gretton, H. (2003). The predictive validity of risk assessment with violent young offenders: A 1-year examination of criminal outcome. *Criminal Justice and Behavior, 30,* 688–708. doi:10.1177/0093854803256455

Centers for Disease Control and Prevention. (2009). *Fastats: Assault or homicide.* Retrieved from http://www.cdc.gov/nchs/fastats/homicide.htm

Chemtob, C. M., Bauer, G., Hamada, R., Pelowski, S., & Muraoka, M. (1989). Patient suicide: Occupational hazard for psychologists and psychiatrists. *Professional Psychology: Research and Practice, 20,* 294–300. doi:10.1037/0735-7028.20.5.294

Chemtob, C. M., Hamada, R., Bauer, G., Torigoe, R., & Kinney, B. (1988). Patient suicide: Frequency and impact on psychologists. *Professional Psychology: Research and Practice, 19,* 416–420. doi:10.1037/0735-7028.19.4.416

Chemtob, C. M., Hamada, R. S., Bauer, G., Kinney, B., & Torigoe, R. Y. (1988). Patients' suicides: Frequency and impact on psychiatrists. *The American Journal of Psychiatry, 145,* 224–228.

Chu, C., Thomas, S., Ogloff, J., & Daffern, M. (2011). The predictive validity of the Short-Term Assessment of Risk and Treatability (START) in a secure forensic hospital: Risk factors and strengths. *International Journal of Forensic Mental Health, 10,* 337–345. doi:10.1080/14999013.2011.629715

Cohen, L. J., Test, M., & Brown, R. (1990). Suicide and schizophrenia: Data from a prospective community study. *The American Journal of Psychiatry, 147,* 602–607.

Cohen, M., Freeman, J., & Thompson, B. (2009). Training the naturalistic decision maker. In C. Zsambok & G. Klein (Eds.), *Naturalistic decision making* (pp. 257–268). New York, NY: Routledge.

Collyer, S., & Malecki, G. (1998). Tactical decision making under stress: History and overview. In J. Canon-Bowers & E. Salas (Eds.), *Making decisions under stress: Implications for individual and team training* (pp. 3–15). Washington, DC: American Psychological Association. doi:10.1037/10278-016

Comstock, B. (1992). Decision to hospitalize and alternatives to hospitalization. In B. Bongar (Ed.), *Suicide: Guidelines for assessment, management, and treatment* (pp. 204–217). New York, NY: Oxford University Press.

Conwell, Y. (1997). Management of suicidal behavior in the elderly. *The Psychiatric Clinics of North America, 20*, 667–683.

Covino, N. (1989). The general hospital emergency ward as a training opportunity for clinical psychologists. *Journal of Training & Practice in Professional Psychology, 3*, 17–32.

Darden, A. J., & Rutter, P. (2011). Psychologists' experiences of grief after client suicide: A qualitative study. *Omega: Journal of Death and Dying, 63*, 317–342.

Deiter, P. J., Nicholls, S., & Pearlman, L. (2000). Self-injury and self-capacities: Assisting an individual in crisis. *Journal of Clinical Psychology, 56*, 1173–1191. doi:10.1002/1097-4679(200009)56:9<1173::AID-JCLP5>3.0.CO;2-P

Desmarais, S., Nicholls, T., Wilson, C., & Brink, J. (2012). Using dynamic risk and protective factors to predict inpatient aggression: Reliability and validity of the START assessments. *Psychological Assessment, 24*, 685–700. doi:10.1037/a0026668

Dexter-Mazza, E. T., & Freeman, K. (2003). Graduate training and the treatment of suicidal clients: The students' perspective. *Suicide and Life-Threatening Behavior, 33*, 211–218. doi:10.1521/suli.33.2.211.22769

Dolan, M., & Rennie, C. (2006). Reliability and validity of the Psychopathy Checklist: Youth Version in a UK sample of conduct disordered boys. *Personality and Individual Differences, 40*, 65–75. doi:10.1016/j.paid.2005.07.001

Douglas, K. S., Blanchard, A., Guy, L., Reeves, K., & Weir, J. (2010). *HCR-20 violence risk assessment scheme: Overview and annotated bibliography.* Retrieved from http://kdouglas.wordpress.com

Douglas, K. S., Hart, S. D., Webster, C. D., & Belfrage, H. (2013). *HCR-20V3: Assessing risk of violence—User guide.* Burnaby, British Columbia, Canada: Simon Fraser University, Mental Health, Law, and Policy Institute.

Douglas, K. S., Ogloff, J., & Hart, S. (2003). Evaluation of a model of violence risk assessment among forensic psychiatric patients. *Psychiatric Services, 54*, 1372–1379. doi:10.1176/appi.ps.54.10.1372

Douglas, K. S., Ogloff, J., Nicholls, T., & Grant, I. (1999). Assessing risk for violence among psychiatric patients: The HCR-20 risk assessment scheme and the Psychopathy Checklist: Screening Version. *Journal of Consulting and Clinical Psychology, 67*, 917–930.

Douglas, K. S., Webster, C., Hart, S., Eaves, D., & Ogloff, J. (2001). *HCR-20 violence risk management companion guide*. Burnaby, British Columbia, Canada: Simon Fraser University, Mental Health, Law, and Policy Institute.

Driskell, J., & Johnston, J. (1998). Stress exposure training. In J. Canon-Bowers & E. Salas (Eds.), *Making decisions under stress: Implications for individual and team training* (pp. 191–217). Washington, DC: American Psychological Association. doi:10.1037/10278-007

Driskell, J. E., Johnston, J., & Salas, E. (2001). Does stress training generalize to novel settings? *Human Factors, 43,* 99–110. doi:10.1518/001872001775992471

Eddy, S., & Harris, E. (1998). Risk management with the violent patient. In P. M. Kleespies (Ed.), *Emergencies in mental health practice: Evaluation and management* (pp. 217–231). New York, NY: Guilford Press.

Ehrensaft, M. K., Cohen, P., Brown, J., Smailes, E., Chen, H., & Johnson, J. (2003). Intergenerational transmission of partner violence: A 20-year prospective study. *Journal of Consulting and Clinical Psychology, 71,* 741–753. doi:10.1037/0022-006X.71.4.741

Elbogen, E. B., Fuller, S., Johnson, S., Brooks, S., Kineer, P., Calhoun, P., & Becham, J. (2010). Improving risk assessment of violence among military veterans: An evidence-based approach for clinical decision-making. *Clinical Psychology Review, 30,* 595–607. doi:10.1016/j.cpr.2010.03.009

Ellis, T., & Dickey, T. (1998). Procedures surrounding the suicide of a trainee's patient: A national survey of psychology internships and psychiatry residency programs. *Professional Psychology: Research and Practice, 29,* 492–497. doi:10.1037/0735-7028.29.5.492

Endsley, M. (2009). The role of situation awareness in naturalistic decision making. In C. Zsambok & G. Klein (Eds.), *Naturalistic decision making* (pp. 269–283). New York, NY: Routledge.

Epstein, R. M., & Hundert, E. (2002). Defining and assessing professional competence. *JAMA, 287,* 226–235. doi:10.1001/jama.287.2.226

Epstein, S., Pacini, R., Denes-Raj, V., & Heier, H. (1996). Individual differences in intuitive-experiential and analytical-rational thinking styles. *Journal of Personality and Social Psychology, 71,* 390–405. doi:10.1037/0022-3514.71.2.390

Evensen, D., & Hmelo, C. (Eds.). (2000). *Problem-based learning: A research perspective on learning interactions.* Mahwah, NJ: Erlbaum.

Fabian, J. (2006). A literature review of the utility of selected violence and sexual violence risk assessment instruments. *Journal of Psychiatry & Law, 34,* 307–350.

Farberow, N. (1993). Bereavement after suicide. In A. Leenaars, A. Berman, P. Cantor, R. Litman, & R. Maris (Eds.), *Suicidology: Essays in honor of Edwin Shneidman* (pp. 337–345). Northvale, NJ: Jason Aronson.

Fawcett, J., Clark, D., & Busch, K. (1993). Assessing and treating the patient at risk for suicide. *Psychiatric Annals, 23,* 244–255.

Fazel, S., Singh, J., Doll, H., & Grann, M. (2012). Use of risk assessment instruments to predict violence and antisocial behavior in 73 samples involving 24 827 people: Systematic review and meta-analysis. *British Medical Journal, 345,* e4692. doi:10.1136/bmj.e4692

Feldman, B. N., & Freedenthal, S. (2006). Social work education in suicide intervention and prevention: An unmet need? *Suicide and Life-Threatening Behavior, 36,* 467–480. doi:10.1521/suli.2006.36.4.467

Figley, C. (1995). Compassion fatigue as secondary traumatic stress disorder: An overview. In C. Figley (Ed.), *Compassion fatigue: Coping with secondary traumatic stress disorder in those who treat the traumatized* (pp. 1–20). New York, NY: Brunner/Mazel.

Flannery, R. B., Fulton, P., Tausch, J., & DeLoffi, A. (1991). A program to help staff cope with psychological sequelae of assaults by patients. *Hospital & Community Psychiatry, 42,* 935–938.

Flannery, R. B., Juliano, J., Cronin, S., & Walker, A. (2006). Characteristics of assaultive psychiatric patients: Fifteen-year analysis of the Assaulted Staff Action Program (ASAP). *Psychiatric Quarterly, 77,* 239–249. doi:10.1007/s11126-006-9011-1

Flannery, R. B., Stone, P., Rego, S., & Walker, A. (2001). Characteristics of staff victims of patient assault: Ten year analysis of the Assaulted Staff Action program (ASAP). *Psychiatric Quarterly, 72,* 237–248. doi:10.1023/A:1010349015108

Gaba, D. M., Howard, S., & Jump, B. (1994). Production pressure in the work environment: California anesthesiologists' attitudes and experiences. *Anesthesiology, 81,* 488–500. doi:10.1097/00000542-199408000-00028

Gammelgard, M., Weitzman-Henelius, G., & Kaltiala-Heino, R. (2008). The predictive validity of the Structured Assessment of Violence Risk in Youth (SAVRY) among institutionalized adolescents. *Journal of Forensic Psychiatry & Psychology, 19,* 352–370. doi:10.1080/14789940802114475

Gawande, A. A., Studdert, D., Orav, E., Brennan, T., & Zinner, M. (2003). Risk factors for retained instruments and sponges after surgery. *The New England Journal of Medicine, 348,* 229–235. doi:10.1056/NEJMsa021721

Gentile, S., Asamen, J., Harmell, P., & Weathers, R. (2002). The stalking of psychologists by their clients. *Professional Psychology: Research and Practice, 33,* 490–494. doi:10.1037/0735-7028.33.5.490

Gore, J., & Sadler-Smith, E. (2011). Unpacking intuition: A process and outcome framework. *Review of General Psychology, 15,* 304–316. doi:10.1037/a0025069

Grad, O. T., Zavasnik, A., & Groleger, U. (1997). Suicide of a patient: Gender differences in bereavement reactions of therapists. *Suicide and Life-Threatening Behavior, 27,* 379–386.

Guy, J., & Brady, J. L. (1998). The stress of violent behavior for the clinician. In P. M. Kleespies (Ed.), *Emergencies in mental health practice: Evaluation and management* (pp. 398–417). New York, NY: Guilford Press.

Guy, J., Brown, C., & Poelstra, P. (1990). Who gets attacked? A national survey of patient violence directed at psychologists in clinical practice. *Professional Psychology: Research and Practice, 21,* 493–495. doi:10.1037/0735-7028.21.6.493

Guy, J., Brown, C., & Poelstra, P. (1991). Living with the aftermath: A national survey of the consequences of patient violence directed at psychotherapists. *Psychotherapy in Private Practice, 9,* 35–44.

Guy, L. S., Douglas, K., & Hendry, M. (2010). The role of psychopathic personality disorder in violence risk assessments using the HCR-20. *Journal of Personality Disorders, 24,* 551–580. doi:10.1521/pedi.2010.24.5.551

Haggard-Grann, U. (2007). Assessing violence risk: A review and clinical recommendations. *Journal of Counseling & Development, 85,* 294–302. doi:10.1002/j.1556-6678.2007.tb00477.x

Hammond, K. (2000). *Judgments under stress.* New York, NY: Oxford University Press.

Harden, R. M., Stevenson, M., Downie, W., & Wilson, G. (1975). Assessment of clinical competence using objective structured examination. *British Medical Journal, 1,* 447–451. doi:10.1136/bmj.1.5955.447

Hare, R. (1991). *Manual for the Hare Psychopathy Checklist–Revised.* Toronto, Ontario, Canada: Multi-Health Systems.

Harris, G. T., Rice, M., & Camilleri, J. (2004). Applying a forensic actuarial assessment (the Violence Risk Appraisal Guide) to nonforensic patients. *Journal of Interpersonal Violence, 19,* 1063–1074. doi:10.1177/0886260504268004

Hart, S., Cox, D., & Hare, R. (1995). *The Hare Psychopathy Checklist: Screening Version (PCL:SV).* North Tonawanda, NY: Multi-Health Systems.

Hendin, H., & Haas, A. (1991). Suicide and guilt as manifestations of PTSD in Vietnam combat veterans. *The American Journal of Psychiatry, 148,* 586–591.

Hendin, H., Haas, A., Maltsberger, J., Szanto, K., & Rabinowicz, H. (2004). Factors contributing to therapists' distress after the suicide of a patient. *The American Journal of Psychiatry, 161,* 1442–1446. doi:10.1176/appi.ajp.161.8.1442

Hilton, N. Z., Harris, G., & Rice, M. (2010). *Risk assessment for domestically violent men: Tools for criminal justice, offender intervention, and victim services.* Washington, DC: American Psychological Association. doi:10.1037/12066-000

Horowitz, M., Wilner, N., & Alvarez, W. (1979). Impact of Event Scale: A measure of subjective stress. *Psychosomatic Medicine, 41,* 209–218.

Hung, E. K., Binder, R., Fordwood, S., Hall, S., Cramer, R., & McNiel, D. (2012). A method for evaluating competency in assessment and management of suicide risk. *Academic Psychiatry, 36,* 23–28. doi:10.1176/appi.ap.10110160

Ilgen, M. A., Bohnert, A., Ignacio, R., McCarthy, J., Valenstein, M., Myra Kim, H., & Blow, F. (2010). Psychiatric diagnoses and risk of suicide in veterans. *Archives of General Psychiatry, 67*, 1152–1158. doi:10.1001/archgenpsychiatry.2010.129

Institute of Medicine. (2002). *Reducing suicide: A national imperative.* Washington, DC: National Academies Press.

Jacobson, J., Osteen, P., Jones, A., & Berman, A. (2012). Evaluation of the Recognizing and Responding to Suicide Risk training. *Suicide and Life-Threatening Behavior, 42*, 471–485. doi:10.1111/j.1943-278X.2012.00105.x

Jacobson, J. M., Ting, L., Sanders, S., & Harrington, D. (2004). Prevalence and reactions to fatal and nonfatal client suicidal behavior: A national study of mental health social workers. *Omega: Journal of Death and Dying, 49*, 237–248.

Jahn, D., Wacha-Montes, A., Drapeau, C., Grant, B., Nadorff, M., & Pusateri, M., ... Cukrowicz, K. (2011). *Suicide-specific courses and training: Prevalence, beliefs, and barriers. Part I: Graduate psychology programs and professional schools of psychology.* Manuscript in preparation.

Janis, I., & Mann, L. (1977). *Decision making: A psychological analysis of conflict, choice, and commitment.* New York, NY: Free Press.

Jayaratne, S., Croxton, T., & Mattison, D. (2004). A national survey of violence in the practice of social work. *Families in Society: The Journal of Contemporary Social Services, 85*, 445–453. doi:10.1606/1044-3894.1833

Jenkins, S. R., & Baird, S. (2002). Secondary traumatic stress and vicarious traumatization: A validational study. *Journal of Traumatic Stress, 15*, 423–432. doi:10.1023/A:1020193526843

Jobes, D. (2006). *Managing suicidal risk: A collaborative approach.* New York, NY: Guilford Press.

Johnston, J., & Cannon-Bowers, J. (1996). Training for stress exposure. In J. Driskell & E. Salas (Eds.), *Stress and human performance* (pp. 223–256). Mahwah, NJ: Erlbaum.

Johnston, J., Driskell, J., & Salas, E. (1997). Vigilant and hypervigilant decision making. *Journal of Applied Psychology, 82*, 614–622. doi:10.1037/0021-9010.82.4.614

Joint Commission. (2010). *Sentinel Event Alert, issue 46: A follow-up report on preventing suicide. Focus on medical/surgical units and the emergency department.* Retrieved from http://www.jointcommission.org/sentinel_event_alert_issue_46_a_followup_report_on_preventing_suicide_focus_on_medicalsurgical_units_and_the_emergency_department/

Joint Commission. (2011). *Sentinel event data: Root causes by event type.* Retrieved from http://www.jointcommission.org/Sentinel_Event_Statistics/

Joint Commission. (2013). *Sentinel event data: Event type by year, 1995–2012.* Retrieved from http://www.jointcommission.org/sentinel_event_statistics_quarterly/

Jones, F., Jr. (1987). Therapists as survivors of client suicide. In E. Dunne, J. McIntosh, & K. Dunne-Maxim (Eds.), *Suicide and its aftermath: Understanding and counseling the survivors* (pp. 126–141). New York, NY: Norton.

Kahneman, D. (2011). *Thinking, fast and slow.* New York, NY: Farrar, Srauss, and Giroux.

Kahneman, D., Slovic, P., & Tversky, A. (Eds.). (1982). *Judgment under uncertainty: Heuristics and biases.* New York, NY: Cambridge University Press. doi:10.1017/CBO9780511809477

Kelly, M., Mufson, M., & Rogers, M. (1999). Medical settings and suicide. In D. Jacobs (Ed.), *The Harvard Medical School guide to suicide assessment and intervention* (pp. 491–519). San Francisco, CA: Jossey-Bass.

Kessler, R. C., Sonnega, A., Bromet, E., Hughes, M., & Nelson, C. (1995). Post-traumatic stress disorder in the National Comorbidity Survey. *Archives of General Psychiatry, 52,* 1048–1060. doi:10.1001/archpsyc.1995.03950240066012

Kilpatrick, D. (2005, August). *The role of trauma in behavioral emergencies: Implications for policy and practice.* Presidential address for Section VII of Division 12, presented at the 113th annual convention of the American Psychological Association, Washington, DC.

Kilpatrick, D. G., Ruggiero, K., Acierno, R., Saunders, B., Resnick, H., & Best, C. (2003). Violence and risk of PTSD, major depression, substance abuse/dependence, and comorbidity: Results from the National Survey of Adolescents. *Journal of Consulting and Clinical Psychology, 71,* 692–700. doi:10.1037/0022-006X.71.4.692

Kleespies, P. M. (1998a). The domain of psychological emergencies: An overview. In P. M. Kleespies (Ed.), *Emergencies in mental health practice: Evaluation and management* (pp. 9–21). New York, NY: Guilford Press.

Kleespies, P. M. (Ed.). (1998b). *Emergencies in mental health practice: Evaluation and management.* New York, NY: Guilford Press.

Kleespies, P. M. (1998c). Introduction. In P. M. Kleespies (Ed.), *Emergencies in mental health practice: Evaluation and management* (pp. 1–6). New York, NY: Guilford Press.

Kleespies, P. M. (2000). Behavioral emergencies and crises: An overview. *Journal of Clinical Psychology, 56,* 1103–1108. doi:10.1002/1097-4679(200009)56:9<1103::AID-JCLP1>3.0.CO;2-L

Kleespies, P. M. (Ed.). (2009). *Behavioral emergencies: An evidence-based resource for evaluating and managing risk of suicide, violence, and victimization.* Washington, DC: American Psychological Association. doi:10.1037/11865-000

Kleespies, P. M., Ahnallen, C., Knight, J., Presskreischer, B., Barrs, K., Boyd, B., & Dennis, J. (2011). A study of self-injurious and suicidal behavior in a veteran population. *Psychological Services, 8,* 236–250. doi:10.1037/a0024881

Kleespies, P. M., Deleppo, J., Gallagher, P., & Niles, B. (1999). Managing suicidal emergencies: Recommendations for the practitioner. *Professional Psychology: Research and Practice, 30,* 454–463. doi:10.1037/0735-7028.30.5.454

Kleespies, P. M., & Dettmer, E. (2000a). An evidence-based approach to evaluating and managing suicidal emergencies. *Journal of Clinical Psychology, 56,* 1109–1130. doi:10.1002/1097-4679(200009)56:9<1109::AID-JCLP2>3.0.CO;2-C

Kleespies, P. M., & Dettmer, E. (2000b). The stress of patient emergencies for the clinician: Incidence, impact, and means of coping. *Journal of Clinical Psychology, 56,* 1353–1369. doi:10.1002/1097-4679(200010)56:10<1353::AID-JCLP7>3.0.CO;2-3

Kleespies, P. M., & Hill, J. (2011). Behavioral emergencies and crises. In D. Barlow (Ed.), *The Oxford handbook of clinical psychology* (pp. 739–761). New York, NY: Oxford University Press.

Kleespies, P. M., Hough, S., & Romeo, A. (2009). Suicide risk in people with medical and terminal illness. In P. M. Kleespies (Ed.), *Behavioral emergencies: An evidence-based resource for evaluating and managing risk of suicide, violence, and victimization* (pp. 103–121). Washington, DC: American Psychological Association. doi:10.1037/11865-005

Kleespies, P. M., Hughes, D., Weintraub, S., & Hart, A. (in press). Evaluating and managing suicide risk and violence risk in the medical setting. In D. Greenberg & B. Fogel (Eds.), *Psychiatric care of the medical patient* (3rd ed.). New York, NY: Oxford University Press.

Kleespies, P. M., Penk, W., & Forsyth, J. (1993). The stress of patient suicidal behavior during clinical training: Incidence, impact, and recovery. *Professional Psychology: Research and Practice, 24,* 293–303. doi:10.1037/0735-7028.24.3.293

Kleespies, P. M., & Ponce, A. (2009). The stress and emotional impact of clinical work with the patient at risk. In P. M. Kleespies (Ed.), *Behavioral emergencies: An evidence-based resource for evaluating and managing risk of suicide, violence, and victimization* (pp. 431–448). Washington, DC: American Psychological Association. doi:10.1037/11865-019

Kleespies, P. M., & Richmond, J. (2009). Evaluating behavioral emergencies: The clinical interview. In P. M. Kleespies (Ed.), *Behavioral emergencies: An evidence-based resource for evaluating and managing risk of suicide, violence, and victimization* (pp. 33–55). Washington, DC: American Psychological Association. doi:10.1037/11865-002

Kleespies, P. M., Smith, M., & Becker, B. (1990). Psychology interns as patient suicide survivors: Incidence, impact, and recovery. *Professional Psychology: Research and Practice, 21,* 257–263. doi:10.1037/0735-7028.21.4.257

Klein, G. (1996). The effect of acute stressors on decision making. In J. Driskell & E. Salas (Eds.), *Stress and human performance* (pp. 49–88). Mahwah, NJ: Erlbaum.

Klein, G. (1999). *Sources of power: How people make decisions*. Cambridge, MA: The MIT Press.

Klein, G. (2009). The recognition-primed decision (RPD) model: Looking back, looking forward. In C. Zsambok & G. Klein (Eds.), *Naturalistic decision making* (pp. 285–292). New York, NY: Routledge.

Koh, R. Y., Park, T., Wickens, C., Ong, L. T., & Chia, S. N. (2011). Differences in attentional strategies by novice and experienced operating theatre scrub nurses. *Journal of Experimental Psychology: Applied, 17,* 233–246. doi:10.1037/a0025171

Kolko, D. (2002). Child physical abuse. In J. Myers, L. Berliner, J. Briere, C. Hendrix, C. Jenny, & T. Reid (Eds.), *The APSAC handbook on child maltreatment* (2nd ed.; pp. 21–54). Thousand Oaks, CA: Sage.

Kolodny, S., Binder, R., Bronstein, A., & Friend, R. (1979). The working through of patients' suicides by four therapists. *Suicide and Life-Threatening Behavior, 9,* 33–46.

Kropp, P. R., & Hart, S. (2000). The Spousal Assault Risk Assessment (SARA) guide: Reliability and validity in adult male offenders. *Law and Human Behavior, 24,* 101–118. doi:10.1023/A:1005430904495

Kropp, P. R., Hart, S., Webster, C., & Eaves, D. (2008). *Manual for the Spousal Assault Risk Assessment Guide*. Vancouver, British Columbia, Canada: Pro-active Resolutions.

Lazarus, R. (1994). *Emotion and adaptation*. New York, NY: Oxford University Press.

LeBlanc, V. R., MacDonald, R., McArthur, B., King, K., & Lepine, T. (2005). Paramedic performance in calculating drug dosages following stressful scenarios in a human patient simulator. *Prehospital Emergency Care, 9,* 439–444. doi:10.1080/10903120500255255

Lerner, U., Brooks, K., McNiel, D., Cramer, R., & Haller, E. (2012). Coping with a patient's suicide: A curriculum for psychiatry residency training programs. *Academic Psychiatry, 36,* 29–33. doi:10.1176/appi.ap.10010006

Linehan, M. (1993). *Skills training manual for treating borderline personality disorder*. New York, NY: Guilford Press.

Linehan, M. M., Armstrong, H., Suarez, A., Allmon, D., & Heard, H. (1991). Cognitive-behavioral treatment of chronically parasuicidal borderline patients. *Archives of General Psychiatry, 48,* 1060–1064. doi:10.1001/archpsyc.1991.01810360024003

Link, B., & Stueve, A. (1994). Psychotic symptoms and the violent/illegal behavior of mental patients compared to community controls. In J. Monahan & H. J. Steadman (Eds.), *Violence and mental disorder: Developments in risk assessment* (pp. 137–159). Chicago, IL: University of Chicago Press.

Lomax, J. W. (1986). A proposed curriculum on suicide for psychiatric residency. *Suicide and Life-Threatening Behavior, 16,* 56–64.

Lutzker, J., & Wyatt, J. (2006). Introduction. In J. Lutzker (Ed.), *Preventing violence: Research and evidence-based intervention strategies* (pp. 3–15). Washington, DC: American Psychological Association. doi:10.1037/11385-013

Maltsberger, J. T., & Buie, D. (1974). Countertransference hate in the treatment of suicidal patients. *Archives of General Psychiatry, 30,* 625–633. doi:10.1001/archpsyc.1974.01760110049005

Mann, J. J., Waternaux, C., Haas, G., & Malone, K. (1999). Toward a clinical model of suicidal behavior in psychiatric patients. *The American Journal of Psychiatry, 156,* 181–189.

Massachusetts General Laws ch. 112, sec. 129A

Massachusetts General Laws ch. 123, sec. 36B

McCann, I., & Pearlman, L. (1990). Vicarious traumatization: A framework for understanding the psychological effects of working with victims. *Journal of Traumatic Stress, 3,* 131–149. doi:10.1007/BF00975140

McIntosh, J. (2012). *U.S.A. suicide: 2010 official final data.* Washington, DC: American Association of Suicidology. Retrieved from http://www.suicidology.org

McNiel, D. E. (2009). Assessment and management of acute risk of violence in adult patients. In P. M. Kleespies (Ed.), *Behavioral emergencies: An evidence-based resource for evaluating and managing risk of suicide, violence, and victimization* (pp. 125–145). Washington, DC: American Psychological Association. doi:10.1037/11865-006

McNiel, D. E., Chamberlain, J., Weaver, C., Hall, S., Fordwood, S., & Binder, R. (2008). Impact of clinical training on violence risk assessment. *The American Journal of Psychiatry, 165,* 195–200. doi:10.1176/appi.ajp.2007.06081396

McNiel, D. E., Fordwood, S., Weaver, C., Chamberlain, J., Hall, J., & Binder, R. (2008). Effects of training on suicide risk assessment. *Psychiatric Services, 59,* 1462–1465. doi:10.1176/appi.ps.59.12.1462

McNiel, D. E., Gregory, A., Lam, J., Sullivan, G., & Binder, R. (2003). Utility of decision support tools for assessing acute risk of violence. *Journal of Consulting and Clinical Psychology, 71,* 945–953. doi:10.1037/0022-006X.71.5.945

McNiel, D. E., Hung, E., Cramer, R., Hall, S., & Binder, R. (2011). An approach to evaluating competence in assessing and managing violence risk. *Psychiatric Services, 62,* 90–92. doi:10.1176/appi.ps.62.1.90

McNiel, D. E., Lam, J., & Binder, R. (2000). Relevance of interrater agreement to violence risk assessment. *Journal of Consulting and Clinical Psychology, 68,* 1111–1115. doi:10.1037/0022-006X.68.6.1111

Meehl, P. (1954). *Clinical versus statistical prediction: A theoretical analysis and review of the evidence.* Minneapolis: University of Minnesota Press. doi:10.1037/11281-000

Meichenbaum, D. (1985). *Stress inoculation training.* New York, NY: Pergamon Press.

Meichenbaum, D. (2007). Stress inoculation training: A preventative and treatment approach. In R. Lehrer, R. Woolfolk, & W. Sime (Eds.), *Principles and practice of stress management* (3rd ed.; pp. 497–516). New York, NY: Guilford Press.

Meloy, J. R., & Gothard, S. (1995). A demographic and clinical comparison of obsessional followers and offenders with mental disorders. *The American Journal of Psychiatry, 152,* 258–263.

Miller, A., & Emanuele, J. (2009). Children and adolescents at risk of suicide. In P. M. Kleespies (Ed.), *Behavioral emergencies: An evidence-based resource for evaluating and managing risk of suicide, violence, and victimization* (pp. 79–101). Washington, DC: American Psychological Association. doi:10.1037/11865-004

Mitchell, J. T. (1983). When disaster strikes . . . The critical incident stress debriefing process. *Journal of Emergency Medical Services, 8,* 36–39.

Monahan, J. (1993). Limiting therapist exposure to Tarasoff liability: Guidelines for risk containment. *American Psychologist, 48,* 242–250. doi:10.1037/0003-066X.48.3.242

Monahan, J., Steadman, H., Silver, E., Appelbaum, P., Robbins, P. C., Mulvey, E., . . . Banks, S. (2001). *Rethinking risk assessment: The MacArthur study of mental disorder and violence.* New York, NY: Oxford University Press.

Munroe, J. (1990). *Therapist traumatization from exposure to clients with combat-related post-traumatic stress disorder: Implications for administration and supervision.* Unpublished doctoral dissertation, Northeastern University, Boston, MA.

Nicholls, T. L., Brink, J., Desmarais, S., Webster, C., & Martin, M.-L. (2006). The Short-Term Assessment of Risk and Treatability (START): A prospective validation study in a forensic psychiatric sample. *Assessment, 13,* 313–327. doi:10.1177/1073191106290559

O'Leary, K., Slep, A., & O'Leary, S. (2000). Co-occurrence of partner and parent aggression: Research and treatment implications. *Behavior Therapy, 31,* 631–648. doi:10.1016/S0005-7894(00)80035-0

O'Leary, K., & Woodin, E. (2006). Bringing the agendas together: Partner and child abuse. In J. Lutzker (Ed.), *Preventing violence: Research and evidence-based intervention strategies* (pp. 239–258). Washington, DC: American Psychological Association.

Omer, H., & Elitzur, A. (2001). What would you say to the person on the roof? A suicide prevention text. *Suicide and Life-Threatening Behavior, 31,* 129–139. doi:10.1521/suli.31.2.129.21509

Oordt, M. S., Jobes, D., Fonseca, V., & Schmidt, S. (2009). Training mental health professionals to assess and manage suicidal behavior: Can provider confidence and practice behaviors be altered? *Suicide and Life-Threatening Behavior, 39,* 21–32. doi:10.1521/suli.2009.39.1.21

Orbach, I. (2001). How would you listen to the person on the roof? A response to H. Omer and A. Elitzur. *Suicide and Life-Threatening Behavior, 31,* 140–143. doi:10.1521/suli.31.2.140.21518

Packman, W., Andalibian, H., Eudy, K., Howard, B., & Bongar, B. (2009). Legal and ethical risk management with behavioral emergencies. In P. M. Kleespies (Ed.), *Behavioral emergencies: An evidence-based resource for evaluating and managing risk of suicide, violence, and victimization* (pp. 405–430). Washington, DC: American Psychological Association. doi:10.1037/11865-018

Payne, J., Bettman, J., & Johnson, E. (1988). Adaptive strategy selection in decision making. *Journal of Experimental Psychology: Learning, Memory, and Cognition, 14,* 534–552. doi:10.1037/0278-7393.14.3.534

Peuskens, J., DeHert, M., Cosyns, P., Pieters, G., Theys, P., & Vermotte, R. (1997). Suicide in young schizophrenic patients during and after inpatient treatment. *International Journal of Mental Health, 25,* 39–44.

Pisani, A. R., Cross, W., & Gould, M. (2011). The assessment and management of suicide risk: State of workshop education. *Suicide and Life-Threatening Behavior, 41,* 255–276. doi:10.1111/j.1943-278X.2011.00026.x

Plutchik, R., Botsis, A., & van Praag, H. (1995). Psychopathology, self-esteem, sexual and ego functions as correlates of suicide and violence risk. *Archives of Suicide Research, 1,* 27–38. doi:10.1080/13811119508258972

Pokorny, A. D. (1983). Prediction of suicide in psychiatric patients. *Archives of General Psychiatry, 40,* 249–257. doi:10.1001/archpsyc.1983.01790030019002

Polic, M. (2009). Decision making: Between rationality and reality. *Interdisciplinary Description of Complex Systems, 7,* 78–89.

Pope, K., & Feldman-Summers, S. (1992). National survey of psychologists' sexual and physical abuse history and their evaluation of training and competence in these areas. *Professional Psychology: Research and Practice, 23,* 353–361. doi:10.1037/0735-7028.23.5.353

Pope, K., & Tabachnick, B. (1993). Therapists' anger, hate, fear, and sexual feelings: National survey of therapist responses, client characteristics, critical events, formal complaints, and training. *Professional Psychology: Research and Practice, 24,* 142–152. doi:10.1037/0735-7028.24.2.142

Pope, K., & Vasquez, M. (1991). *Ethics in psychotherapy and counseling.* San Francisco, CA: Jossey-Bass.

Preston, S. D., Buchanan, T., Stansfield, R., & Bechara, A. (2007). Effects of anticipatory stress on decision making in a gambling task. *Behavioral Neuroscience, 121,* 257–263. doi:10.1037/0735-7044.121.2.257

Purcell, R., Powell, M., & Mullen, P. (2005). Clients who stalk psychologists: Prevalence, methods, and motives. *Professional Psychology: Research and Practice, 36,* 537–543. doi:10.1037/0735-7028.36.5.537

Quinsey, V., Harris, G., Rice, M., & Cormier, C. (1998). *Violent offenders: Appraising and managing risk.* Washington, DC: American Psychological Association. doi:10.1037/10304-000

Randel, J., Pugh, H., Reed, S., Schuler, J., & Wyman, B. (1994). *Methods for analyzing cognitive skills for a technical task.* San Diego, CA: Navy Personnel Research and Development Center.

Raquepaw, J., & Miller, R. (1989). Psychotherapist burnout: A componential analysis. *Professional Psychology: Research and Practice, 20,* 32–36. doi:10.1037/0735-7028.20.1.32

Resnick, H., Acierno, R., Holmes, M., Dammeyer, M., & Kilpatrick, D. (2000). Emergency evaluation and intervention with female victims of rape and other violence. *Journal of Clinical Psychology, 56,* 1317–1333. doi:10.1002/1097-4679(200010)56:10<1317::AID-JCLP5>3.0.CO;2-H

Rice, M., & Harris, G. (1995). Violent recidivism: Assessing predictive validity. *Journal of Consulting and Clinical Psychology, 63,* 737–748

Riggs, D., Caulfield, M., & Fair, K. (2009). Risk for intimate partner violence: Factors associated with perpetration and victimization. In P. M. Kleespies (Ed.), *Behavioral emergencies: An evidence-based resource for evaluating and managing risk of suicide, violence, and victimization* (pp. 189–208). Washington, DC: American Psychological Association. doi:10.1037/11865-009

Riggs, D., Kilpatrick, D., & Resnick, H. (1992). Long-term psychological distress associated with marital rape and aggravated assault: A comparison to other crimes. *Journal of Family Violence, 7,* 283–296. doi:10.1007/BF00994619

Rodolfa, E., Kraft, W., & Reilley, R. (1988). Stressors of professionals and trainees at APA-approved counseling and VA medical center internship sites. *Professional Psychology: Research and Practice, 19,* 43–49. doi:10.1037/0735-7028.19.1.43

Roy, A. (1982). Risk factors for suicide in psychiatric patients. *Archives of General Psychiatry, 39,* 1089–1095. doi:10.1001/archpsyc.1982.04290090071014

Ruben, H. (1990). Surviving a suicide in your practice. In S. Blumenthal & D. Kupfer (Eds.), *Suicide over the life cycle: Risk factors, assessment, and treatment of suicidal patients* (pp. 619–636). Washington, DC: American Psychiatric Press.

Rudd, M. D., Berman, A., Joiner, T., Nock, M., Silverman, M., Mandrusiak, M., . . . Witte, T. (2006). Warning signs for suicide: Theory, research, and clinical applications. *Suicide and Life-Threatening Behavior, 36,* 255–262. doi:10.1521/suli.2006.36.3.255

Rudd, M. D., Cukrowicz, K. C., & Bryan, C. J. (2008). Core competencies in suicide risk assessment and management: Implications for supervision. *Training and Education in Professional Psychology, 2*, 219–228. doi:10.1037/1931-3918.2.4.219

Rudd, M. D., & Joiner, T. (1998). The assessment, management, and treatment of suicidality: Toward clinically informed and balanced standards of care. *Clinical Psychology: Science and Practice, 5*, 135–150. doi:10.1111/j.1468-2850.1998.tb00140.x

Rudd, M. D., Joiner, T., & Rajab, M. H. (2001). *Treating suicidal behavior: An effective, time-limited approach.* New York, NY: Guilford Press.

Rudd, M. D., Joiner, T., Trotter, D., Williams, B., & Cordero, L. (2009). The psychological and behavioral treatment of suicidal behavior: A critique of what we know (and don't know). In P. M. Kleespies (Ed.), *Behavioral emergencies: An evidence-based resource for evaluating and managing risk of suicide, violence, and victimization* (pp. 339–350). Washington, DC: American Psychological Association. doi:10.1037/11865-015

Ruskin, R., Sakinofsky, I., Bagby, R., Dickens, S., & Sousa, G. (2004). Impact of patient suicide on psychiatrists and psychiatry trainees. *Academic Psychiatry, 28*, 104–110. doi:10.1176/appi.ap.28.2.104

Saakvitne, K. W., & Pearlman, L. A. (1996). *Transforming the pain: A workbook on vicarious traumatization.* New York, NY: Norton.

Sandberg, D. A., McNiel, D., & Binder, R. (2002). Stalking, threatening, and harassing behavior by psychiatric patients toward clinicians. *The Journal of the American Academy of Psychiatry and the Law, 30*, 221–229.

Sanders, S., Jacobson, J., & Ting, L. (2005). Reactions of mental health social workers following a client suicide completion: A qualitative investigation. *Omega: Journal of Death and Dying, 51*, 197–216.

Sanders, S., Jacobson, J., & Ting, L. (2008). Preparing for the inevitable: Training social workers to cope with client suicide. *Journal of Teaching in Social Work, 28*, 1–18. doi:10.1080/08841230802178821

Schauben, L., & Frazier, P. (1995). Vicarious trauma: The effects on female counselors of working with sexual violence survivors. *Psychology of Women Quarterly, 19*, 49–64. doi:10.1111/j.1471-6402.1995.tb00278.x

Schmitz, W., Jr., Allen, M., Feldman, B., Gutin, N., Jahn, D., Kleespies, P., . . . Simpson, S. (2012). Preventing suicide through improved training in suicide risk assessment and care: An American Association of Suicidology Task Force Report addressing serious gaps in U.S. mental health training. *Suicide and Life-Threatening Behavior, 42*, 292–304.

Schulman, K. A., Berlin, J., Harless, W., Kerner, J., Sistrunk, S., Gersh, B., . . . Escarce, J. (1999). The effect of race and sex on physician's recommendations for cardiac catheterization. *The New England Journal of Medicine, 340,* 618–626. doi:10.1056/NEJM199902253400806

Schwartz, T. L., & Park, T. (1999). Assaults by patients on psychiatric residents: A survey and training recommendations. *Psychiatric Services, 50,* 381–383.

Shaban, R. (2005). Theories of clinical judgment and decision-making: A review of the theoretical literature. *Journal of Emergency Primary Health Care, 3,* 1–13.

Silverman, M., Berman, A., Bongar, B., Litman, R., & Maris, R. (1998). Inpatient standards of care and the suicidal patient: Part II. An integration with clinical risk management. In B. Bongar, A. Berman, R. Maris, M. Silverman, E. Harris, & W. Packman (Eds.), *Risk management with suicidal patients* (pp. 83–109). New York, NY: Guilford Press.

Simon, H. (1957). *Models of man: Social and rational, mathematical essays on rational human behavior in a social setting.* New York, NY: Wiley.

Simon, R. I. (2006). Imminent suicide: The illusion of short-term prediction. *Suicide and Life-Threatening Behavior, 36,* 296–301. doi:10.1521/suli.2006. 36.3.296

Singh, J. P., Grann, M., & Fazel, S. (2011). A comparative study of violence risk assessment tools: A systematic review and metaregression analysis of 68 studies involving 25,980 participants. *Clinical Psychology Review, 31,* 499–513. doi:10.1016/j.cpr.2010.11.009

Smedley, B., Stith, A., & Nelson, A. (Eds.). (2003). *Unequal treatment: Confronting racial and ethnic disparities in health care.* Washington, DC: National Academies Press.

Sommers-Flanagan, R., Sommers-Flanagan, J., & Welfel, E. R. (2009). The duty to protect and the ethical standards of professional organizations. In J. Werth, Jr., E. R. Welfel, & G. A. Benjamin (Eds.), *The duty to protect: Ethical, legal, and professional considerations for mental health professionals* (pp. 29–40). Washington, DC: American Psychological Association. doi:10.1037/11866-003

Spiegelman, J., & Werth, J., Jr. (2005). Don't forget about me: The experiences of therapists-in-training after a client has attempted or died by suicide. *Women and Therapy, 28,* 35–57.

Stanley, B., & Brown, G. (2012). Safety planning intervention: A brief intervention to mitigate suicide risk. *Cognitive and Behavioral Practice, 19,* 256–264. doi:10.1016/j.cbpra.2011.01.001

Stanton, A., & Schwartz, M. (1954). *The mental hospital: A study of institutional participation in psychiatric illness and treatment.* New York, NY: Basic Books. doi:10.1037/10670-000

Starcke, K., Wolf, O., Markowitsch, H., & Brand, M. (2008). Anticipatory stress influences decision making under explicit risk conditions. *Behavioral Neuroscience, 122,* 1352–1360. doi:10.1037/a0013281

Stokols, D. (1992). Establishing and maintaining healthy environments: Towards a social ecology of health promotion. *American Psychologist, 47,* 6–22. doi:10. 1037/0003-066X.47.1.6

Storey, J., Gibas, A., Reeves, K., & Hart, S. (2011). Evaluation of a violence risk (threat) assessment training program for police and other criminal justice professionals. *Criminal Justice and Behavior, 38,* 554–564. doi:10.1177/0093854811403123

Suicide Prevention Resource Center. (2006). *Core competencies in the assessment and management of suicidality.* Waltham, MA: Author.

Suicide Prevention Resource Center. (2011). *Assessing and managing suicide risk: Core competencies for mental health professionals.* Retrieved from http://sprc. org/traininginstitute/amsr/clincomp.asp

Suicide Prevention Resource Center and Suicide Prevention Action Network USA. (2010, August). *Charting the future of suicide prevention: A 2010 progress review of the national strategy and recommendations for the decade ahead.* Retrieved from http://www.sprc.org/library/ChartinThe Future_Fullbook.pdf

Sullivan, G., & Bongar, B. (2009). Assessing suicide risk in the adult patient. In P. M. Kleespies (Ed.), *Behavioral emergencies: An evidence-based resource for evaluating and managing risk of suicide, violence, and victimization* (pp. 59–78). Washington, DC: American Psychological Association. doi:10.1037/11865-003

Tanney, B. (1992). Mental disorders, psychiatric patients, and suicide. In R. Maris, A. Berman, J. Maltsberger, & R. Yufit (Eds.), *Assessment and prediction of suicide* (pp. 277–320). New York, NY: Guilford Press.

Tarasoff v. Regents of University of California, 13 Cal. 3d 177 (1974).

Tarasoff v. Regents of University of California, 17 Cal. 3d 425 (1976).

Teasdale, B., Silver, E., & Monahan, J. (2006). Gender, threat/control override delusions and violence. *Law and Human Behavior, 30,* 649–658. doi:10.1007/s10979-006-9044-x

Teo, A. R., Holly, S., Leary, M., & McNiel, D. (2012, November). The relationship between level of training and accuracy of violence risk assessment. *Psychiatric Services, 63*(11). doi:10.1176/appi.ps.201200019

Ting, L., Sanders, S., Jacobson, J., & Power, J. (2006). Dealing with the aftermath: A qualitative analysis of mental health social workers' reactions after a client suicide. *Social Work, 51,* 329–341. doi:10.1093/sw/51.4.329

Tjaden, P., & Thoennes, N. (2000). *Prevalence, nature, and consequences of violence against women: Findings from the National Violence Against Women Survey.* Washington, DC: U.S. Department of Justice.

Trippany, R. L., White Kress, V. E., & Wilcoxin, S. A. (2004). Preventing vicarious trauma: What counselors should know when working with trauma survivors. *Journal of Counseling & Development, 82,* 31–37. doi:10.1002/j.1556-6678.2004. tb00283.x

Tuckey, M. (2007). Issues in the debriefing debate for emergency services: Moving research outcomes forward. *Clinical Psychology: Science and Practice, 14,* 106–116. doi:10.1111/j.1468-2850.2007.00069.x

Tversky, A., & Kahneman, D. (1974). Judgments under uncertainty: Heuristics and biases. *Science, 185,* 1124–1131. doi:10.1126/science.185.4157.1124

United Nations/World Health Organization. (1996). *Prevention of suicide: Guidelines for the formulation and implementation of national strategies* (ST/ESA/245). Geneva, Switzerland: World Health Organization.

U.S. Department of Health and Human Services. (2001). *National strategy for suicide prevention: Goals and objectives for action.* Rockville, MD: Author. Retrieved from http://store.samhsa.gov/shin/content/SMA01-3517/SMA01-3517.pdf

U.S. Department of Justice. (2011). *Homicides fall to lowest rates in four decades.* Retrieved on from http://www.bjs.gov/index.cfm?ty=pbdetail&iid=2221

U.S. Public Health Service. (1999). *The Surgeon General's call to action to prevent suicide.* Retrieved from http://www.surgeongeneral.gov/library/calltoaction/calltoaction.pdf

VandeCreek, L., & Knapp, S. (2000). Risk management and life-threatening behaviors. *Journal of Clinical Psychology, 56,* 1335–1351. doi:10.1002/1097-4679(200010)56:10<1335::AID-JCLP6>3.0.CO;2-A

VanDeusen, K. M., & Way, I. (2006). Vicarious trauma: An exploratory study of the impact of providing sexual abuse treatment on clinicians' trust and intimacy. *Journal of Child Sexual Abuse, 15,* 69–85. doi:10.1300/J070v15n01_04

van Meer, J., & Theunissen, N. (2009). Prospective educational applications of mental simulation: A meta-review. *Educational Psychology Review, 21,* 93–112. doi:10.1007/s10648-009-9097-8

Van Orden, K. A., Joiner, T., Hollar, D., Rudd, M. D., Mandrusiak, M., & Silverman, M. (2006). A test of the effectiveness of a list of suicide warning signs for the public. *Suicide and Life-Threatening Behavior, 36,* 272–287. doi:10.1521/suli.2006.36.3.272

Vincent, G., Guy, L., Fusco, S., & Gershenson, B. (2012). Field reliability of the SAVRY with juvenile probation officers: Implications for training. *Law and Human Behavior, 36,* 225–236.

Way, B. B., Allen, M., Mumpower, J., Stewart, T., & Banks, S. (1998). Interrater agreement among psychiatrists in psychiatric emergency assessments. *The American Journal of Psychiatry, 155,* 1423–1428.

Webster, C., Bloom, H., & Augimeri, L. (2009, December 14). Violence risk assessment in everyday psychiatric practice. *Psychiatric Times,* 40–43. Retrieved from www.psychiatrictimes.com

Webster, C., Douglas, K., Eaves, D., & Hart, S. (1997). *HCR-20: Assessing risk for violence* (Version 2). Burnaby, British Columbia, Canada: Simon Fraser University, Mental Health, Law, and Policy Institute.

Webster, C., Martin, M., Brink, J., Nicholls, T., & Desmarais, S. (2009). *Manual for the Short-Term Assessment of Risk and Treatability (START)* (Version 1.1). Coquitlam, British Columbia, Canada: British Columbia Mental Health and Addiction Services.

Welfel, E. R., Werth, J., Jr., & Benjamin, G. A. (2009). Introduction to the duty to protect. In J. Werth, Jr., E. R. Welfel, & G. A. Benjamin (Eds.), *The duty to protect: Ethical, legal, and professional considerations for mental health professionals* (pp. 3–8). Washington, DC: American Psychological Association. doi:10.1037/11866-001

Westen, D., & Weinberger, J. (2004). When clinical description becomes statistical prediction. *American Psychologist, 59,* 595–613. doi:10.1037/0003-066X.59.7.595

White, S., & Meloy, J. R. (2007). *The WAVR-21: A structured professional guide for the workplace assessment of violence risk.* San Diego, CA: Specialized Training Resources.

Whitman, R. M., Armao, B. B., & Dent, O. (1976). Assault on the therapist. *American Journal of Psychiatry, 133,* 426–429.

Wilson, R. (2007). *Eliminating healthcare disparities in America: Beyond the IOM Report.* Totowa, NJ: Humana Press.

Woolfolk, R., Lehrer, P., & Allen, L. (2007). Conceptual issues underlying stress management. In P. Lehrer, R. Woolfolk, & W. Sime (Eds.), *Principles and practice of stress management* (3rd ed.; pp. 3–15). New York, NY: Guilford Press.

Yang, M., Wong, S., & Coid, J. (2010). The efficacy of violence prediction: A meta-analytic comparison of nine risk assessment tools. *Psychological Bulletin, 136,* 740–767. doi:10.1037/a0020473

Yudofsky, S. C., Silver, J., Jackson, W., Endicott, J., & Williams, D. (1986). The Overt Aggression Scale for the objective rating of verbal and physical aggression. *The American Journal of Psychiatry, 143,* 35–39.

Zellman, G., & Fair, C. C. (2002). Preventing and reporting abuse. In J. Myers, L. Berliner, J. Briere, C. T. Hendrix, C. Jenny, & T. Reid (Eds.), *The APSAC handbook on child maltreatment* (2nd ed.; pp. 449–475). Thousand Oaks, CA: Sage.

Zimet, C., & Weissberg, M. (1979). The emergency service: A setting for internship training. *Psychotherapy: Theory, Research, & Practice, 16,* 334–336. doi:10.1037/h0085898

Zsambok, C. (2009). Naturalistic decision making: Where are we now? In C. Zsambok & G. Klein (Eds.), *Naturalistic decision making* (pp. 3–16). New York, NY: Routledge.

Index

"Experience near," 125. *See also*
    Behavioral emergency evaluation
    and management training

Fair, C. C., 28
Fair, K., 29, 69–70
Farberow, N., 166
Fazel, S., 106–107
Feasibility (assessment), 134–135
Feature matching, 35
Feldman, B. N., 15
Feldman-Summers, S., 19
Fidelity (assessment), 134–135
Firearms, 148
Flannery, R. B., 163, 164, 169
Fonseca, V., 56
Forensic patients, 107–108
"Foreseeable victim" standard, 155
Forsyth, J., 18, 49–50, 130
Foundational competencies, 124
Frazier, P., 165, 170
Freedenthal, S., 15
Freeman, K., 18
Friend, R., 168
Fulton, P., 163
Functional competencies, 124

Gaba, D. M., 54
Gallagher, P., 23
Gawande, A. A., 53
Gender biases, 45
Gentile, S., 16
Gibas, A., 118
Glick, R., 131
Gore, J., 35
Gothard, S., 16
Gould, M., 58
Grann, M., 106–107
Greaney, S., 144
Gregory, A., 110
Guns, 148
Guy, J., 16, 19, 44, 164, 170
Guy, L. S., 113

Haas, G., 14
Haller, E., 166
Hammond, K., 51
"Hardening the target," 24, 25
Hare Psychopathy Checklist-Revised
    (PCL-R), 106–108
Harmatz, M., 18, 123
Harmell, P., 16
Harris, G. T., 107
Hart, S., 105, 117, 118
HCR-20. *See* Historical-Clinical-Risk
    Management-20
*HCR-20 Violence Risk Management
    Companion Guide,* 113
Hendin, 162–163
Hendry, M., 113
Heuristics, 34, 44, 45
High-risk patients, 5
Historical-Clinical-Risk
    Management-20 (HCR-20),
    106, 110–113, 119
Holly, S., 55, 112
Homicide, 12, 144, 148
Hospitalization, 149–150
    for incapacitating violent patient,
        25, 27
    making decisions about, 23–24
    voluntary and involuntary, 156
Hospital settings, 131–132, 172.
    See also Inpatient settings;
    Outpatient settings
Howard, B., 141
Howard, S., 54
Hypervigilant decision-making, 5,
    39–40

Imminent risk, 11
Impact of Event Scale (IES), 49–50,
    162
Incapacitation, of patient, 24–27
Incompleteness (recognition/
    metacognition model), 36
Information processing, 33–35

About the Author

Phillip M. Kleespies, PhD, was awarded his doctoral degree in clinical psychology from Clark University in 1971. He is a clinical psychologist in the Department of Veterans Affairs (DVA) Boston Healthcare System and an assistant clinical professor of psychiatry at Boston University School of Medicine. Dr. Kleespies has over 40 years of experience in working in emergency department, urgent care clinic, and inpatient psychiatry settings with patients who are at risk of such behavioral emergencies as suicidal behavior, violence, and interpersonal victimization. In 2013, he was recognized with the Outstanding Clinician Award presented by the VA Section of the American Psychological Association's Division of Psychologists in Public Service (APA Division 18). Dr. Kleespies has also been an active supervisor and teacher to psychology interns and psychology postdoctoral fellows with an interest in evaluating and managing patients at risk to self and others. His research interests have included the development of a database for the study of self-injurious and suicidal behavior in veterans and the impact of patient suicide and suicidal behavior on the treating clinicians.

Dr. Kleespies has authored and coauthored many publications, and he has made numerous presentations on behavioral emergencies and related topics. He is a contributing author and the editor of the books *Emergencies in Mental Health Practice: Evaluation and Management* (1998) and *Behavioral Emergencies: An Evidence-Based Resource for Evaluating and*

Managing Risk of Suicide, Violence, and Victimization (2009). In addition, he is the author of the book *Life and Death Decisions: Psychological and Ethical Considerations in End-of-Life Care* (2004). He has served as a member of the VA Boston Ethics Case Consultation Team, the VA Boston Palliative Care Consult Team, and the VA Boston Violence Threat Assessment Committee.

Dr. Kleespies is a diplomate in clinical psychology of the American Board of Professional Psychology and an APA fellow. He was the founding president of the Section on Clinical Emergencies and Crises, Section VII of APA Division 12 (Society of Clinical Psychology), and he remains involved with the section as advisor to the Executive Board.